寿宁贯木拱廊桥

鸾峰桥 Luanfeng Bridge

航拍片（2019.10）

西立面（2019.10）

北立面（2011.3）

西立面局部（2019.10）

廊屋内部（2011.3）

拱架（2011.3）

杨溪头桥 Yangxitou Bridge

航拍片（2019.10）

南立面（2019.10）

西立面（2019.10）

北立面（2019.10）

廊屋内部（2019.10）

拱架（2019.10）

廊屋外神龛（2019.10）

长濑溪桥 Changlaixi Bridge

廊屋内部（2005.8）
拱架（2005.8）
西立面（2005.8）
东立面（2005.8）
南立面（2005.8）
北立面（2005.8）

杨梅州桥 Yangmeizhou Bridge

廊屋内部（2019.10）
航拍片（2019.10）
拱架（2010.2）
北立面正中窗口（2019.10）
南立面（2006.12）

福寿桥 Fushou Bridge

廊屋内部（2019.10）

航拍片（2019.10）

西立面（2019.10）

北立面（2019.10）

拱架（2019.10）

南立面（2011.3）

张坑桥 Zhangkeng Bridge

西立面（2005.8）

西侧仰视（2005.8）

北侧端部（2005.8）

廊屋梁架局部（2005.8）

廊屋内梁上墨书（2005.8）

拱架（2005.8）

红军桥 Hongjun Bridge

廊屋内部（2019.10）

航拍片（2019.10）

北立面（2019.10）

东立面（2011.3）

西立面（2019.10）

大宝桥 Dabao Bridge

船形桥台（2019.10）

航拍片（2019.10）

西南立面（2019.10）

东北立面（2019.10）

东南立面（2006.12）

仙宫桥 Xiangong Bridge

航拍片（2019.10）

廊屋内藻井（2019.10）

北立面（2019.10）

廊屋梁架局部（2019.10）

拱架（2019.10）

东立面（2019.10）

登云桥 Dengyun Bridge

西立面（2006.12）

廊屋内部（2006.12）

东立面（2006.12）

拱架构件（2008.5）

东南部仰视（2008.5）

里仁桥 Liren Bridge

廊屋内部（2019.10）

航拍片（2019.10）

北立面（2010.2）

东立面（2019.10）

西立面（2010.2）

升平桥 Shengping Bridge

廊屋内藻井（2011.3）

航拍片（2019.10）

廊屋梁架局部（2019.10）

北立面（2019.10）

上层屋檐局部（2019.10）

西立面（2019.10）

回澜桥 Huilan Bridge

拱架构件（2011.3）

航拍片（2019.10）

西立面（2019.10）

廊屋南端坐靠（2019.10）

北立面（2011.3）

飞云桥 Feiyun Bridge

西立面（2011.3）

廊屋内藻井（2019.10）

上层屋顶局部（2019.10）

三节苗与垫苗石（2011.3）

廊屋内西南侧神龛（2019.10）

尤溪上桥 Youxishang Bridge

廊屋内部（2019.10）

航拍片（2019.10）

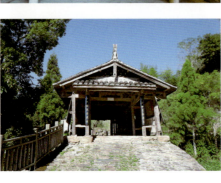
拱架（2019.10）

东立面中部（2019.10）

北立面（2010.2）

小东上桥 Xiaodongshang Bridge

廊屋内部（2019.10）

航拍片（2019.10）

东立面（2019.10）

南立面仰视（2019.10）

北立面（2019.10）

溪南桥 Xi'nan Bridge

航拍片（2019.10）

北立面（2011.3）

南立面（2019.10）

廊屋内部（2019.10）

西侧南立面局部（2019.10）

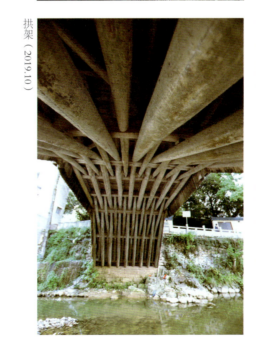
拱架（2019.10）

单桥 Dan Bridge

航拍片（2019.10）

东立面（2011.3）

构架局部（2019.10）

廊屋内部（2019.10）

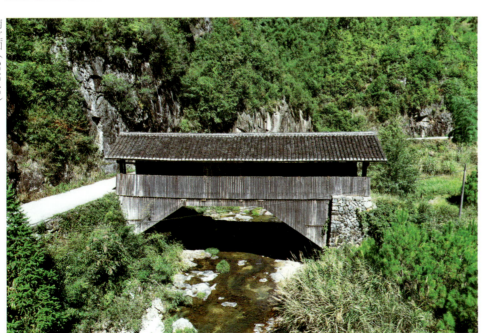
南立面（2019.10）

寿春桥 Shouchun Bridge

廊屋梁架局部（2011.3）

航拍片（2019.10）

北立面（2011.3）

西立面（2011.3）

东立面（2011.3）

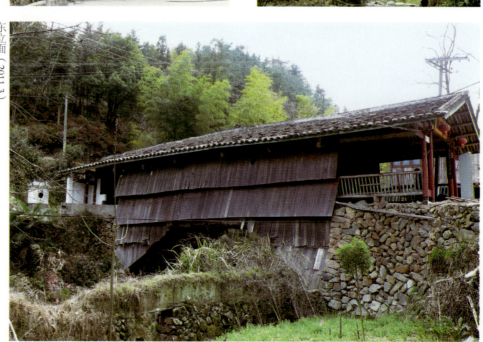

屏南贯木拱廊桥

百祥桥 Baixiang Bridge

廊屋内部（2019.10）

航拍片（2019.10）

西立面与北立面（2019.10）

东立面（2019.10）

南立面（2019.10）

金造桥 Jinzao Bridge

西立面与南立面（2005.3）

南立面（2005.3）

廊屋内梁上墨书（2005.3）

拱架（2005.3）

屋檐局部（2005.3）

北立面（2005.3）

千乘桥 Qiansheng Bridge

航拍片（2019.10）

廊屋内部（2019.10）

西立面（2008.10）

拱架（2019.10）

南立面（2019.10）

西立面桥墩部位（2019.10）

北立面（2019.10）

广福桥 Guangfu Bridge

航拍片（2019.10）

廊屋内部（2008.1）

拱架（2019.10）

西立面与南立面（2019.10）

东立面和北立面（2019.10）

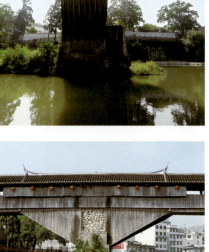
从廊屋内看西立面（2019.10）

龙津桥 Longjin Bridge

廊屋内部（2019.10）

航拍片（2019.10）

拱架（2019.10）

西立面屋檐局部（2019.10）

北立面（2019.10）

惠风桥 Huifeng Bridge

廊屋内部（2019.10）

航拍片（2019.10）

东南立面（2019.10）

东北立面（2019.10）

西南立面（2019.10）

清晏桥 Qingyan Bridge

鸟瞰（2005.3）

屋檐局部（2005.3）

拱架（2005.3）

翼角（2005.3）

西南立面与东南立面（2005.3）

龙井桥 Longjing Bridge

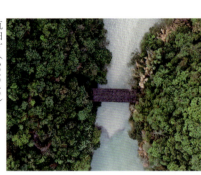
廊屋内部（2019.10）

航拍片（2019.10）

廊屋内砖铺地面（2019.10）

北立面与西立面（2019.10）

东立面（2019.10）

溪里桥 Xili Bridge

廊屋内部（2019.10）

航拍片（2019.10）

拱架（2019.10）

西立面（2008.11）

北立面（2019.10）

西侧仰视（2019.10）

广利桥 Guangli Bridge

廊屋内部（2019.10）

航拍片（2019.10）

拱架局部（2019.10）

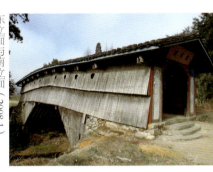
东立面与南立面（2008.1）

南立面（2008.1）

樟口桥 Zhangkou Bridge

航拍片（2019.10）

廊屋内部（2019.10）

东南立面（2019.10）

拱架（2019.10）

东北立面（2019.10）

西南立面（2019.10）

万安桥 Wan'an Bridge

航拍片（2019.10）

廊屋内部（2019.10）

北立面（2019.10）

南立面（2008.10）

东立面（2019.10）

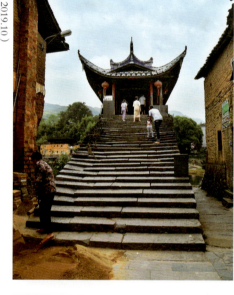
西立面（2019.10）

西立面屋顶局部（2019.10）

迎风桥 Yingfeng Bridge

廊屋内部（2019.10）

航拍片（2019.10）

拱架（2008.11）

构架局部（2019.10）

南立面（2019.10）

中国古建筑测绘大系·古桥建筑

福建贯木拱廊桥

肖东 姚洪峰 程霏 编著

Traditional Chinese Architecture Surveying and
Mapping Series:
Ancient Bridges

THE INTERLOCKED TIMBER-ARCHED
COVERED BRIDGES IN FUJIAN
PROVINCE

Edited by XIAO Dong, YAO Hongfeng, CHENG Fei

China Architecture & Building Press

中国建筑工业出版社

Editorial Board of the Traditional Chinese Architecture Surveying and Mapping Series

Editorial Advisory Board: FU Xinian, HOU Youbin
Editorial Director: SHEN Yuanqin
Deputy Editorial Director: WANG Lihui
Editors in Chief: WANG Qiheng, WANG Guixiang, CHEN Wei, CHANG Qing

Editorial Team Members (Characters arranged according to stroke counts):
DING Yao, WANG Nan, WANG Wei, WANG Mo, BAI Ying, BAI Chengjun,
FENG Di, ZHU Lei, ZHU Yuhui, LIU Chang, LIU Yang, LIU Daping,
LIU Tongtong, LI Luke, YANG Jing, XIAO Dong, WU Cong, WU Xiaomin,
HE Jie, HE Beijie, WANG Zhiyang, ZHANG Long, ZHANG Shiqing,
ZHANG Fengwu, ZHANG Xingguo, ZHANG Chunyan, LIN Yuan, YUE Yanmin,
SHI Fei, YAO Hongfeng, HE Congrong, JIA Jun, GUO Xuan, GUO Huazhan,
ZHUGE Jing, CAO Peng, YU Mengzhe, CHENG Fei, LIAO Huinong

『中国古建筑测绘大系』编委会

顾问 傅熹年 侯幼彬
主任 沈元勤
副主任 王莉慧
主编（以姓氏笔画为序）王其亨 王贵祥 陈薇 常青
编委（以姓氏笔画为序）
丁垚 王南 王蔚 王莫 白颖 白成军 冯棣
朱蕾 朱宇晖 刘畅 刘洋 刘大平 刘彤彤 李路珂
杨菁 肖东 吴葱 吴晓敏 何捷 何蓓洁 汪智洋
张龙 张十庆 张凤梧 张兴国 张春彦 林源 岳岩敏
是霏 姚洪峰 贺从容 贾珺 郭璇 郭华瞻 诸葛净
曹鹏 喻梦哲 程霏 廖慧农

目　录

导言——〇〇一

图版——〇〇九

寿宁贯木拱廊桥——〇一一
鸾峰桥——〇一三
杨溪头桥——〇二一
杨梅州桥——〇二九
长濑溪桥——〇三七
张坑桥——〇四五
福寿桥——〇五三
大宝桥——〇六一
红军桥——〇六九
登云桥——〇七七
仙宫桥——〇八五
升平桥——〇九七
里仁桥——一〇七
飞云桥——一一五
回澜桥——一二三
尤溪上桥——一三一
小东上桥——一三九
溪南桥——一四七
单桥——一五五
寿春桥——一六三

屏南贯木拱廊桥——一七一
百祥桥——一七三
金造桥——一八一
千乘桥——一八九
广福桥——二〇五
惠风桥——二一三
龙津桥——二二一
清晏桥——二二九
龙井桥——二三七
广利桥——二四五
溪里桥——二五三
樟口桥——二六一
万安桥——二六九
迎风桥——二七九

参与测绘及相关工作的单位及人员名单——二八七

Contents

Introduction 001

Figure 009

The Interlocked Timber-Arched Covered Bridges in Shouning County 011

    Luanfeng Bridge 013
    Yangxitou Bridge 021
    Yangmeizhou Bridge 029
    Changlaixi Bridge 037
    Zhangkeng Bridge 045
    Fushou Bridge 053
    Dabao Bridge 061
    Hongjun Bridge 069
    Dengyun Bridge 077
    Xiangong Bridge 085
    Shengping Bridge 097
    Liren Bridge 107
    Feiyun Bridge 115
    Huilan Bridge 123
    Youxishang Bridge 131
    Xiaodongshang Bridge 139
    Xi'nan Bridge 147
    Dan Bridge 155
    Shouchun Bridge 163

The Interlocked Timber-Arched Covered Bridges in Pingnan County 171

    Baixiang Bridge 173
    Jinzao Bridge 181
    Qiansheng Bridge 189
    Guangfu Bridge 205
    Huifeng Bridge 213
    Longjin Bridge 221
    Qingyan Bridge 229
    Longjing Bridge 237
    Guangli Bridge 245
    Xili Bridge 253
    Zhangkou Bridge 261
    Wan'an Bridge 269
    Yingfeng Bridge 279

List of Participants Involved in Surveying and Related Works 288

Introduction

The interlocked timber-arched covered bridges (*Guan mugong langqiao*) are known as the "living fossils of old Chinese bridges", and, according to *Zhongguo Kexue Jishu Shi* (History of Chinese science and technology), they are a treasure unique to China among the historical bridges of the world. In light of today's knowledge, the interlocked timber-arched bridge first appeared in Zhang Zeduan's masterpiece *Qingming Shanghe Tu* (Along the River During the Qingming Festival) in the Northern Song Dynasty. The scroll depicts a huge timber-arched bridge spanning across the Bian River without piers. Because of its delicate structure, graceful form, and resemblance to a rainbow, the bridge was known as Hongqiao (Rainbow Bridge). The whole painting reaches its climax in the striking image of the Rainbow Bridge scene. Today, the timber-arched construction with bundled joints shown in the painting has advanced into a construction with mortise and tenon joints.

Key to understanding the interlocked timber-arched covered bridges is the technology of arched-system of the timber interlocked together. A typical arched-system is taken as an example. The first system is called *Sanjiemiao* (the three-sided arch) and formed by the two latitudinal squared-timbers (*Daniutou*) interlocked with three groups of longitudinal logs, i.e. one group of horizontal beams and two groups of sloping beams. The second system is called *Wujiemiao* (the five-sided arch) and composed of the four latitudinal squared-timbers (*Xiaoniutou*) interlocked with five groups of longitudinal logs, i.e. one group of horizontal beams and four groups of sloping beams. In addition, the third system may consist of *Jiangjun* [commander] columns, erected at the corner position at both ends of the timber arched system with *Paijia* columns (the smaller columns in-between *Jiangjun* [commander] columns), crossbeams and *Qiaobanmiao* (the beams linked *ShangXiaoniutou* and the crossbeams). The interlocking of compartments of the first and second system, with the mortise and tenon joints, longitudinal and latitudinal interlocking, continuous force transmitting and the

导言

贯木拱廊桥被称为『中国古桥的活化石』，《中国科学技术史》称其『在世界桥梁史上唯中国有之』。目前所知，贯木拱桥最初出现在北宋画家张择端的《清明上河图》巨作中，是一座横跨汴河的宏大木拱桥，结构精巧，形式优美，宛如飞虹，故名『虹桥』，构成了此画的一个高潮和显著画面，桥体拱架中的捆绑结构已发展为现在技术成熟的榫卯结构。

贯木拱廊桥的核心技术是拱架系统，在一个典型拱架系统中，纵向『一平两斜』三根拱杆与横向两根牛头纵横相贯形成的『三节苗』被称为『第一系统』；纵向『一平四斜』五根拱杆与横向四根牛头纵横形成的『五节苗』被称为『第二系统』；在两个系统之外，由将军柱与排架柱、横梁、桥板苗，共同组成了第三系统』。第一系统与第二系统构件的交错搭构，充分体现了榫卯节点、纵横相贯、接续传力、挤压支撑，从而形成了多边拱廊的大跨度桥梁的特质。加之

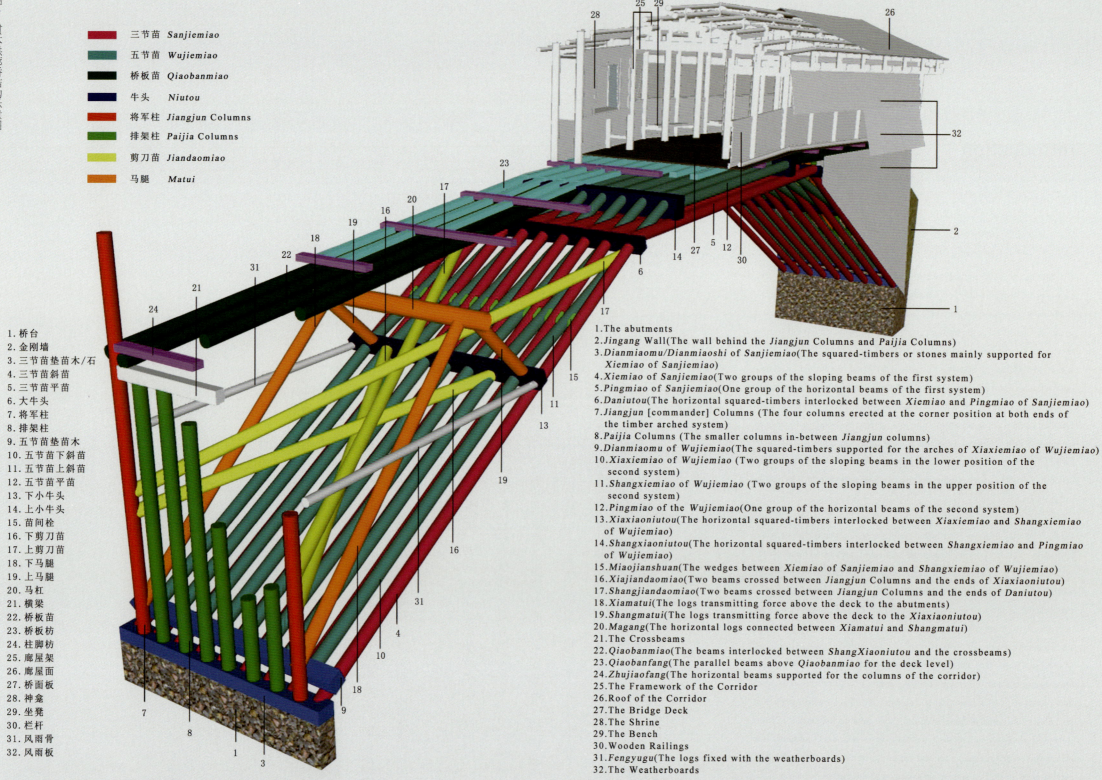

图一 贯木拱廊桥结构示意图

- 三节苗 *Sanjiemiao*
- 五节苗 *Wujiemiao*
- 桥板苗 *Qiaobanmiao*
- 牛头 *Niutou*
- 将军柱 *Jiangjun Columns*
- 排架柱 *Paijia Columns*
- 剪刀苗 *Jiandaomiao*
- 马腿 *Matui*

1. 桥台
2. 金刚墙
3. 三节苗垫苗木/石
4. 三节苗斜苗
5. 三节苗平苗
6. 大牛头
7. 将军柱
8. 排架柱
9. 五节苗垫苗木
10. 五节苗下斜苗
11. 五节苗上斜苗
12. 五节苗平苗
13. 下小牛头
14. 上小牛头
15. 苗间栓
16. 下剪刀苗
17. 上剪刀苗
18. 下马腿
19. 上马腿
20. 马杠
21. 横梁
22. 桥板苗
23. 桥板枋
24. 柱脚枋
25. 廊屋架
26. 廊屋面
27. 桥面板
28. 神龛
29. 坐凳
30. 栏杆
31. 风雨骨
32. 风雨板

1. The abutments
2. *Jingang* Wall (The wall behind the *Jiangjun* Columns and *Paijia* Columns)
3. *Dianmiaomu/Dianmiaoshi* of *Sanjiemiao* (The squared-timbers or stones mainly supported for *Xiemiao* of *Sanjiemiao*)
4. *Xiemiao* of *Sanjiemiao* (Two groups of the sloping beams of the first system)
5. *Pingmiao* of *Sanjiemiao* (One group of the horizontal beams of the first system)
6. *Daniutou* (The horizontal squared-timbers interlocked between *Xiemiao* and *Pingmiao* of *Sanjiemiao*)
7. *Jiangjun* [commander] Columns (The four columns erected at the corner position at both ends of the timber arched system)
8. *Paijia* Columns (The smaller columns in-between *Jiangjun* columns)
9. *Dianmiaomu* of *Wujiemiao* (The squared-timbers supported for the arches of *Xiaxiemiao* of *Wujiemiao*)
10. *Xiaxiemiao* of *Wujiemiao* (Two groups of the sloping beams in the lower position of the second system)
11. *Shangxiemiao* of *Wujiemiao* (Two groups of the sloping beams in the upper position of the second system)
12. *Pingmiao* of the *Wujiemiao* (One group of the horizontal beams of the second system)
13. *Xiaxiaoniutou* (The horizontal squared-timbers interlocked between *Xiaxiemiao* and *Shangxiemiao* of *Wujiemiao*)
14. *Shangxiaoniutou* (The horizontal squared-timbers interlocked between *Shangxiemiao* and *Pingmiao* of *Wujiemiao*)
15. *Miaojianshuan* (The wedges between *Xiemiao* of *Sanjiemiao* and *Shangxiemiao* of *Wujiemiao*)
16. *Xiajiandaomiao* (Two beams crossed between *Jiangjun* Columns and the ends of *Xiaxiaoniutou*)
17. *Shangjiandaomiao* (Two beams crossed between *Jiangjun* Columns and the ends of *Daniutou*)
18. *Xiamatui* (The logs transmitting force above the deck to the abutments)
19. *Shangmatui* (The logs transmitting force above the deck to the *Xiaxiaoniutou*)
20. *Magang* (The horizontal logs connected between *Xiamatui* and *Shangmatui*)
21. The Crossbeams
22. *Qiaobanmiao* (The beams interlocked between *ShangXiaoniutou* and the crossbeams)
23. *Qiaobanfang* (The parallel beams above *Qiaobanmiao* for the deck level)
24. *Zhujiaofang* (The horizontal beams supported for the columns of the corridor)
25. The Framework of the Corridor
26. Roof of the Corridor
27. The Bridge Deck
28. The Shrine
29. The Bench
30. Wooden Railings
31. *Fengyugu* (The logs fixed with the weatherboards)
32. The Weatherboards

Fig.1 Schematic drawing of the structure of the interlocked timber-arched covered bridge

logs pressing and supporting, gives a unique characteristic of the large-span polygonal arch. Stone abutments are added at either side of the bridge to help bear the weight of the bridge and the load of the three systems (pressure or thrust). Finally, an enclosed passageway or covered corridor is built in *Chuandou* (column-and-tie-beam) style on top of the bridge (Fig. 1).

The interlocked timber-arched covered bridges are concentrated in a mountainous landscape with many streams in the borders of Fujian and Zhejiang provinces. The region includes the Yandang, Kuocang, Donggong, and Jiufeng mountains, as well as the Minjiang, Oujiang, Feiyunjiang, Huotongxi, and Jiaoxi rivers. A few bridges are also found in the Daiyun Mountains around Fuzhou and Quanzhou in Fujian province. The high mountains and numerous rivers impeded the development of convenient traffic networks, but conversely spurred the production of the Chinese fir, a high quality construction material. This led to the popularity of the interlocked timber-arched covered bridges in the region.

In 2001, the State Council of China began to acknowledge the interlocked timber-arched covered bridges in Zhejiang and Fujian provinces as National Priority Protected Sites. The "Traditional Design and Practices for Building Chinese Wooden Arch Bridges", jointly proposed by Shouning and Pingnan counties, was inscribed on China's National Intangible Cultural Heritage List (announced in the second batch) in 2008, and in 2009, it was officially included in the UNESCO List of Intangible Cultural Heritage in Need of Urgent Safeguarding. This marks a historically significant step towards the preservation of China's interlocked timber-arched covered bridges at both the national and international level. In 2012, some of the interlocked timber-arched covered bridges in Fujian and Zhejiang provinces were officially included in the updated version of China's World Cultural Heritage Tentative List by the National Cultural Heritage Administration.

The interlocked timber-arched covered bridges are well preserved in Shouning county (19 examples) and Pingnan county (13 examples) of Fujian province (Fig.2, Fig.3). The largest number and best-documented the interlocked timber-arched covered bridges in China has survived in Shouning county, and among them, Luanfeng Bridge stands out with the largest single arch span (37.08m). In Pingnan county, Wan'an Bridge is outstanding because it is the longest of all the Chinese interlocked timber-arched covered bridges measuring 111.90 m (including bridge steps and approach); furthermore Pingnan's Qiansheng Bridge and Longjing Bridge are all both listed in the 1986 edition of *Zhongguo Guqiao Jishu Shi* (*History of Chinese Historical Bridge Technology*), with Longjing Bridge described as the steepest bridge in southeastern China.

两端的石桥台抵挡挤靠，就形成了坚固一体的贯木拱桥体；桥上再建木结构长廊，此即为贯木拱廊桥（图1）。

现存贯木拱廊桥主要分布在闽浙两省交界的雁荡、括苍、洞宫、鹫峰以及闽江、瓯江、飞云江、霍童溪、交溪等山峰和溪流密集地区，在位于福建省属于福州和泉州山区的戴云山脉中也有少量留存。这些区域山高水深，溪流纵横，交通极为不便，却因盛产南方杉木这种优质的建桥木材，而造就了只有在这些区域才能流传的特有贯木拱桥。

自2001年起，国务院开始将浙江省和福建省的部分木拱廊桥公布为全国重点文物保护单位。2008年，福建省寿宁县和屏南县联合申报的『中国木拱桥传统营造技艺』被列入第二批国家级非物质文化遗产名录，于2009年又被联合国教科文组织列入急需保护的非物质文化遗产名录，迈出了中国贯木拱廊桥保护的历史性一步。2012年，国家文物局将闽、浙两省的部分贯木拱廊桥列入中国世界文化遗产预备名单。

福建寿宁与屏南两县是贯木拱廊桥非常集中的地区之一，现分别主要有19座和13座保存完整、各具特色的贯木拱廊桥（图2、图3）。在全国范围内，寿宁是贯木拱廊桥数量最多的县，造桥年代序列也最为齐全，其中鸾峰桥以单拱跨度37.08米为拱跨最大者。在屏南贯木拱廊桥中，包含台阶和引桥，加起来达111.90米长的万安桥是最长者；千乘桥和龙井桥被录入1986年版的《中国古桥技术史》，龙井桥在该书中又被称为『中国东南第一险桥』。

虽然贯木拱廊桥比较容易被飓风、洪水、火灾、战争等外力毁坏，但是为了满足人们通行和休闲等生产、生活需求，修缮与重建活动从古代以至近年从未中断，造桥传承人、贯木拱廊桥营造技

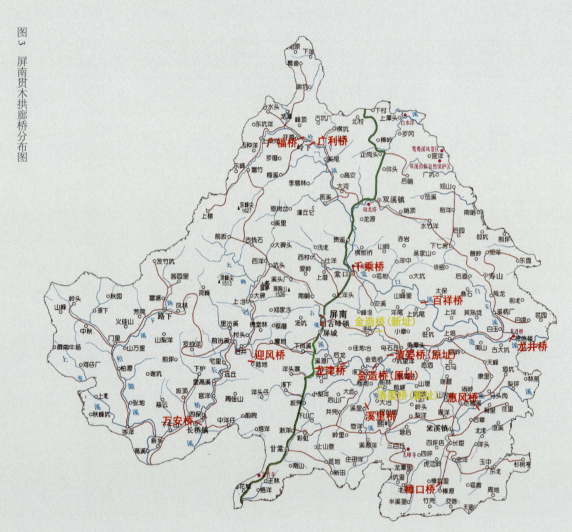

Fig.2 Distribution of the interlocked timber-arched covered bridges in Shouning county
Fig.3 Distribution of the interlocked timber-arched covered bridges in Pingnan county

Although the interlocked timber-arched covered bridges are relatively vulnerable to natural and manmade disasters like hurricanes, floods, fire, and war, these bridges have been restored and rebuilt on numerous occasions since ancient times to meet people's needs for transportation and daily life. This guaranteed the continuation of the bridges building tradition that has relied on skilled craftsmen, established techniques handed down for generations, and Chinese firs grown in the forest near to the bridges. These factors may also serve to explain why the traditional bridge construction techniques have been included in the Intangible Cultural Heritage List.

Included in this volume of the *Traditional Chinese Architecture Surveying and Mapping Series* are thirty-two the interlocked timber-arched covered bridges situated in Shouning and Pingnan counties and dating from the Song Dynasty to the present. The survey also includes modern bridges that are precisely built according to the traditional construction techniques still used in modern times. Bridges are listed in the order of their single span size, from the largest to the smallest, and are always shown in the following sequence of plans to provide in-depth knowledge of the basic form of each bridge and reduce repetition of information (Tab.1, Tab.2): surface floor plan, drawing of the interlocked timber arch system as seen from below and above, drawing of the beam framework of the corridor as seen from below and above, two asymmetric elevations, two cross-sections, longitude section, elevation and section of the shrine inside the corridor, detail drawings of bracket sets (*Dougong*), detail drawings of cushion timbers for the arches (*Dianmiaomu*), and detail drawings of caisson ceilings (*Zaojing*). Some of the names of the components not shown on all the drawings can be found on partial cross-sectional views in the introduction, which are varied depended on regions or the inheritance of the bridge builders. In addition, site plans and maps showing the geographical distribution of the thirty-two the interlocked timber-arched bridges are presented in the introduction of the book, and each bridge is briefly introduced in a short text supplemented by a group of photos.

艺以及专用杉木桥林等因素，都为此提供了非常齐备的保障，这些也是其能够被列入非物质文化遗产名录的充要条件。

本测绘图集纳入的寿宁与屏南贯木拱廊桥共32座，从宋代延续至今，包括严格按照上述非物质文化遗产要素的古法于近现代建造之桥。以两地单拱跨度自大到小者为标准排序，主要包括桥面层平面图、桥体拱架系统仰视与俯视图、廊屋梁架仰视与俯视图，非对称的2个立面图、2个横剖面图、一个纵剖面图、神龛立面图与剖面图，斗栱大样图、垫苗木大样图、藻井大样图，以期尽可能多样且详实地展现各座贯木拱廊桥的基本形制，同时也要减少相同构造的信息重复（表1、表2）。鉴于画面效果，各图上未标注的构部件名称，可对照所绘制的局部剖视示意图辅助查阅；其中，有的名称在不同地区或不同桥匠传承中有所差异。此外，制作了本书涉及的32座贯木拱廊桥分布图，对每座木拱廊桥撰写了简短的中英文介绍，并选取了一组典型的点位照片作为参照。

Tab.1 The Dimensions of the interlocked timber-arched covered bridges in Shouning County

No.	Bridge name	Span length of timber arch (i.e. the distance between the two *Jiangjun* columns at span end) (m)	Corridor length of corridor (i.e. intercolumnar distance at corridor end) (m)	Corridor width (i.e. distance between two edges of surface floor) (m)
1	Luanfeng Bridge	37.08	44.66	5.16
2	Yangxitou Bridge	36.36	47.37	5.29
3	Yangmeizhou Bridge	33.80	39.91	4.93
4	Changlaixi Bridge	33.42	37.03	5.20
5	Zhangkeng Bridge	32.92	37.20	5.26
6	Fushou Bridge	32.45	38.92	5.33
7	Dabao Bridge	32.37	42.35	5.49
8	Hongjun Bridge	31.45	38.68	5.41
9	Dengyun Bridge	29.04	33.65	4.50
10	Xiangong Bridge	23.57	29.18	5.31
11	Shengping Bridge	22.59	22.59	6.08
12	Liren Bridge	20.02	24.59	5.09
13	Feiyun Bridge	17.91	26.79	5.42
14	Huilan Bridge	16.89	23.58	5.13
15	Youxishang Bridge	16.22	20.90	4.49
16	Xiaodongshang Bridge	15.81	19.37	5.11
17	Xi'nan Bridge	15.80	23.33	5.23
18	Dan Bridge	15.72	17.92	4.40
19	Shouchun Bridge	12.36	19.72	5.08

Note: The total lengths of the covered timber-arched bridges, including the lengths of the bridge approaches and the lengths of the steps, cannot be accurately measured, because of the environment changes on the both sides of the bridges. There are not the total lengths in the table.

Tab.2 The Dimensions of the interlocked timber-arched covered bridges in Pingnan County

No.	Bridge name	Span length of timber arch (i.e. the distance between the two *Jiangjun* columns at span end) (m)	Corridor length (i.e. intercolumnar distance at corridor end) (m)	Corridor width (i.e. distance between two edges of surface floor) (m)
1	Baixiang Bridge	34.64	36.14	4.92
2	Jinzao Bridge	31.84	38.71	5.21
3	Qiansheng Bridge	North: 26.38; South: 25.56	59.88	5.25
4	Guangfu Bridge	25.22	29.35	5.00
5	Huifeng Bridge	23.37	30.01	5.07

寿宁贯木拱廊桥尺寸一览表　　表1

序号	桥名	桥体拱跨轴距（两侧桥台将军柱轴距）（米）	廊屋长度（面阔方向）边柱轴距（米）	桥面宽度（进深方向桥面板边缘距）（米）
1	鸾峰桥	37.08	44.46	5.16
2	杨溪头桥	36.36	47.37	5.29
3	杨梅州桥	33.80	39.91	4.93
4	长濑溪桥	33.42	37.03	5.20
5	张坑桥	32.92	37.20	5.26
6	福寿桥	32.45	38.92	5.33
7	大宝桥	32.37	42.35	5.49
8	红军桥	31.45	38.68	5.41
9	登云桥	29.04	33.65	4.50
10	仙宫桥	23.57	29.18	5.31
11	升平桥	22.59	22.59	6.08
12	里仁桥	20.02	24.59	5.09
13	飞云桥	17.91	26.79	5.42
14	回澜桥	16.89	23.58	5.13
15	尤溪上桥	16.22	20.90	4.49
16	小东上桥	15.81	19.37	5.11
17	溪南桥	15.80	23.33	5.23
18	单桥	15.72	17.92	4.40
19	寿春桥	12.36	19.72	5.08

注：因多数贯木拱廊桥桥头环境有变化，包含引桥和台阶长度的廊桥总长度无法准确测算，本表未予统计。

No.	Bridge name	Span length of timber arch (i.e. the distance between the two *Jiangjun* columns at span end) (m)	Corridor length (i.e. intercolumnar distance at corridor end) (m)	Corridor width (i.e. distance between two edges of surface floor) (m)
6	Longjin Bridge	22.11	32.20	5.07
7	Qingyan Bridge	20.79	24.25	5.21
8	Longjing Bridge	19.92	24.73	5.23
9	Guangli Bridge	19.11	28.29	4.75
10	Xili Bridge	18.88	35.45	4.52
11	Zhangkou Bridge	17.98	23.06	3.97
12	Wan'an Bridge	(Measured from west to east) 14.09、13.55、14.25、13.46、12.76、9.90	96.32	4.70
13	Yingfeng Bridge	13.41	26.52	4.42

Note: The total lengths of the covered timber-arched bridges, including the lengths of the bridge approaches and the lengths of the steps, cannot be accurately measured, because of the environment changes on the both sides of the bridges. There are not the total lengths in the table.

The drawings are the achievement of the surveying and mapping conducted by an energetic research team between 2005-2008 and 2011-2015. Team members were enthusiastic about the interlocked timber-arched covered bridges and dedicated their time to the measurement and drawing of these landmarks. Included here is the information gathered through their restoration projects and special field investigations. The work has been supported both conceptually and financially by local governments, craftsmen and village communities. In the progress of Publishing, it is also given backing by "Study on Cultural Value of Traditional Design and Practices for the Construction of Chinese Interlocked Timber-Arched Covered Bridges", one of the Art Projects of the National Social Science Fund of China.The successful documentation of these endangered, world famous bridges of outstanding value that are unique to China was a goal shared by all parties involved, and adheres to the international standards of cultural heritage survey and mapping. We hope that the data collected will facilitate future research, protection, application, inheritance and communication of China's interlocked timber-arched covered bridges.

We apologize for any (occasionally) incorrect or incomplete information resulting from the precarious location of most interlocked timber-arched covered bridges, situated on the steep slopes of a gully or somewhere on a remote mountainside. Nevertheless, despite these challenges, we finished the work using conventional methods in conjunction with new, creative means. Your feedback on the work presented in book is greatly appreciated, and we look forward to hearing from you to improve this publication and our future work.

该套图纸是由一个长期热衷于贯木拱廊桥研究与保护的团队，于2005—2008年、2011—2015年期间，分多次结合专项调查研究和保护修缮工程开展的测绘与校核工作，并得到了当地有关部门、造桥工匠以及社区民众等的大力支持甚至资助，在本次整理出版过程中，还受到了『国家社科基金艺术学一般项目：贯木拱廊桥传统营造的文化价值研究』课题的支持。能够将这些闻名世界、中国独有、价值突出、易于损毁的贯木拱廊桥，按照文化遗产勘测的深度标准记录成图，是以上所有参与人的真诚心愿和倾力而为，我们希望该实测性资料能够为从事中国贯木拱廊桥的研究、保护、利用、传承、交流等方面的各界所用。

还请读者理解的是，由于绝大多数贯木拱廊桥位于沟壑陡坎之上，更有处于偏远山区之中者，尽最大可能开展工作，因而未必做到图文尺寸的绝对准确无误，恳请不吝赐教反馈，以助于我们择机完善再一并致谢。

我们克服各种困难，利用许多巧妙方法，

屏南贯木拱廊桥尺寸一览表　　表2

序号	桥名	桥体拱跨轴距（两侧桥台将军柱轴距）（米）	廊屋长度（面阔方向）边柱轴距（米）	桥面宽度（进深方向桥面板边缘距）（米）
1	百祥桥	34.64	36.14	4.92
2	金造桥	31.84	38.71	5.21
3	千乘桥	北跨：26.38；南跨：25.56	59.88	5.25
4	广福桥	25.22	29.35	5.00
5	惠风桥	23.37	30.01	4.85
6	龙津桥	22.11	32.20	5.07
7	清晏桥	20.79	24.25	5.21
8	龙井桥	19.92	24.73	5.23
9	广利桥	19.11	28.29	4.75
10	溪里桥	18.88	35.45	4.52
11	樟口桥	17.89	23.06	3.97
12	万安桥	自西向东各跨：14.09、13.55、14.25、13.46、12.76、9.90	96.32	4.70
13	迎风桥	13.41	26.52	4.42

注：因多数贯木拱廊桥桥头环境有变化，包含引桥和台阶长度的廊桥总长度无法准确测算，本表未予统计。

图版

Figure

寿宁贯木拱廊桥

The Interlocked
Timber-Arched
Covered Bridges in
Shouning County

鸾峰桥

Luanfeng Bridge

Luanfeng Bridge, also known as Xiadang Bridge, was first built in the Ming dynasty and rebuilt in 1800, the fifth year of the Jiaqing period of the Qing Dynasty. Located at the end of Xiuzhu Stream next to Xiadang village in Xiadang township, the bridge crosses north to south across the stream in a single span. It is generally acknowledged as the largest known the interlocked timber-arched covered bridge with single span. Wooden boards are mounted above the arched-system to form a deck, and a shrine dedicated to Guanyin is installed in the middle of the covered corridor. Upstream from the bridge is a dam, over which the water of the stream flows making a curtain of water. On the southern hillside of the bridge stands Wenchang Pavilion opposite of Luanfeng Bridge.

鸾峰桥，又称『下党桥』，始建于明代，现桥建于清代嘉庆五年（1800年），位于下党乡下党村水尾，单孔跨越修竹溪，南北走向，是现有已知贯木拱廊桥中单孔拱跨距离最大的一座。桥体拱架系统上铺木板为桥面，廊屋中部设神龛，祀观音。桥的上游不远处被修建拦水坝，溪水越坝形成水帘，桥南山冈上的文昌阁与其相望。

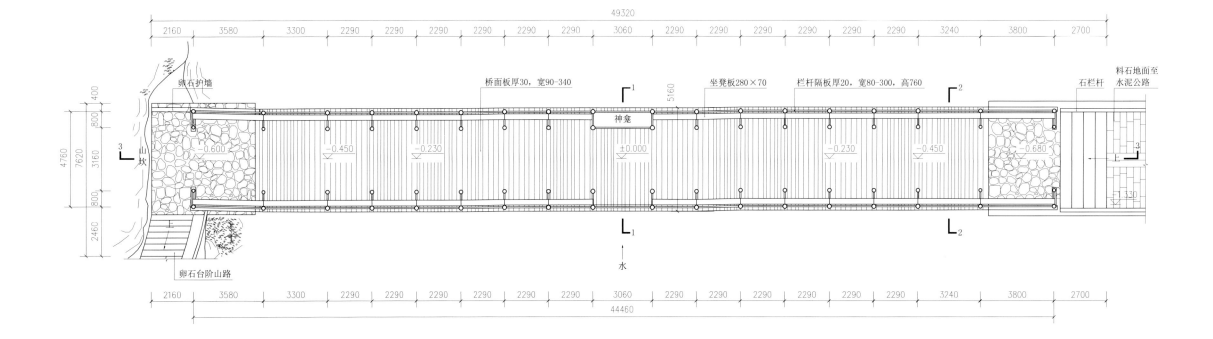

鸾峰桥平面图
Surface floor plan of Luanfeng Bridge

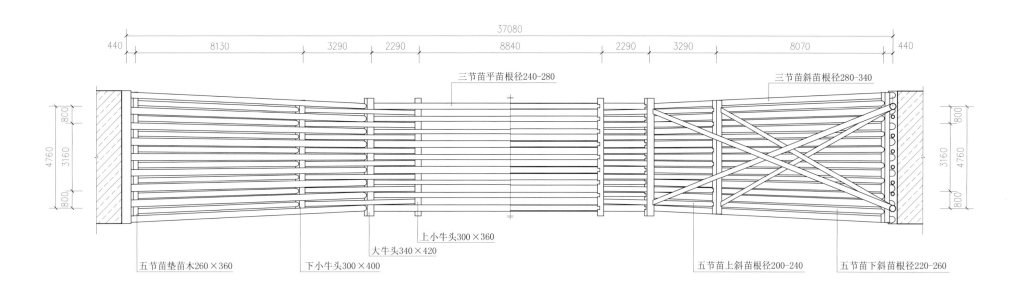

鸾峰桥桥梁拱骨系统仰视（左）与俯视（右）图
Plan of timber arch system of Luanfeng Bridge as seen from below (left) and above (right)

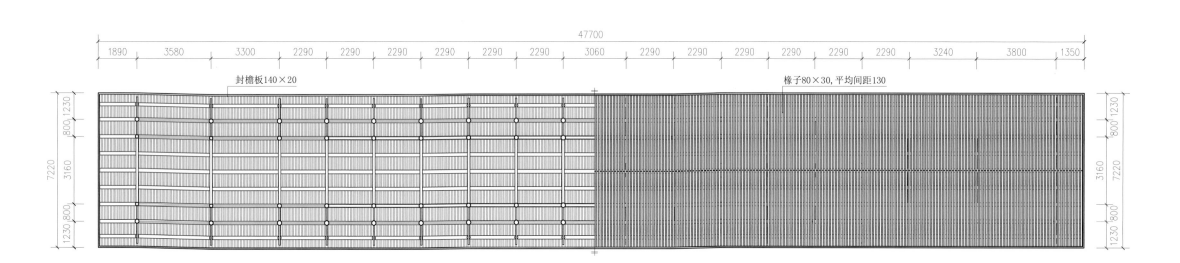

鸾峰桥廊屋梁架仰视（左）与俯视（右）图
Plan of corridor beam framework of Luanfeng Bridge as seen from below (left) and above (right)

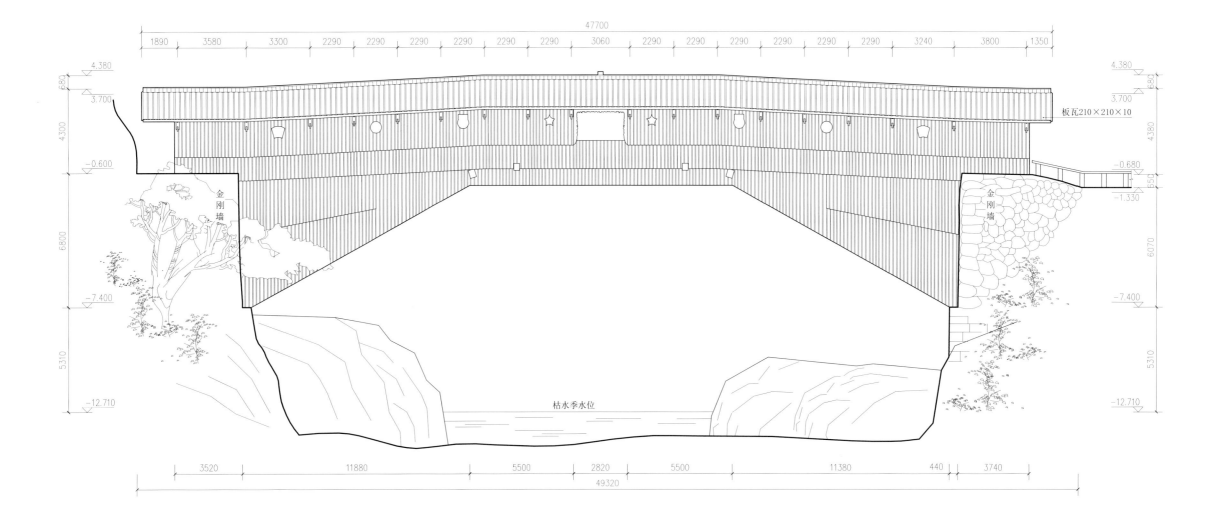

鸾峰桥西立面图
West elevation of Luanfeng Bridge

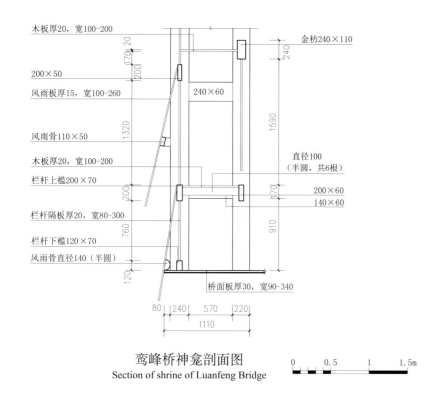

鸾峰桥神龛剖面图
Section of shrine of Luanfeng Bridge

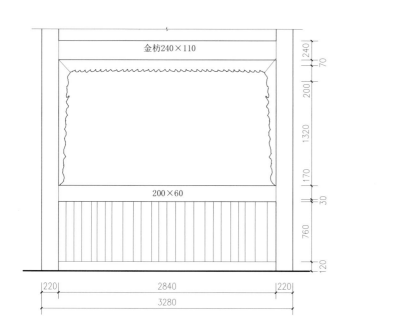

鸾峰桥神龛立面图
Elevation of shrine of Luanfeng Bridge

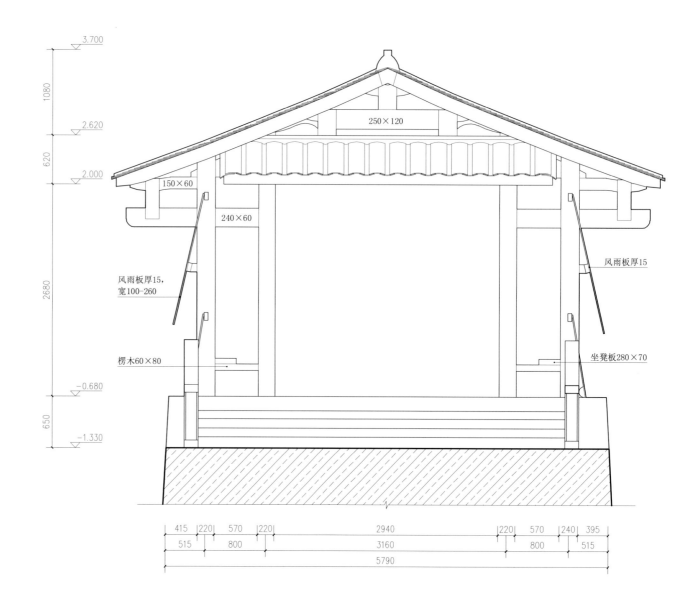

鸾峰桥南立面图
South elevation of Luanfeng Bridge

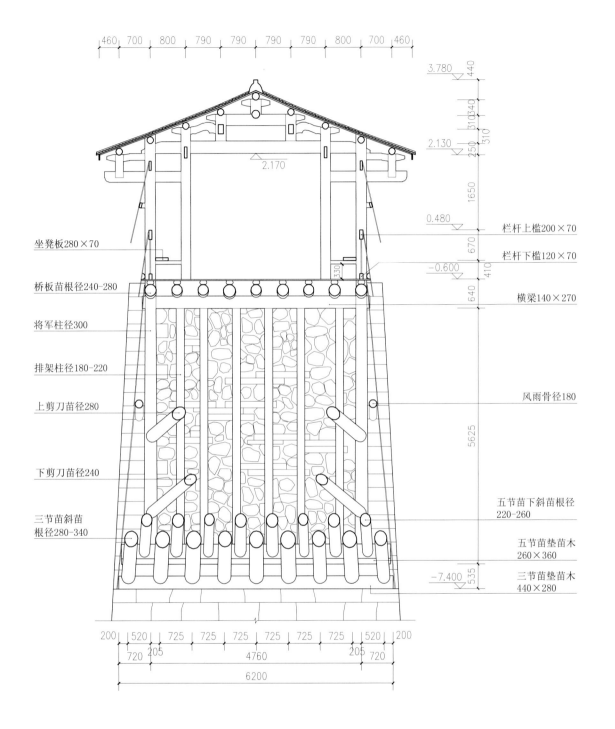

鸾峰桥 2-2 剖面图
Section 2-2 of Luanfeng Bridge

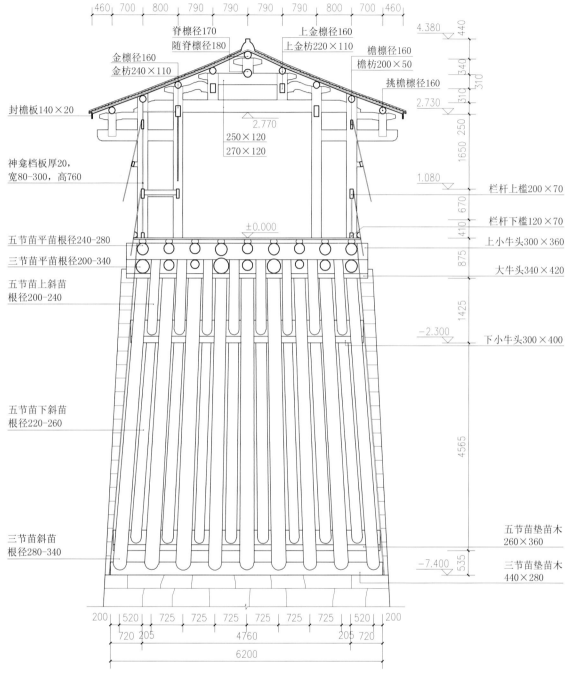

鸾峰桥 1-1 剖面图
Section 1-1 of Luanfeng Bridge

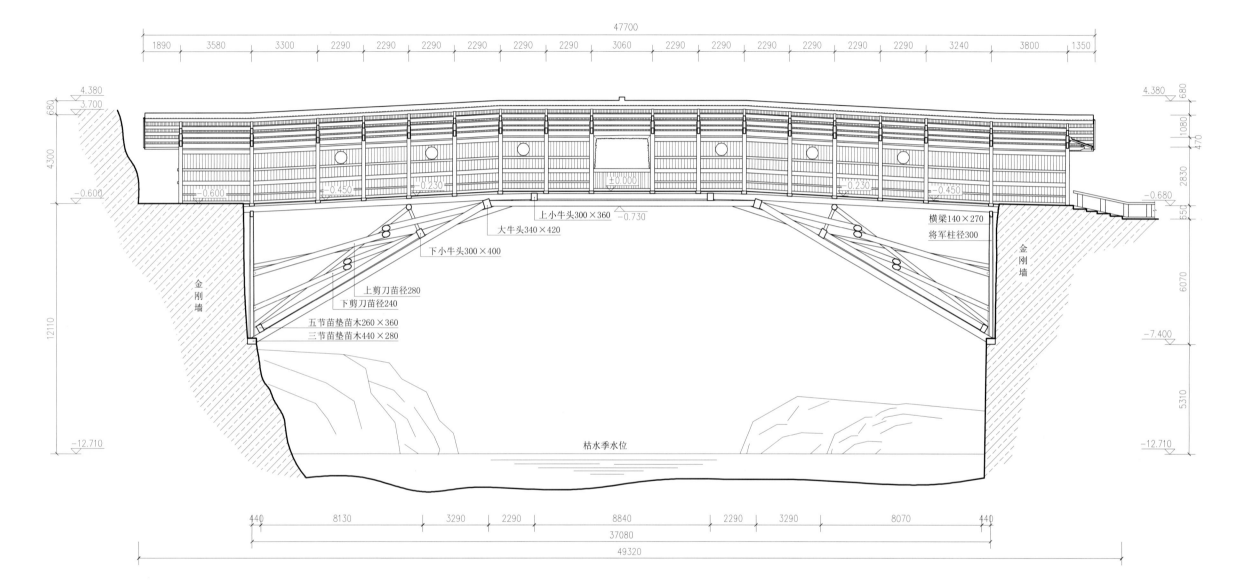

鸾峰桥 3-3 剖面图
Section 3-3 of Luanfeng Bridge

杨溪头桥

Yangxitou Bridge

Yangxitou Bridge is located in Yangxitou village of Xiadang township. According to hearsay, the first bridge on this site was built in the Qing Dynasty but later destroyed. In 1967, the current bridge was built. The plaques containing quotations of Chairman Mao were installed at the ceiling beam and the slogans were inscribed on the columns in the covered corridor, which dated to the "Cultural Revolution". The bridge extends from east to west across Xiuzhu Stream in a single span. Wooden boards are mounted to form a deck, and a shrine is installed in the middle of the corridor to worship Guanyin.

杨溪头桥，位于下党乡杨溪头村，据说此处原有一座建于清代的桥，后被毁，现桥建于1967年。廊屋梁上仍挂有『毛主席语录』牌，梁柱上残留『文革』时书写的标语口号，具有很强的时代性。该桥单孔跨越修竹溪，东西走向。桥体拱架系统上铺木板为桥面，廊屋中部设神龛，祀观音。

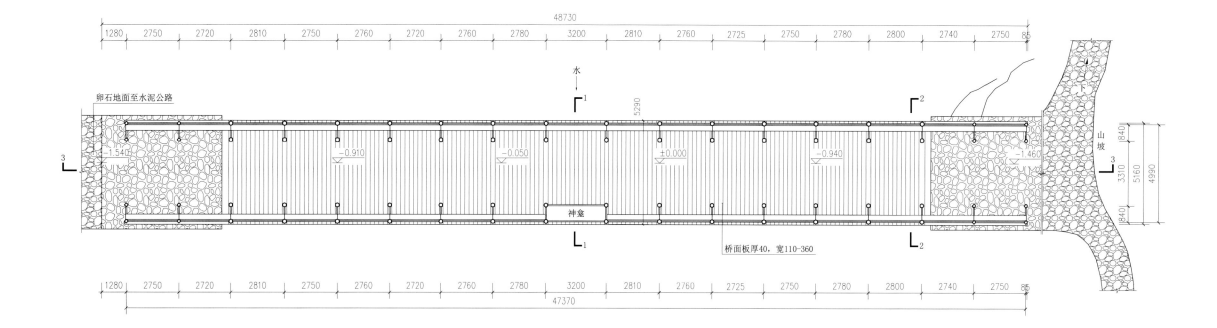

杨溪头桥平面图
Surface floor plan of Yangxitou Bridge

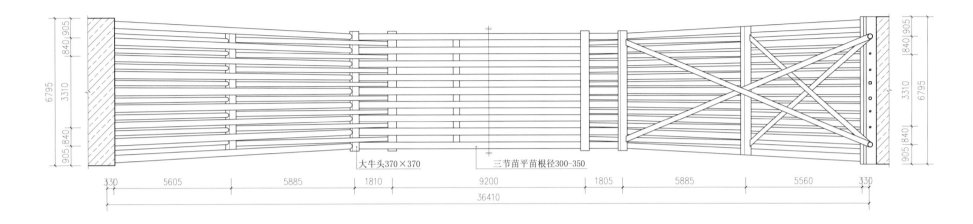

杨溪头桥桥梁拱骨系统仰视（左）与俯视（右）图

Plan of timber arch system of Yangxitou Bridge as seen from below (left) and above (right)

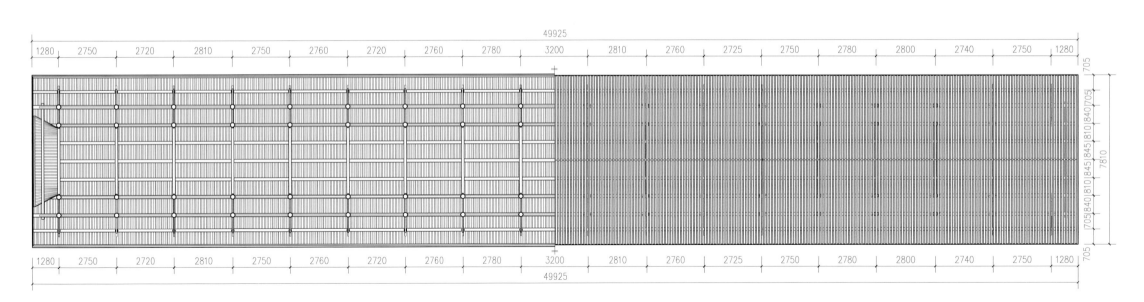

杨溪头桥廊屋梁架仰视（左）与俯视（右）图

Plan of corridor beam framework of Yangxitou Bridge as seen from below (left) and above (right)

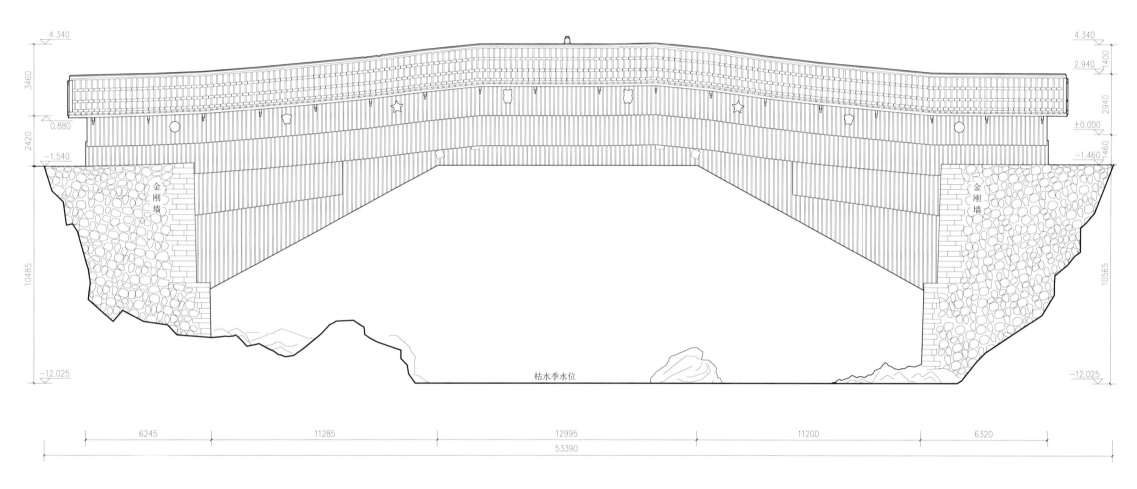

杨溪头桥南立面图
South elevation of Yangxitou Bridge

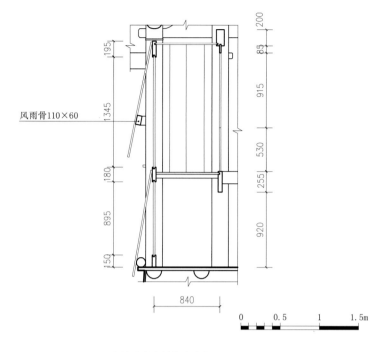

杨溪头桥神龛剖面图
Section of shrine of Yangxitou Bridge

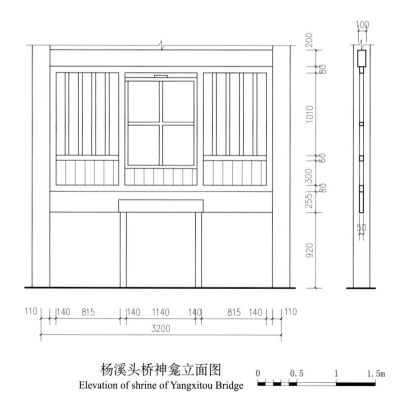

杨溪头桥神龛立面图
Elevation of shrine of Yangxitou Bridge

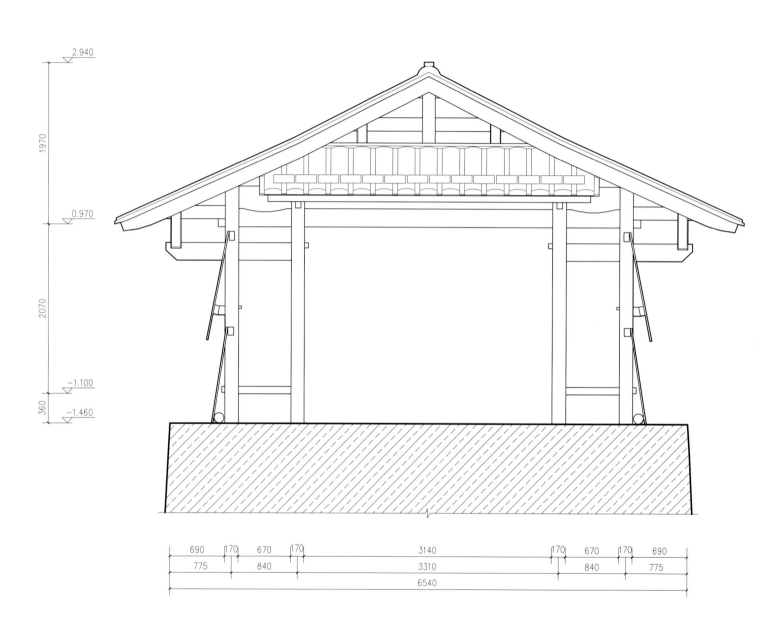

杨溪头桥东立面图
East elevation of Yangxitou Bridge

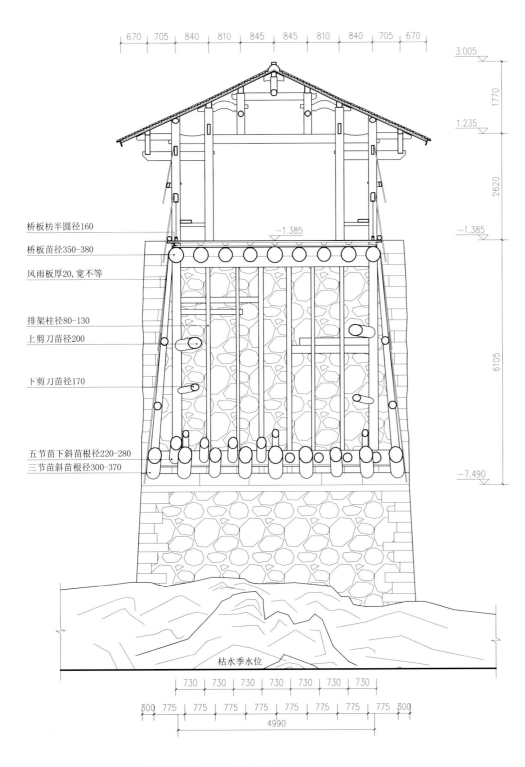

杨溪头桥 2-2 剖面图

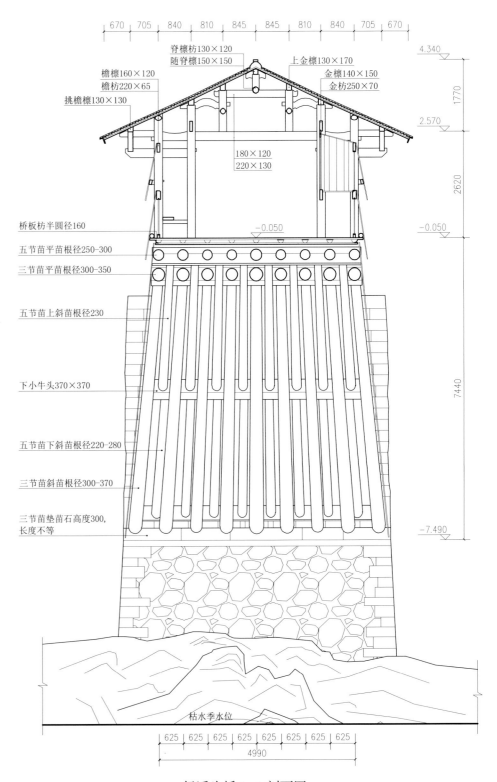

杨溪头桥 1-1 剖面图

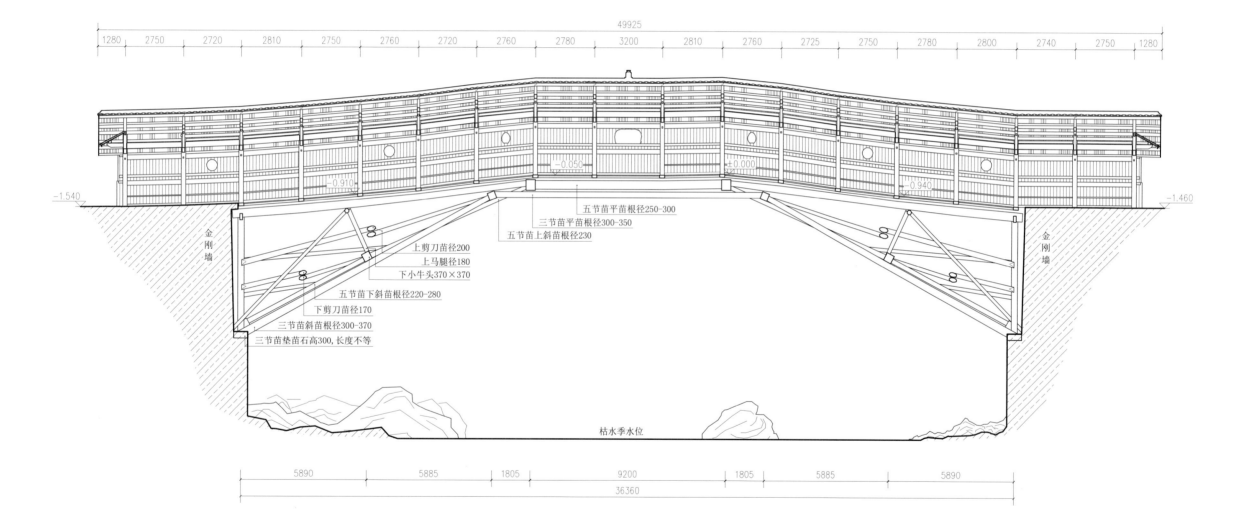

杨溪头桥 3-3 剖面图
Section 3-3 of Yangxitou Bridge

杨梅州桥

Yangmeizhou Bridge

Yangmeizhou Bridge was first built in 1791, the fifty-sixth reign year of the Qing emperor Qianlong and rebuilt in 1937, the twenty-sixth year of the Republic of China. Located about 1km from Yangmeizhou village of Kengdi township down an ancient path on the northeastern mountain, the bridge crosses east to west across Tiegeng Stream in a single span and has a wooden deck, and a shrine is located in the center of the covered corridor, which is now gone.

杨梅州桥，始建于清代乾隆五十六年（1791年），中华民国26年（1937年）重建，位于坑底乡杨梅州村东北山间古道下行约1公里处，单孔跨越铁梗溪，东西走向，桥体拱架系统上铺木板为桥面。原有神龛，现无存。

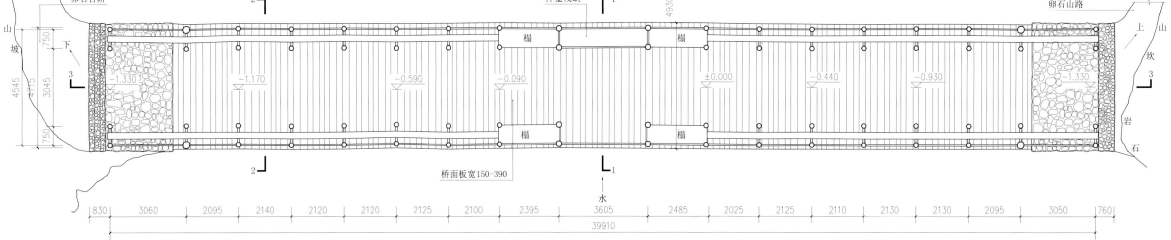

杨梅州桥平面图
Surface floor plan of Yangmeizhou Bridge

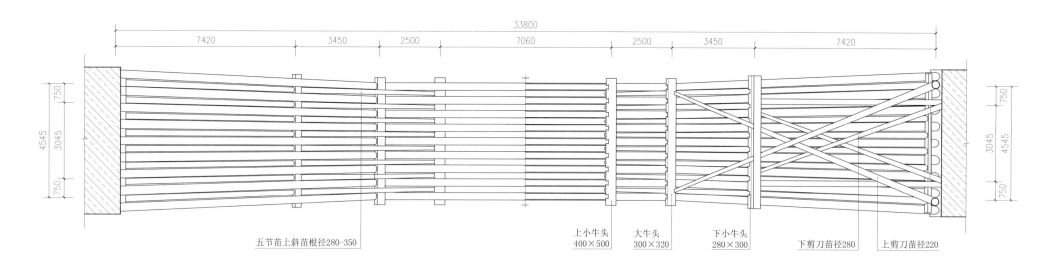

杨梅州桥桥梁拱骨系统仰视（左）与俯视（右）图

Plan of timber arch system of Yangmeizhou Bridge as seen from below (left) and above (right)

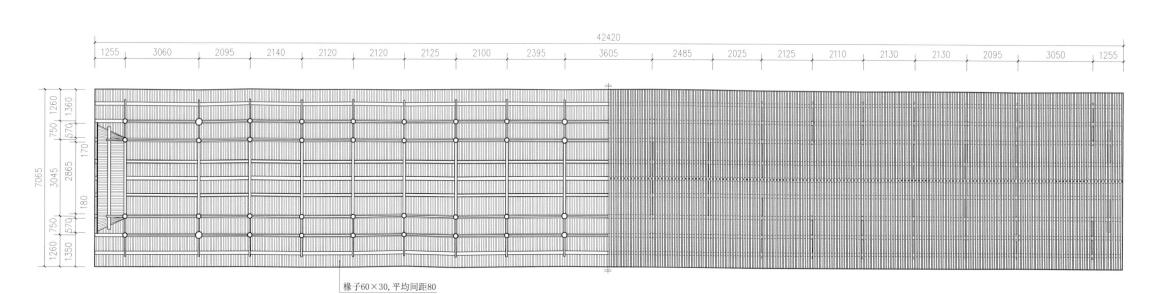

杨梅州桥廊屋梁架仰视（左）与俯视（右）图

Plan of corridor beam framework of Yangmeizhou Bridge as seen from below (left) and above (right)

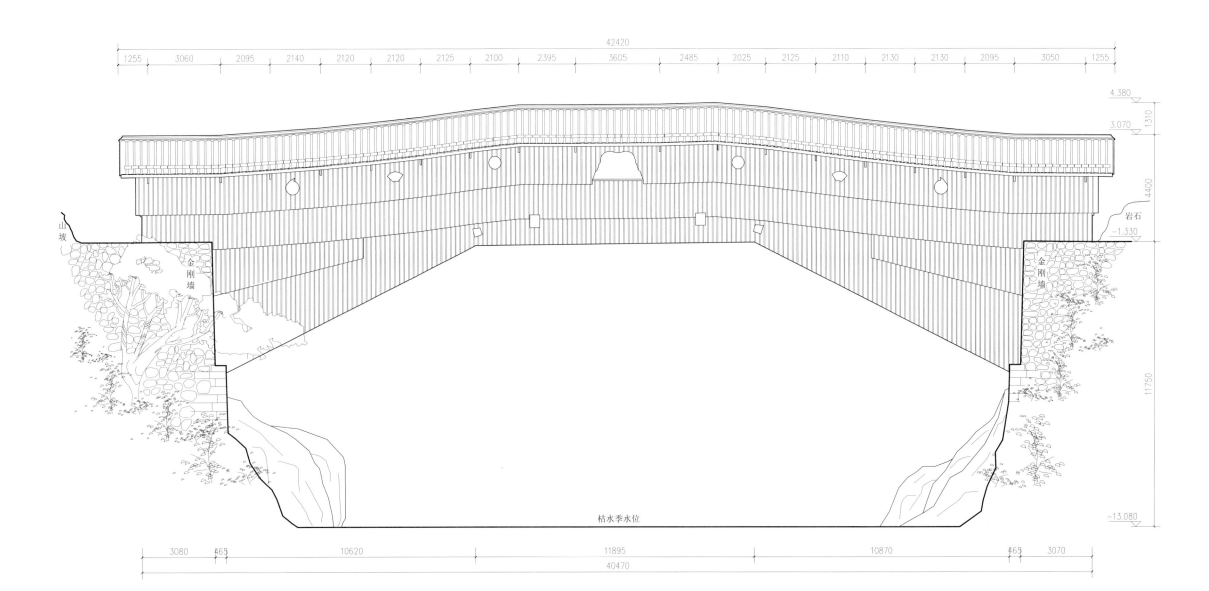

杨梅州桥北立面图
North elevation of Yangmeizhou Bridge

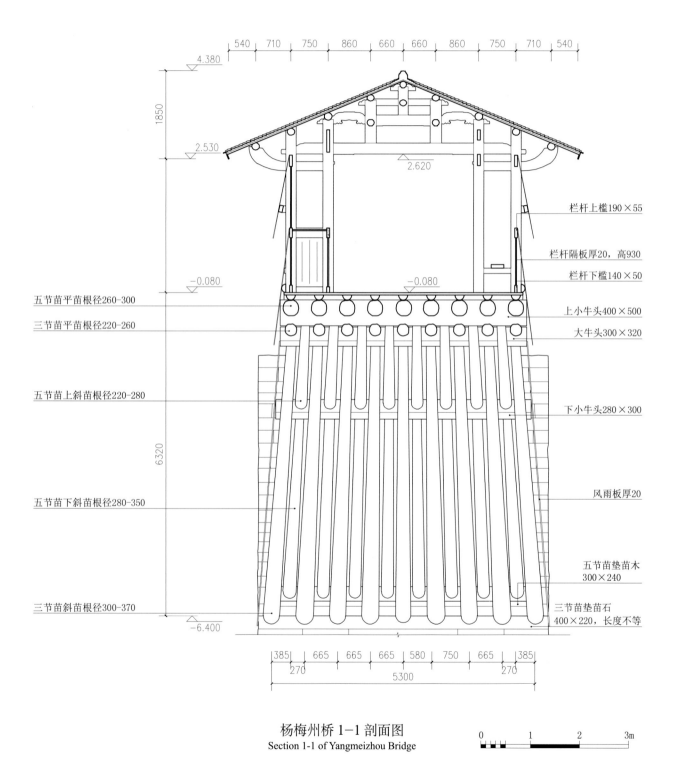

杨梅州桥 1-1 剖面图
Section 1-1 of Yangmeizhou Bridge

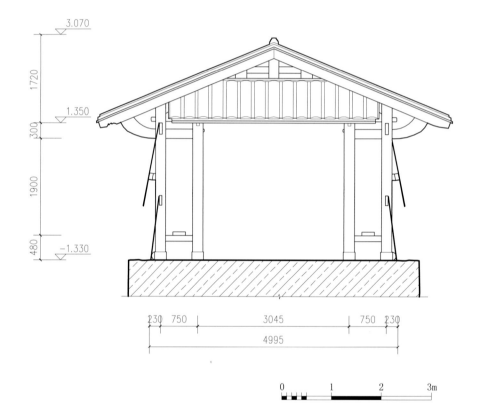

杨梅州桥西立面图
West elevation of Yangmeizhou Bridge

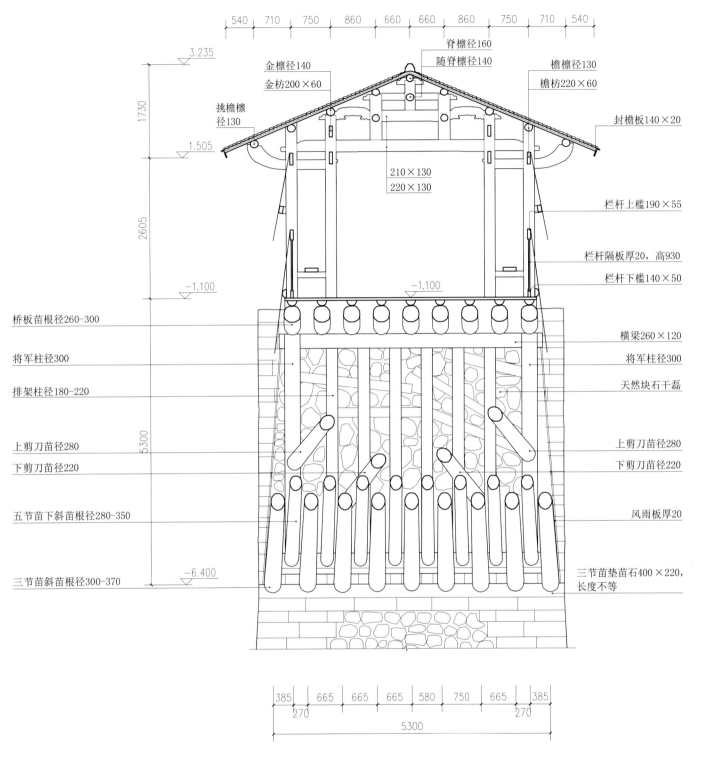

杨梅州桥 2-2 剖面图

Section 2-2 of Yangmeizhou Bridge

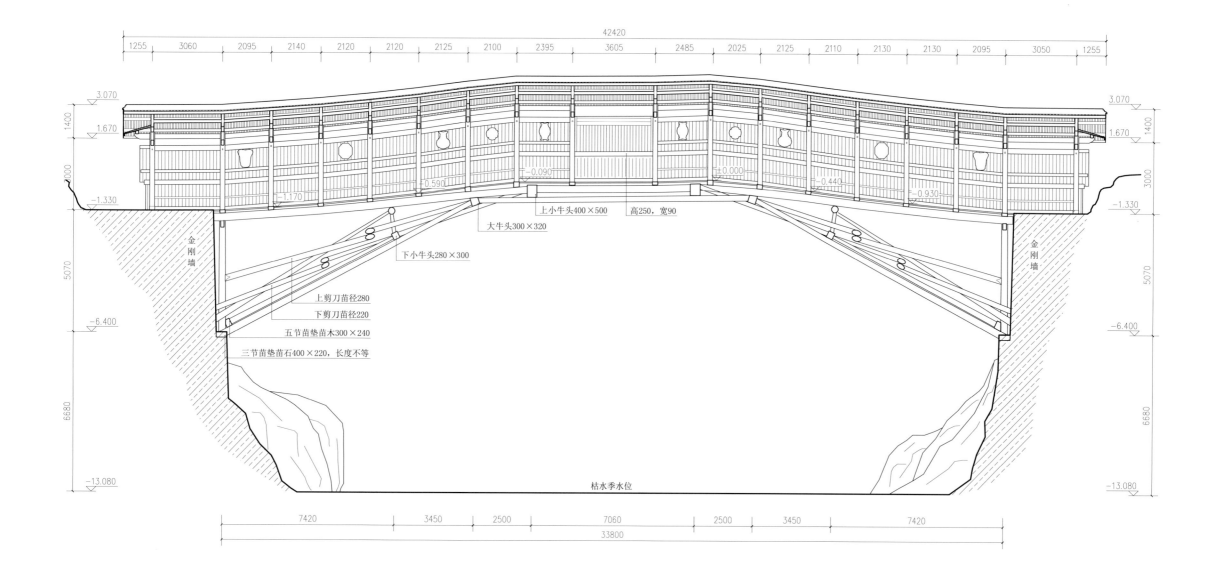

杨梅州桥 3-3 剖面图
Section 3-3 of Yangmeizhou Bridge

长濑溪桥

Changlaixi Bridge

长濑溪桥，又称"同心桥"，建于清代道光九年（1829年），原位于寿宁县芹洋乡长濑溪村，因建设牛头山水电站，被迁建于芹洋村水尾。该桥单孔跨越长濑溪，南北走向。桥体拱架系统上铺木板为桥面，廊屋中部设神龛，祀观音。

Changlaixi Bridge, also known as Tongxin Bridge, was built in 1829, the ninth year of the Daoguang reign period (in the Qing Dynasty). Originally located in Changlaixi village of Qinyang township in Shouning county, the bridge was relocated to the end of Qinyang village during the construction of Niutoushan Hydropower Station. The bridge crosses north to south across Changlai River in a single span. Wooden boards are mounted to form a deck, and a shrine is located in the center of the covered corridor to worship Guanyin.

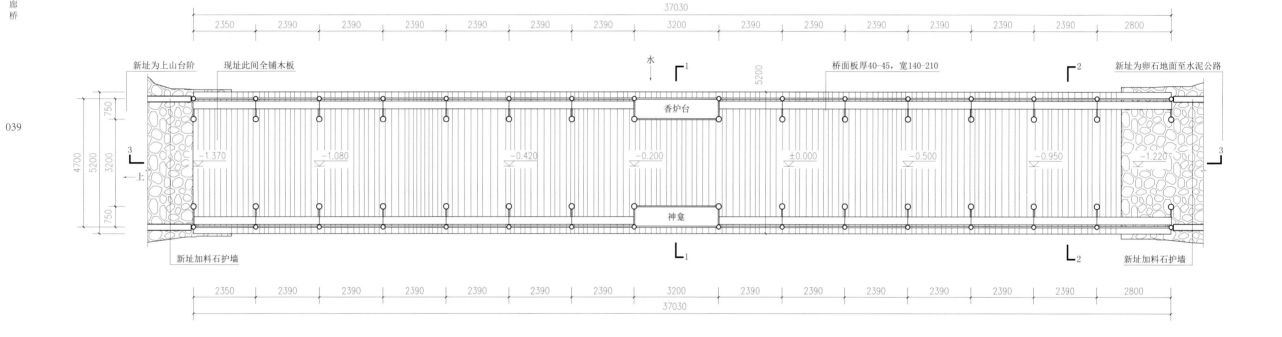

长濑溪桥平面图
Surface floor plan of Changlaixi Bridge

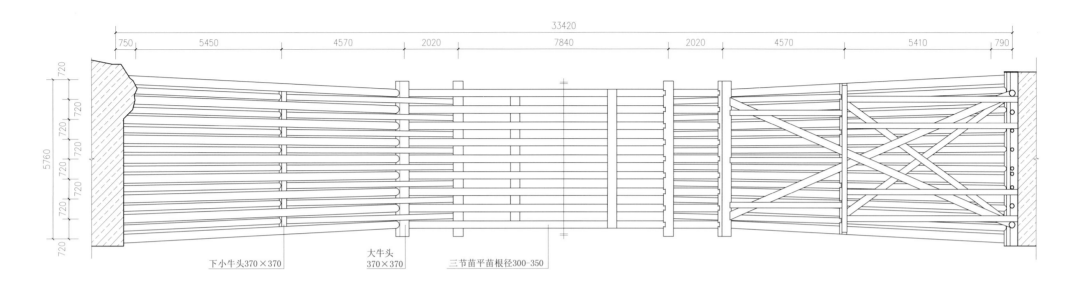

长濑溪桥桥梁拱骨系统仰视（左）与俯视（右）图

Plan of timber arch system of Changlaixi Bridge as seen from below (left) and above (right)

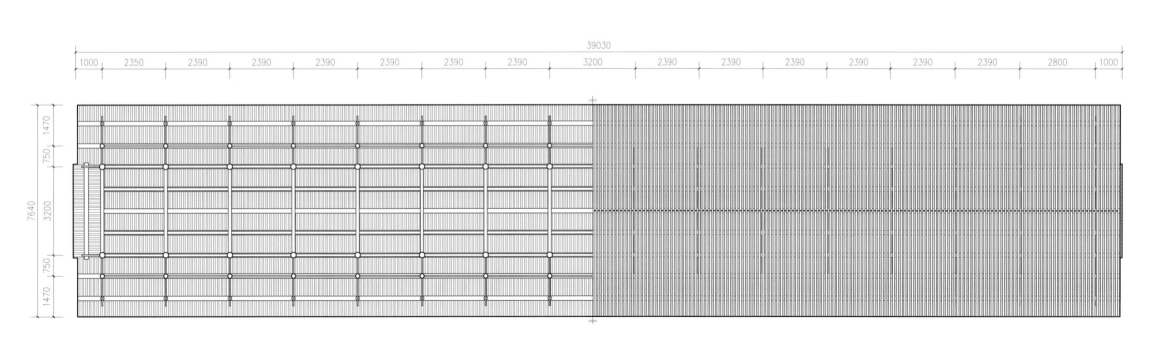

长濑溪桥廊屋梁架仰视（左）与俯视（右）图

Plan of corridor beam framework of Changlaixi Bridge as seen from below (left) and above (right)

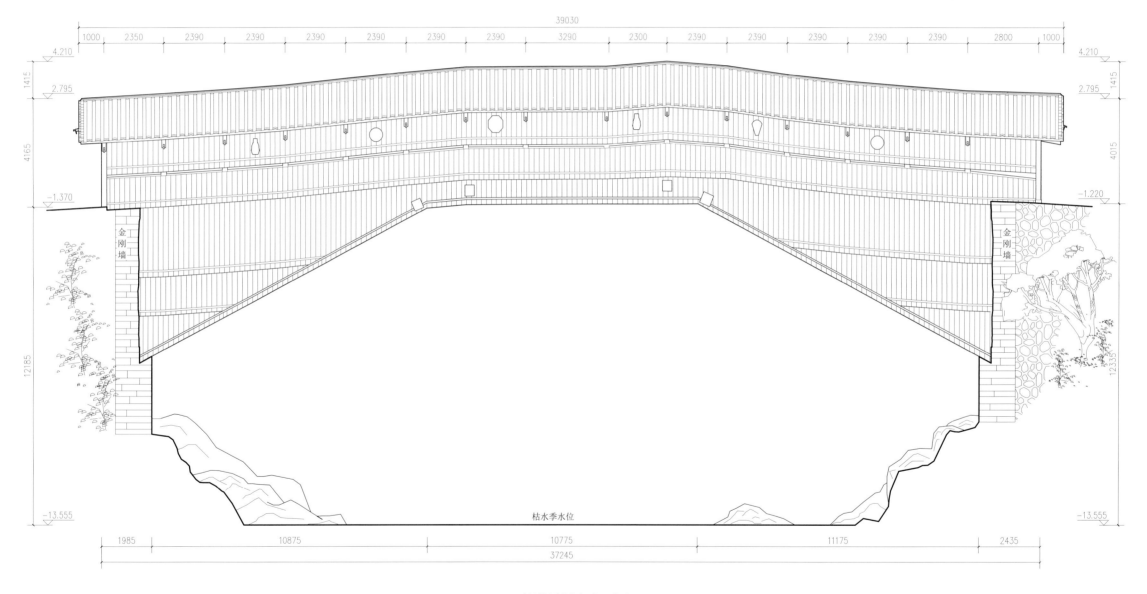

长濑溪桥东立面图
East elevation of Changlaixi Bridge

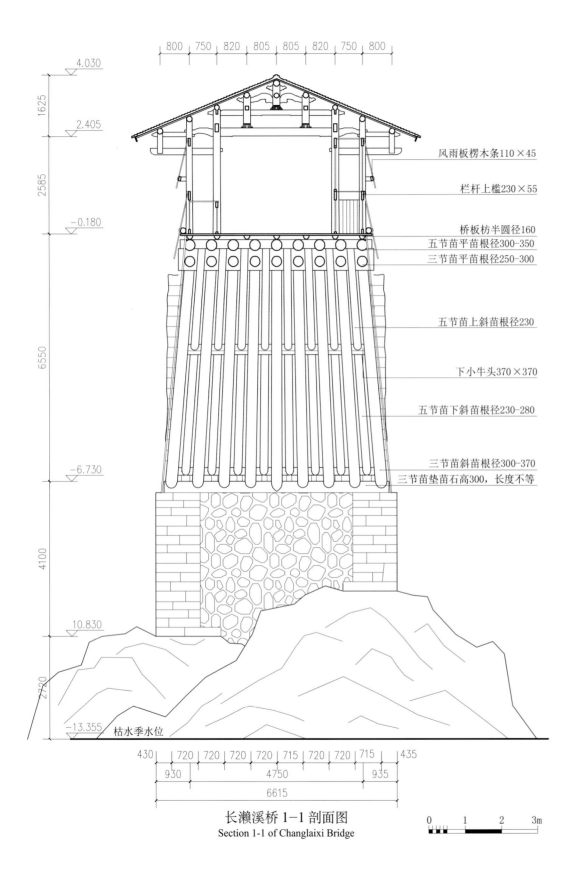

长濑溪桥 1-1 剖面图
Section 1-1 of Changlaixi Bridge

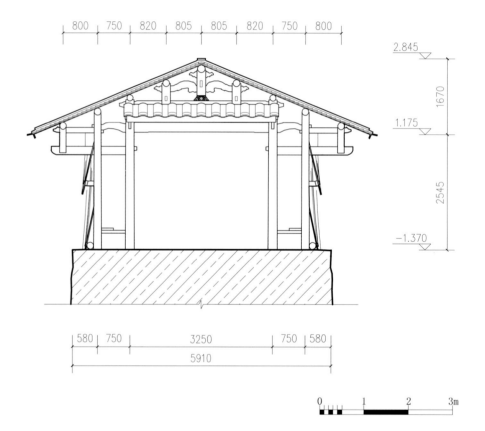

长濑溪桥南立面图
South elevation of Changlaixi Bridge

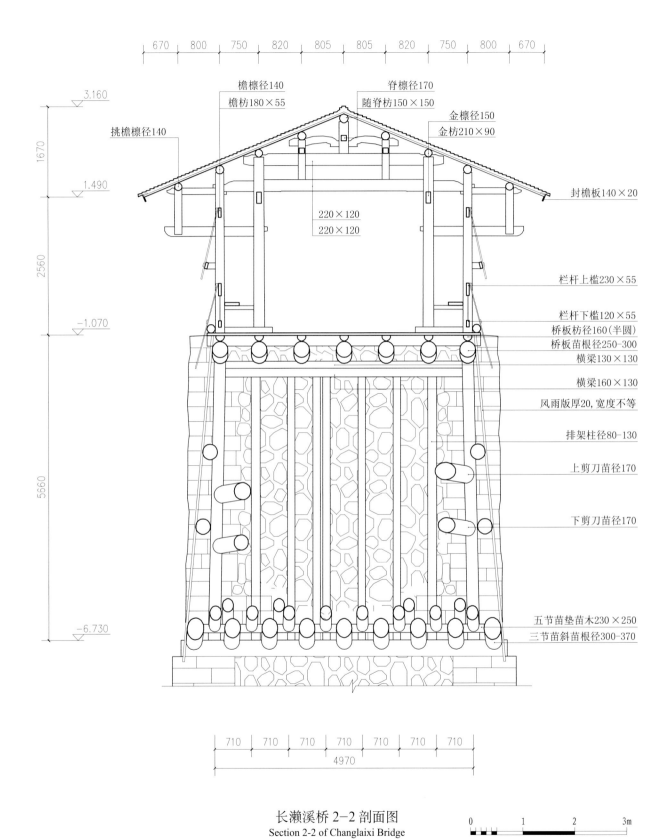

长濑溪桥 2-2 剖面图
Section 2-2 of Changlaixi Bridge

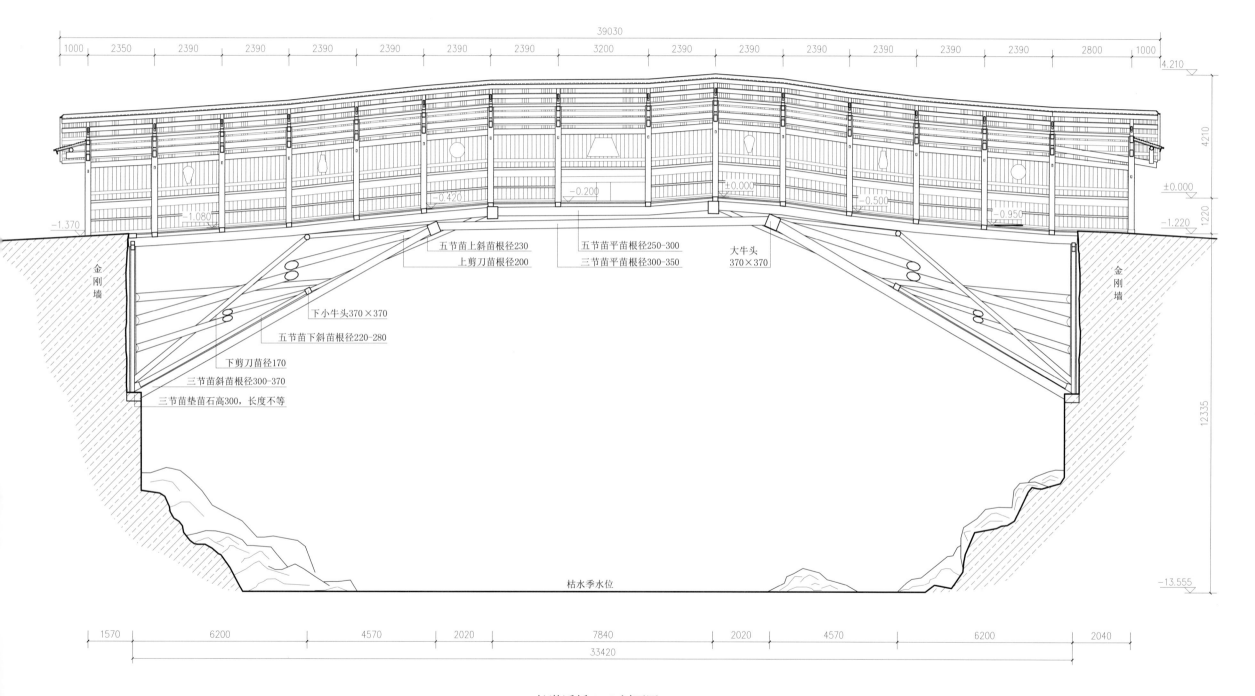

长濑溪桥 3-3 剖面图
Section 3-3 of Changlaixi Bridge

张坑桥

Zhangkeng Bridge

The time of construction of Zhangkeng Bridge is unknown, but it was rebuilt in 1828, the eighth year of the Daoguang reign period in the Qing Dynasty. Originally located in Zhangkeng village of Qinyang township, the bridge was relocated to the east of Youxi village, 500m away downstream of Liren Bridge, because of the construction of Niutoushan Hydropower Station. The bridge extends from north to south across Jiuling Stream in a single span. Wooden boards are mounted to form a deck, and a shrine is installed in the middle of the covered corridor.

张坑桥，始建年代不详，清代道光八年（1828年）重建，原位于芹洋乡张坑村，因建设牛头山水电站，被迁建于尤溪村东侧里仁桥下游约500m。该桥单孔跨越九岭溪，南北走向。桥体拱架系统上铺木板为桥面，廊屋中部设神龛。

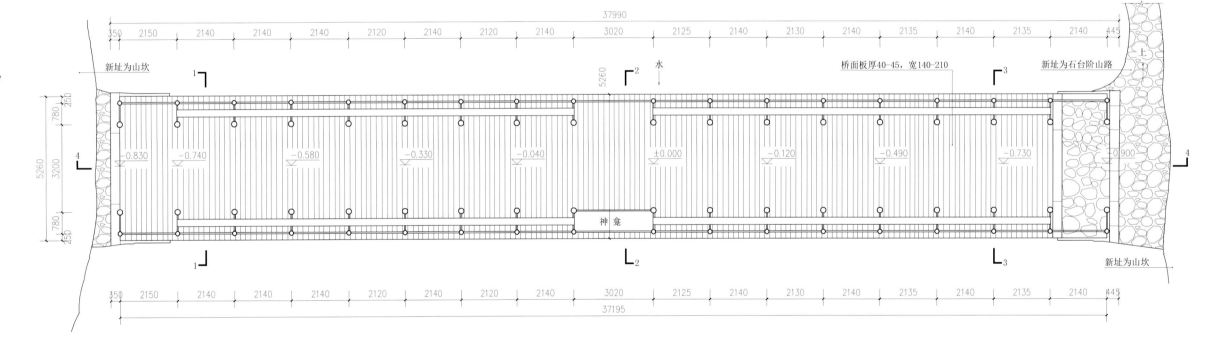

张坑桥平面图
Surface floor plan of Zhangkeng Bridge

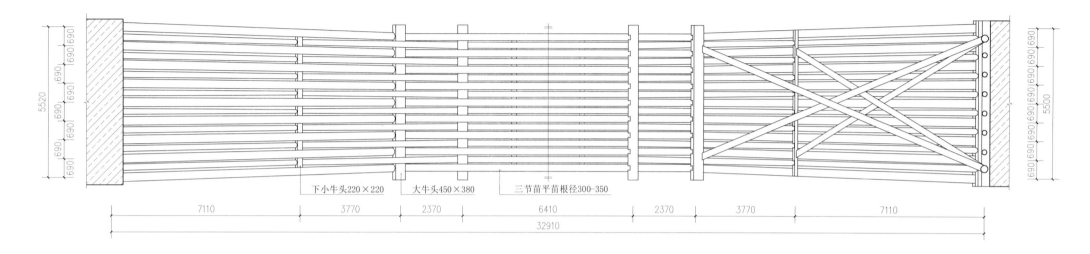

张坑桥桥梁拱骨系统仰视（左）与俯视（右）图
Plan of timber arch system of Zhangkeng Bridge as seen from below (left) and above (right)

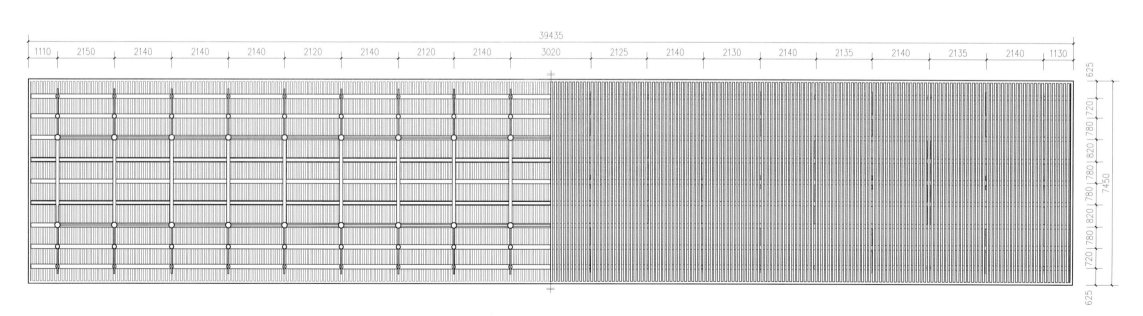

张坑桥廊屋梁架仰视（左）与俯视（右）图
Plan of corridor beam framework of Zhangkeng Bridge as seen from below (left) and above (right)

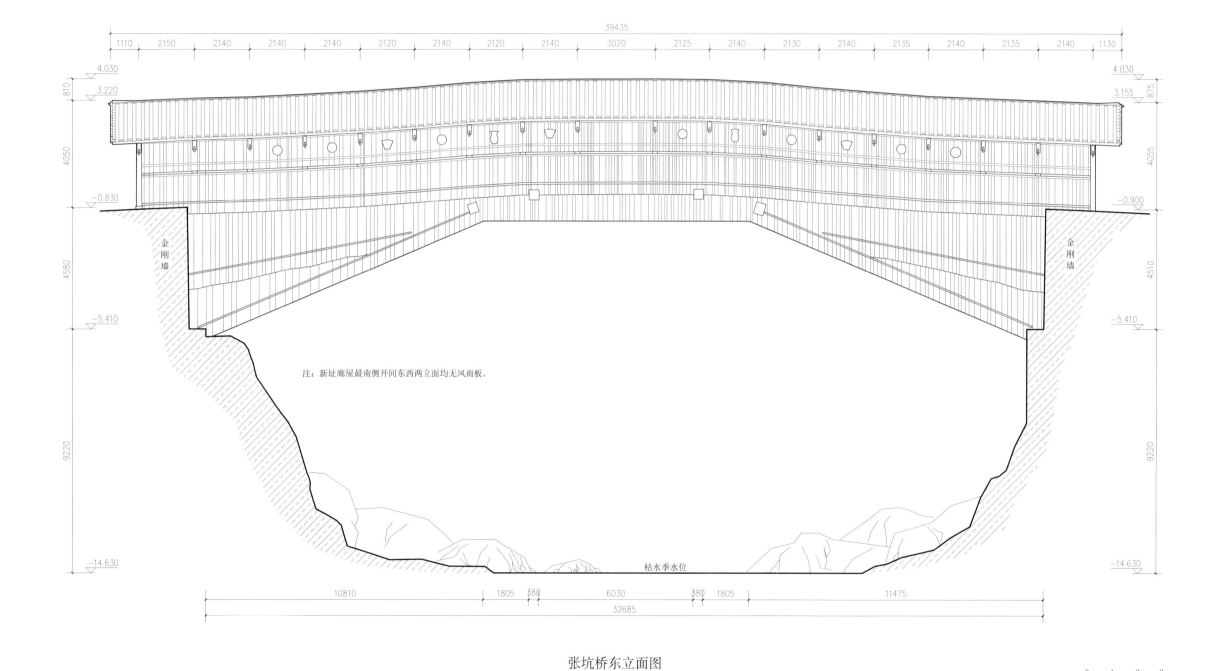

张坑桥东立面图
East elevation of Zhangkeng Bridge

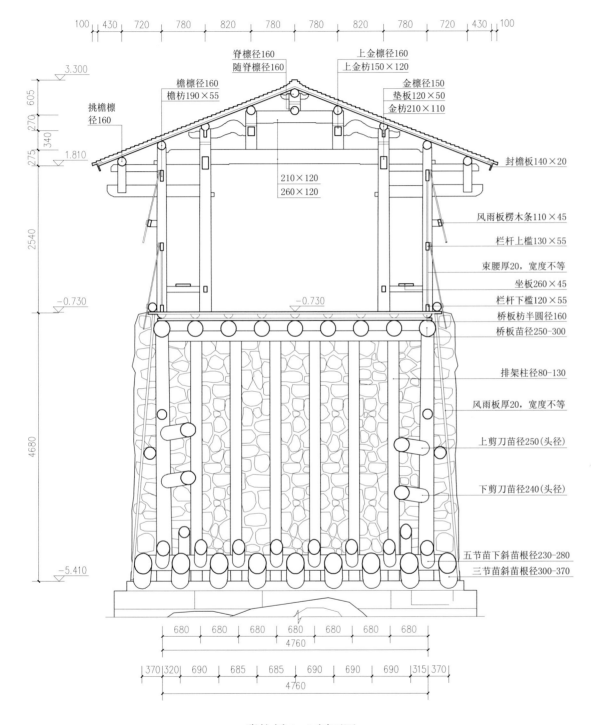

张坑桥 1-1 剖面图

Section 1-1 of Zhangkeng Bridge

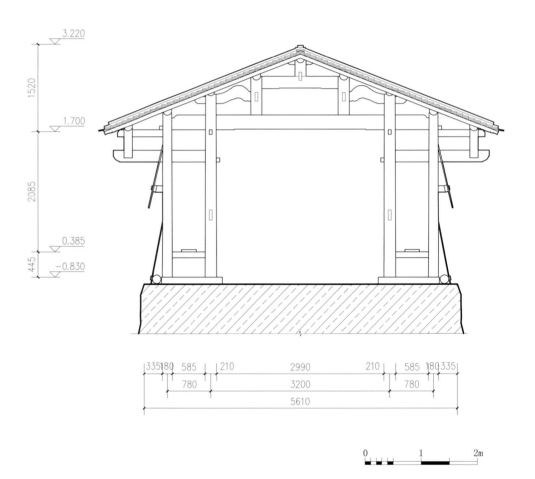

张坑桥南立面图

South elevation Zhangkeng Bridge

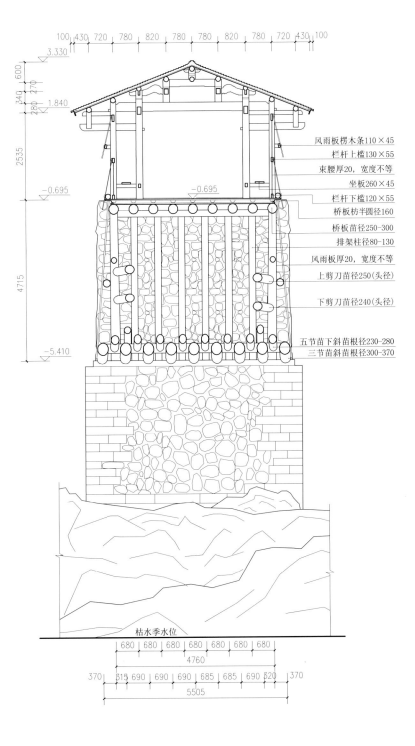

张坑桥 3-3 剖面图
Section 3-3 of Zhangkeng Bridge

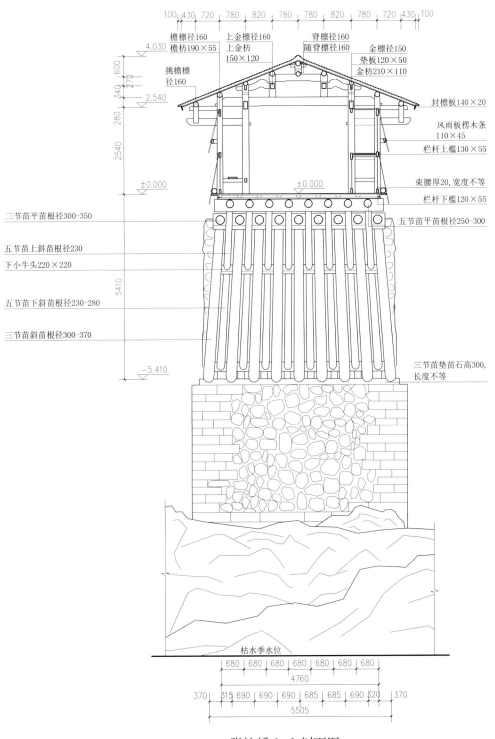

张坑桥 2-2 剖面图
Section 2-2 of Zhangkeng Bridge

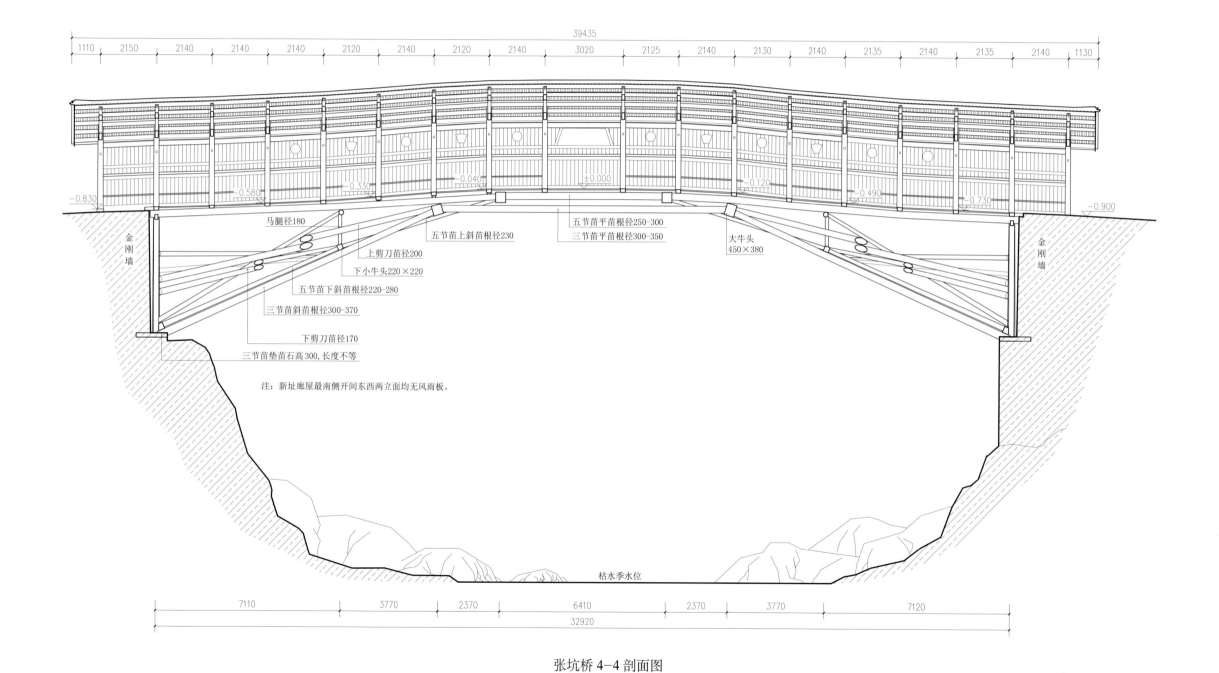

张坑桥 4-4 剖面图
Section 4-4 of Zhangkeng Bridge

福寿桥

Fushou Bridge

Fushou Bridge, also known as Batouxi Bridge, was built in 1814, the nineteenth year of the Jiaqing reign period of the Qing Dynasty. Located in Xixi township of Xixi district, Fushou Bridge spans north to south across Xixi Stream in a single span. Wooden boards are mounted to form a deck, and a shrine is installed in the middle of the covered corridor in honor of the Buddhist bodhisattva Avalokiteśvara (Guanyin) and deities of Chinese popular religion— Zhenwudi (Emperor Zhenwu; True Warrior also known as Xuanwu, Xuandi) and Linshui Furen (Lady Linshui or Waterside Dame). To the north of the bridge stands Zuanxian Pavilion dedicated to local gods.

福寿桥，又称「坝头溪桥」，建于清代嘉庆十九年（1814年），位于犀溪乡犀溪村，单孔跨越犀溪，南北走向。桥体拱架系统上铺木板为桥面，廊屋中部设神龛，祀观音、真武帝以及临水夫人。桥北有一座缵先亭，内祀神灵。

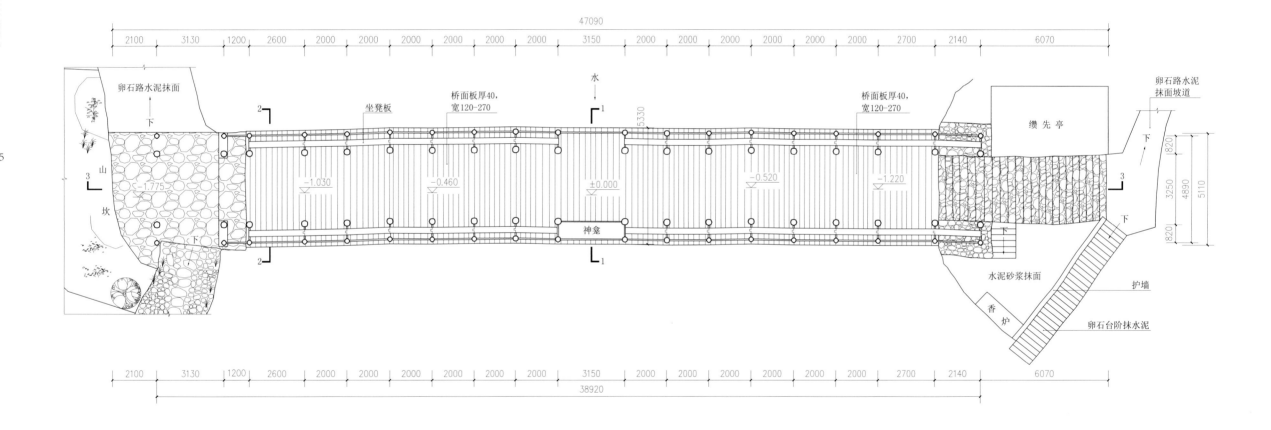

福寿桥平面图
Surface floor plan of Fushou Bridge

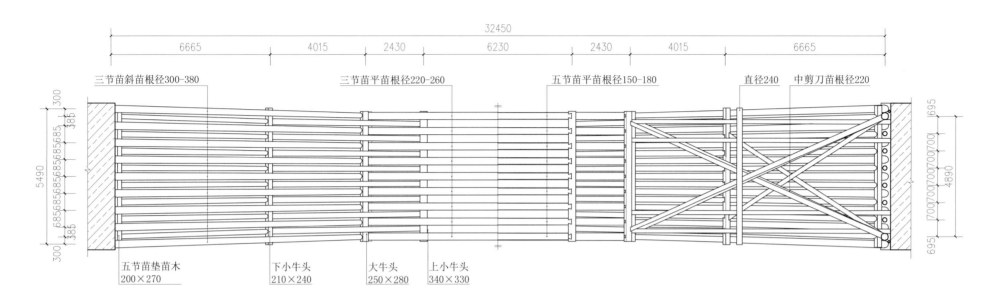

福寿桥桥梁拱骨系统仰视（左）与俯视（右）图

Plan of timber arch system of Fushou Bridge as seen from below (left) and above (right)

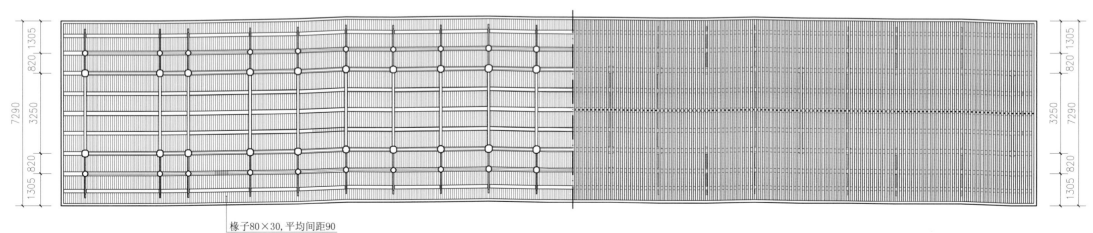

福寿桥廊屋梁架仰视（左）与俯视（右）图

Plan of corridor beam framework of Fushou Bridge as seen from below (left) and above (right)

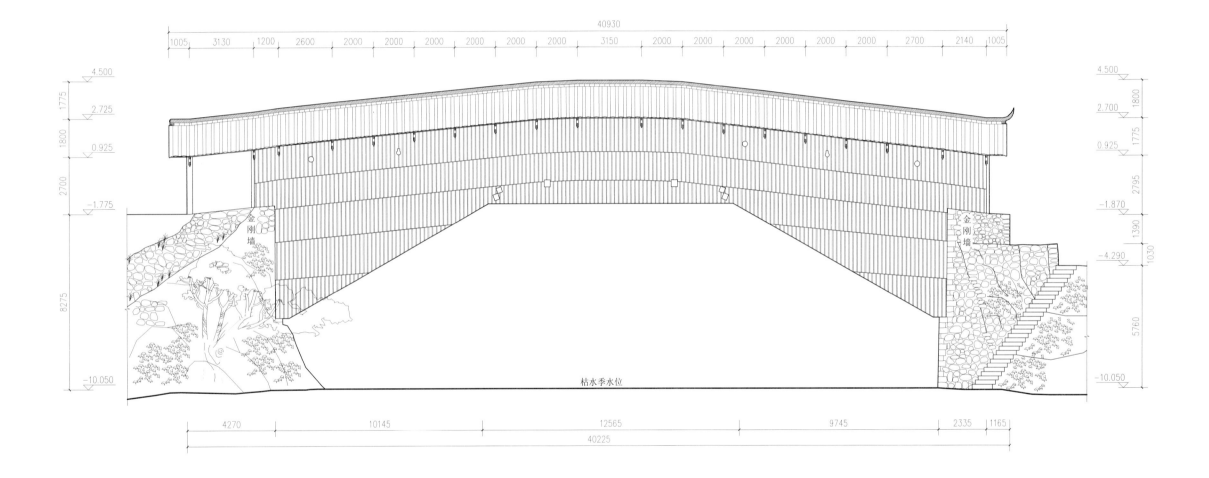

福寿桥东立面图
East elevation of Fushou Bridge

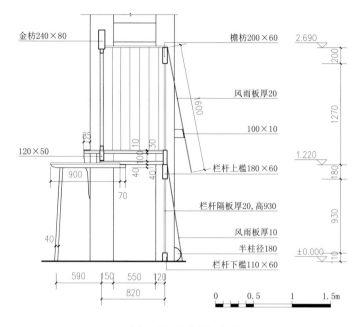

福寿桥神龛剖面图
Section of shrine of Fushou Bridge

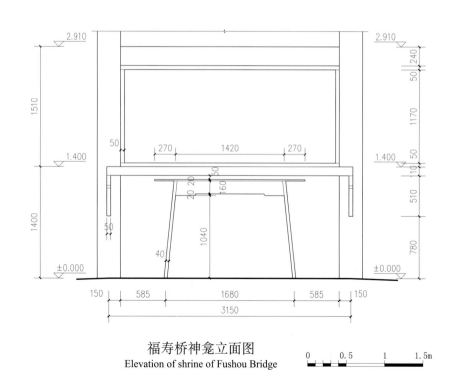

福寿桥神龛立面图
Elevation of shrine of Fushou Bridge

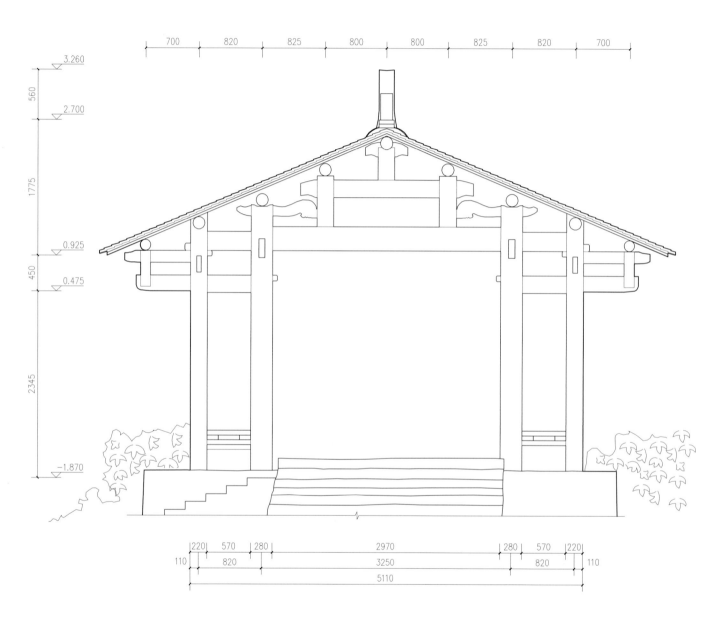

福寿桥北立面图
North elevation of Fushou Bridge

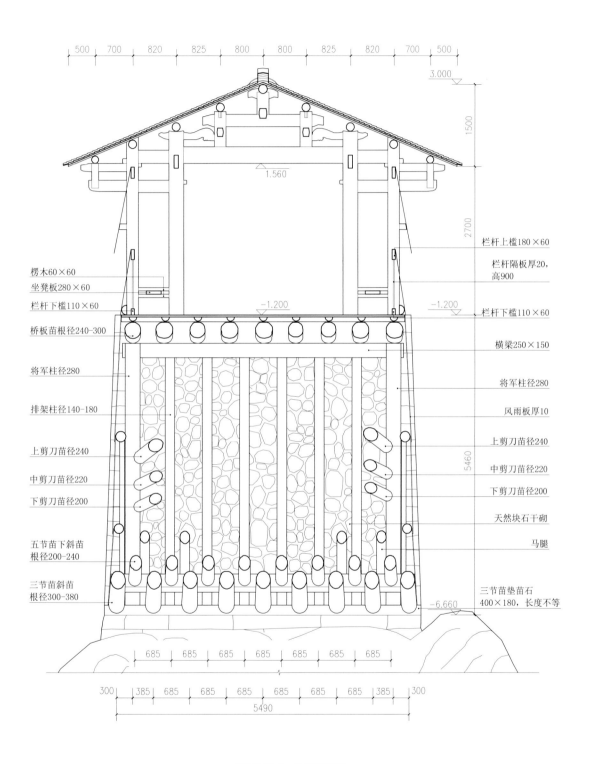

福寿桥 2-2 剖面图
Section 2-2 of Fushou Bridge

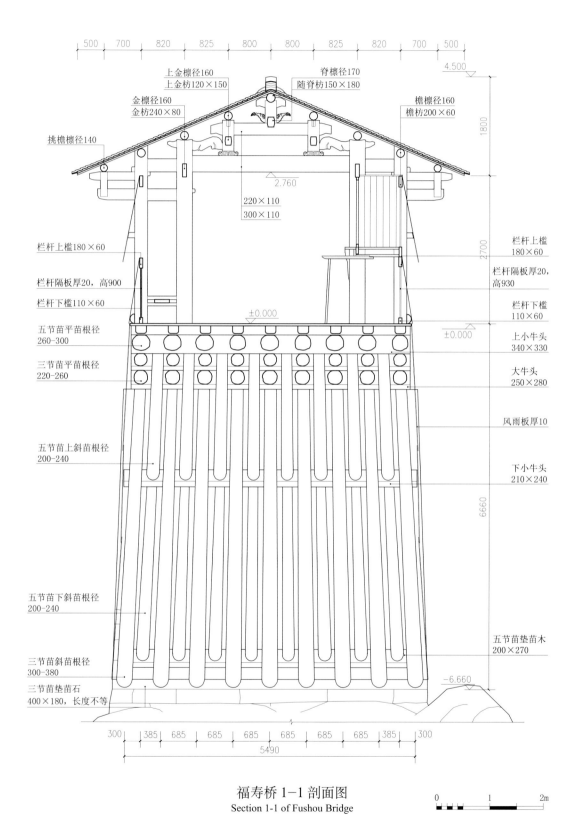

福寿桥 1-1 剖面图
Section 1-1 of Fushou Bridge

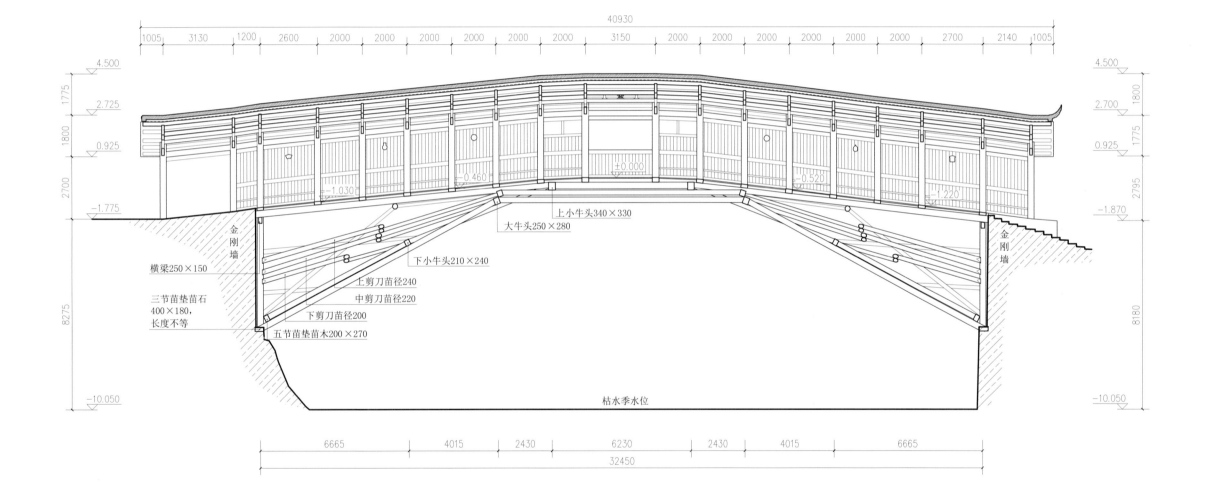

福寿桥 3-3 剖面图
Section 3-3 of Fushou Bridge

大宝桥

Dabao Bridge

Dabao Bridge, also known as Xiaodongxia Bridge, was first built in the Ming Dynasty but rebuilt in 1878, the fourth year of the Guangxu reign period of the Qing Dynasty. Located in Xiaodong village, Kengdi township, the single-span bridge extends from northeast to southwest across the stream that runs through the village. That stream is a tributary of the Houxi River that forms the border between Shouning County in Fujian Province and Taishun County in Zhejiang Province. Wooden boards are mounted as a deck, and a shrine is set up in the middle of the covered corridor to worship Lady Linshui. At both sides of the shrine are wooden benches for people to store their belongings or to rest. To the northwest of the bridge stands a Guanyin Pavilion.

Five interlocked timber-arched covered bridges stretch across the Houxi River and its tributaries, including Danqiao Bridge, Xiaodongshang Bridge, Dabao Bridge and Yangmeizhou Bridge all located in Kengdi township and Hongjun Bridge in Xixi township. The village is the hometown of the Dongshanlou (Xiaodong) family of craftsmen. Members of this family have passed on the technology of the interlocked timber-arched covered bridges for six generations over 140 years.

大宝桥，又称『小东下桥』，始建于明代，清代光绪四年（1878年）重建，位于坑底乡小东村水尾，东北—西南走向，单孔跨越流经小东村的溪流，此溪流为寿宁县与浙江泰顺县界河后溪的支流。桥体拱架系统上铺木板为桥面，廊屋中部设神龛，祀临水夫人。神龛左右设榻，供人放物和躺卧休息。桥西北不远处有观音阁。

在后溪上游和支流上，共分布了坑底乡的单桥、小东上桥、大宝桥、杨梅州桥以及犀溪乡的红军桥5座贯木拱廊桥，这里是造桥群体『东山楼（小东）』的家乡，其造桥技术共传承六代工匠、140多年。

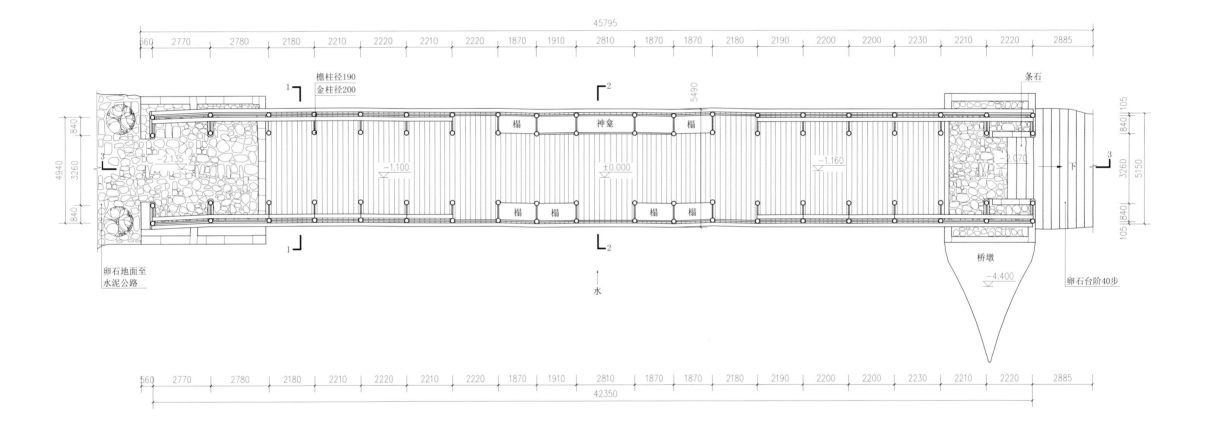

大宝桥平面图
Surface floor plan of Dabao Bridge

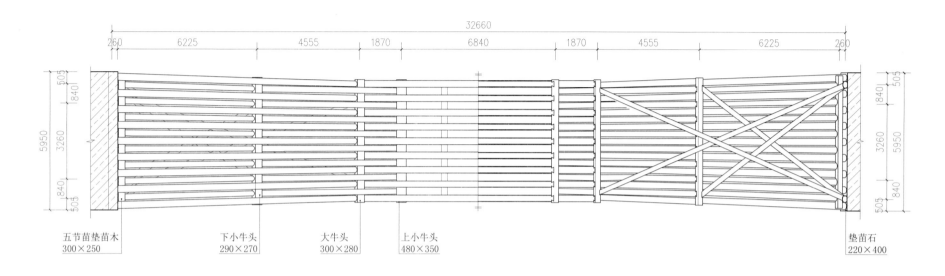

大宝桥桥梁拱骨系统仰视（左）与俯视（右）图
Plan of timber arch system of Dabao Bridge as seen from below (left) and above (right)

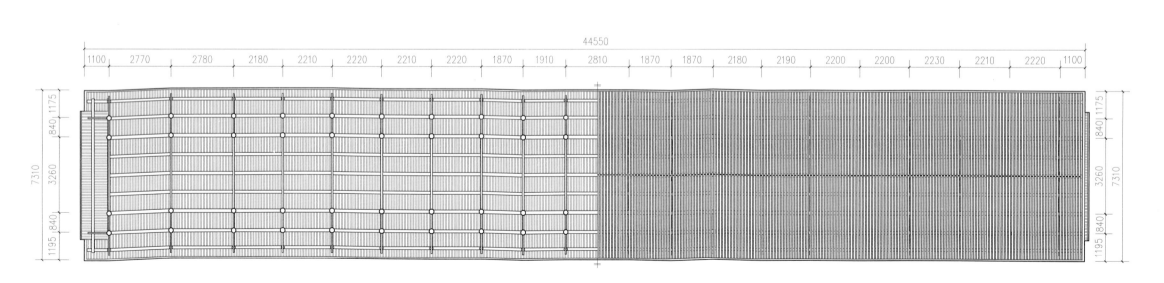

大宝桥廊屋梁架仰视（左）与俯视（右）图
Plan of corridor beam framework of Dabao Bridge as seen from below (left) and above (right)

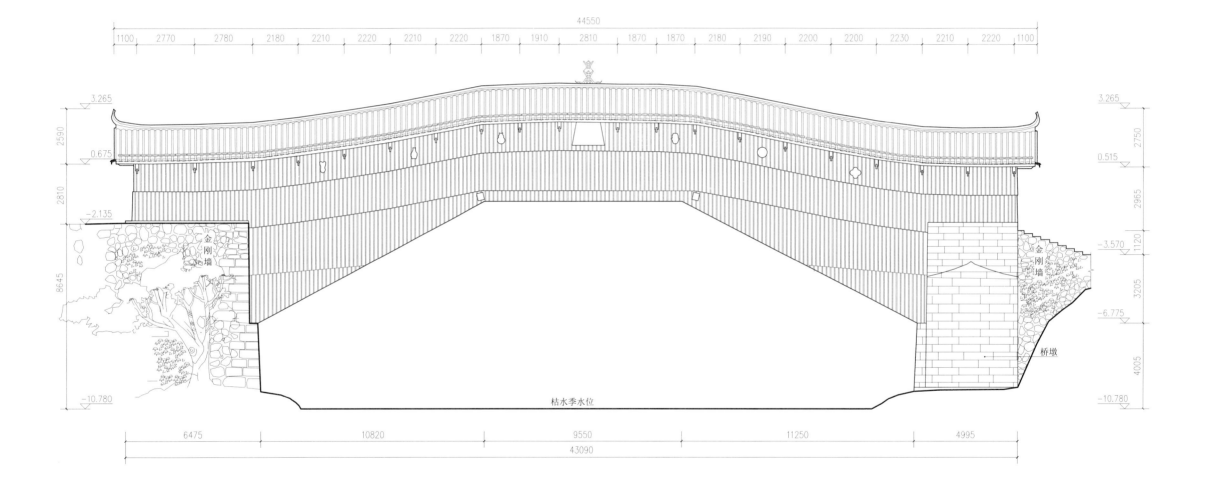

大宝桥西北立面图
Northwest elevation of Dabao Bridge

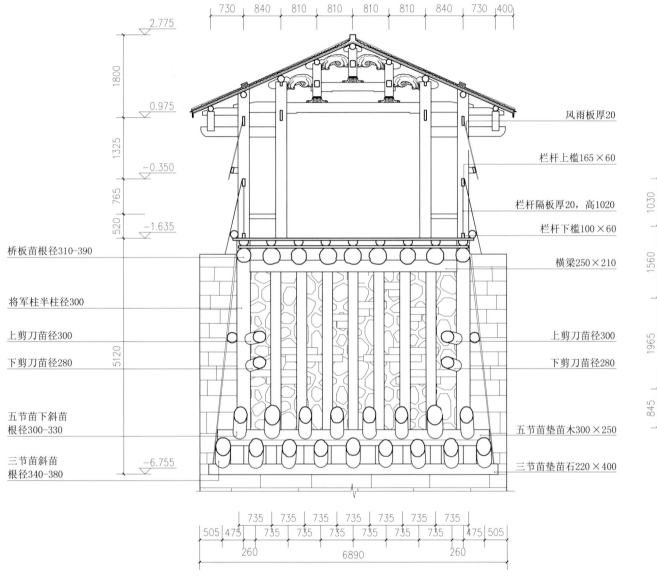

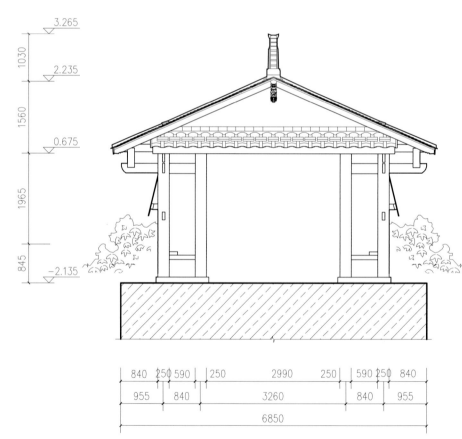

大宝桥 1-1 剖面图
Section 1-1 of Dabao Bridge

大宝桥东北立面图
Northeast elevation of Dabao Bridge

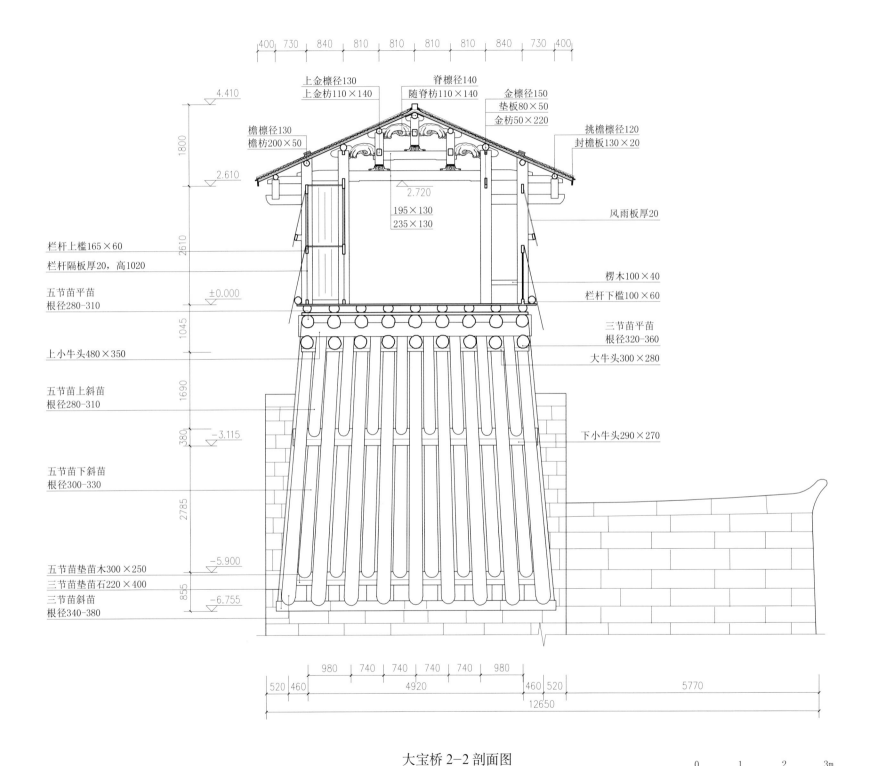

大宝桥 2-2 剖面图
Section 2-2 of Dabao Bridge

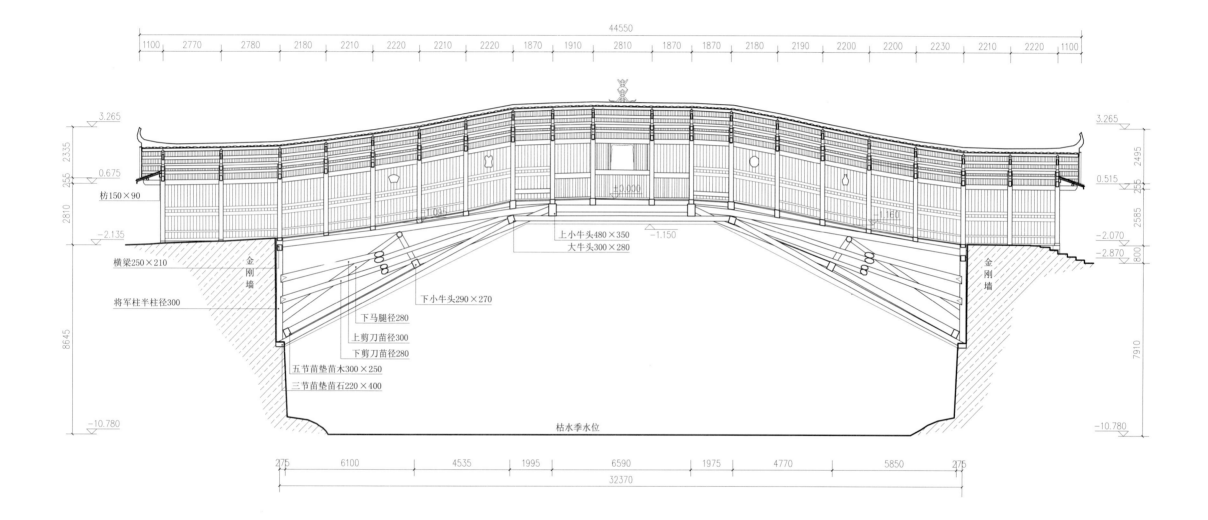

大宝桥 3-3 剖面图
Section 3-3 of Dabao Bridge

红军桥

Hongjun Bridge

Hongjun Bridge crosses Houxi River running about one km from Lijiashan village of Xixi township down an ancient path. The original wooden bridge was destroyed by a flood that ravaged the area on March 12, 1937. At that time, the Red Army was surrounded by Guomindang troops at Lijiashan village but then evacuated with the help of local secret agents. Hongjun (Red Army) Bridge was built in 1954 to commemorate the event.

Hongjun Bridge spans north to south across Hou Stream the boundary river between Shouning county in Fujian Province and Taishun county in Zhejiang Province. Wooden boards are mounted to form a deck. The top layer of the weatherboards of the covered corridor has five-star-shaped lighting holes, a characteristic feature of that time.

红军桥，位于犀溪乡李家山村沿古道下行1km处的后溪上，此地原有一木桥，于1937年3月12日被山洪冲毁。当时李家山村的红军被国民党军队包围，后在当地地下交通员的帮助下安全撤离。1954年建此桥并称"红军桥"以纪念。

红军桥单孔跨越福建寿宁与浙江泰顺的分界溪流后溪上，南北走向，桥体拱架系统上铺木板为桥面，廊屋风雨板最上层五星等形状的采光孔，显示了时代特征。

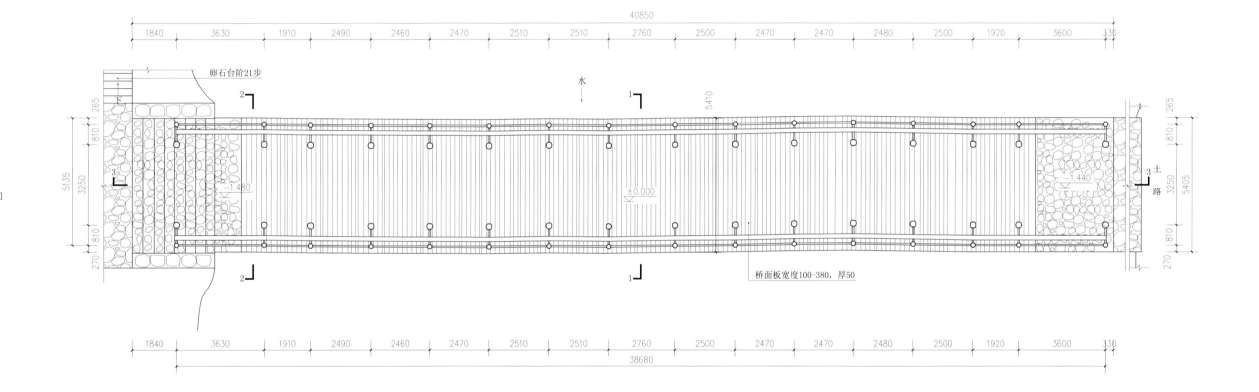

红军桥平面图
Surface floor plan of Hongjun Bridge

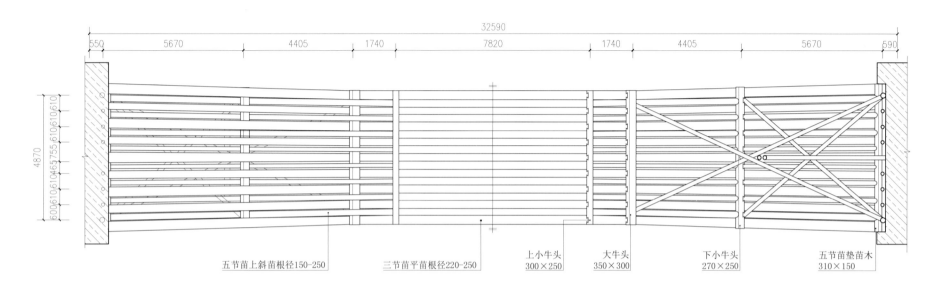

红军桥桥梁拱骨系统仰视（左）与俯视（右）图
Plan of timber arch system of Hongjun Bridge as seen from below (left) and above (right)

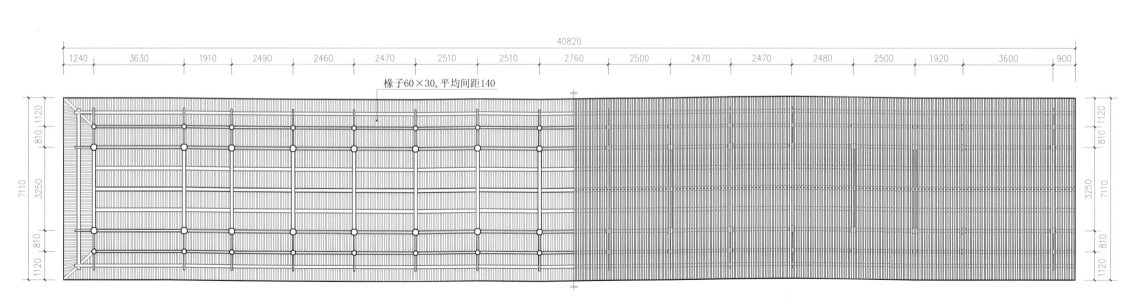

红军桥廊屋梁架仰视（左）与俯视（右）图
Plan of corridor beam framework of Hongjun Bridge as seen from below (left) and above (right)

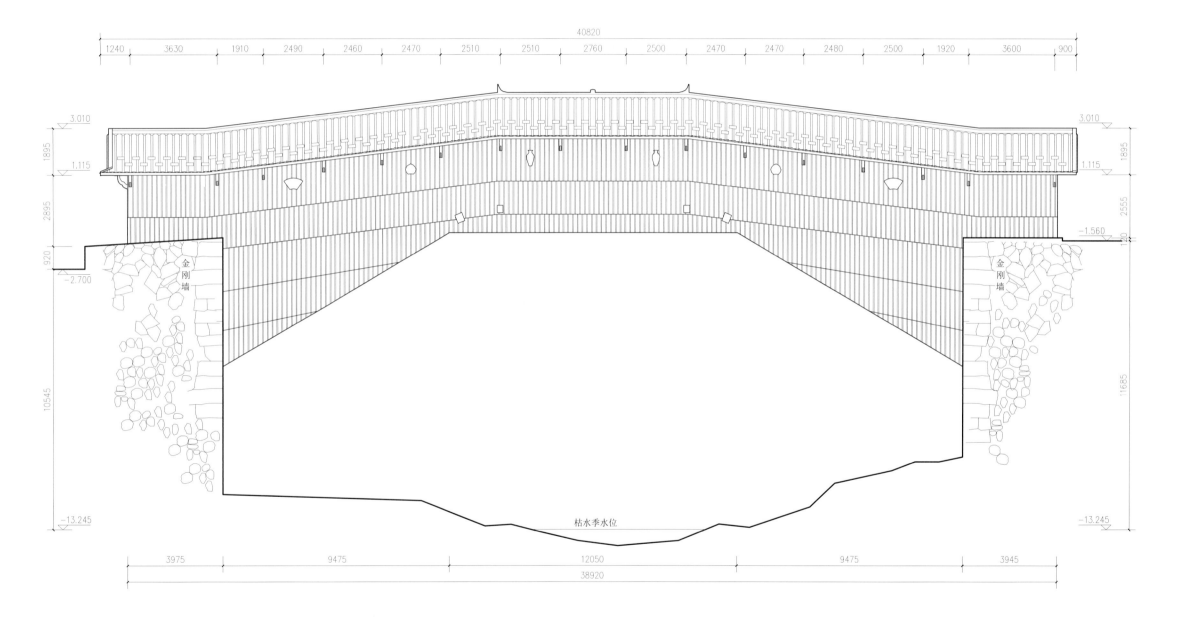

红军桥东立面图
East elevation of Hongjun Bridge

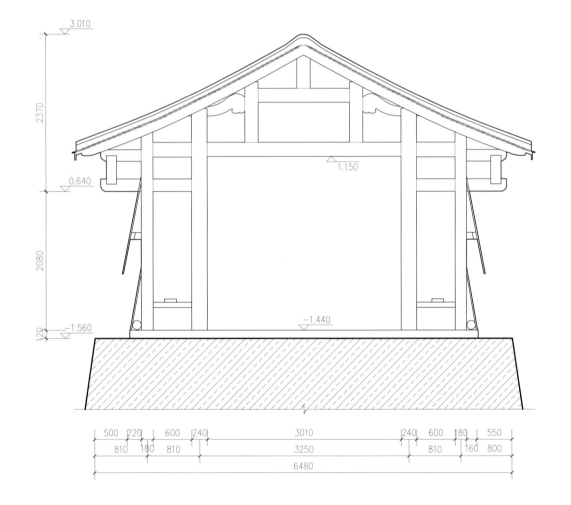
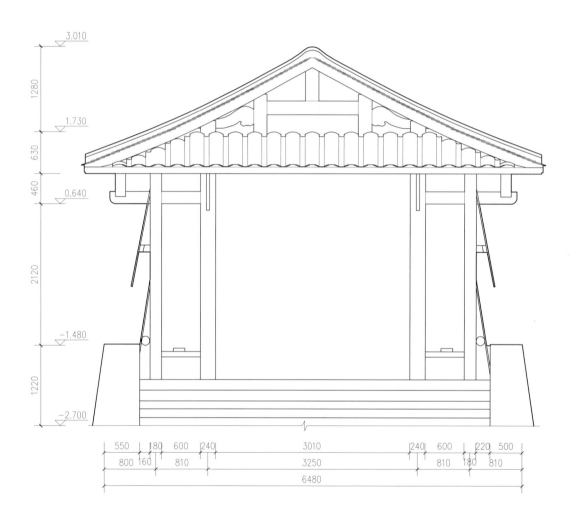

红军桥北立面图
North elevation of Hongjun Bridge

红军桥南立面图
South elevation of Hongjun Bridge

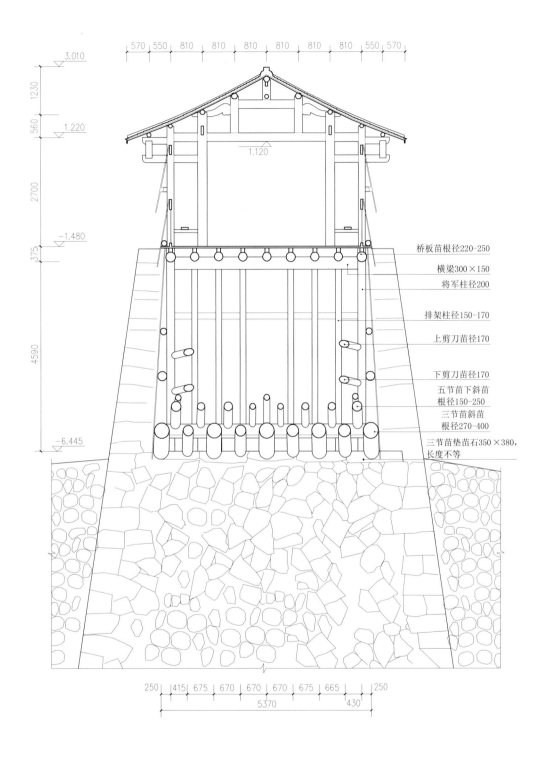

红军桥 2-2 剖面图
Section 2-2 of Hongjun Bridge

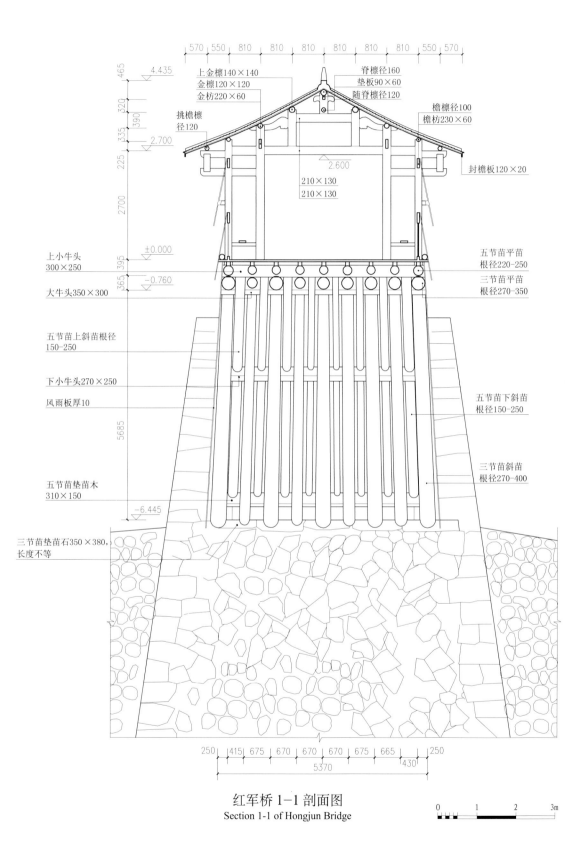

红军桥 1-1 剖面图
Section 1-1 of Hongjun Bridge

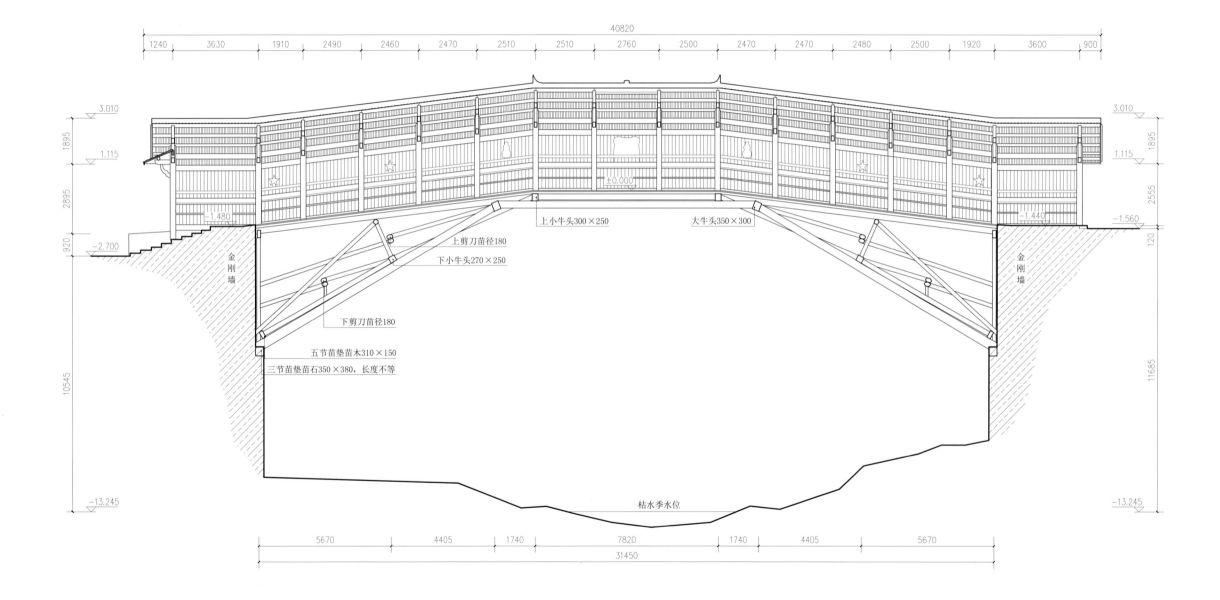

红军桥 3-3 剖面图
Section 3-3 of Hongjun Bridge

登云桥

Dengyun Bridge

The construction date of Dengyun Bridge, also known as Yangmei Bridge, remains unknown, but a record in the local gazetteer of Shouning county confirms its existence as early as 1685, the twenty-fifth year of the Qing emperor Kangxi's reign. From 1771 to 1773, the thirty-sixth year to the thirty-eighth reign year of the Qing emperor Qianlong, the bridge was rebuilt. Originally located in Yangmei village of Aoyang township, the single-span bridge crossed Chanxi River but during the expansion of Shouning's downtown area, it was moved to a new location upstream along the Chanxi River, nearby Shouning No.6 High School, spanning from north to south. Wooden boards are mounted to form a deck, and a shrine is installed in the middle of the covered corridor dedicated to Lady Linshui.

登云桥，又称「杨梅桥」，始建年代不详，清代康熙二十五年（1685年）的《寿宁县志》已记载此桥，清代乾隆三十六至三十八年（1771—1773年）重建。此桥原位于鳌阳镇杨梅村，单孔跨越蟾溪。现因寿宁县城扩建，被沿蟾溪迁到距原址几百米的上游寿宁县第六中学附近，南北走向。桥体拱架系统上铺木板以为桥面，廊屋中部设神龛，祀临水夫人。

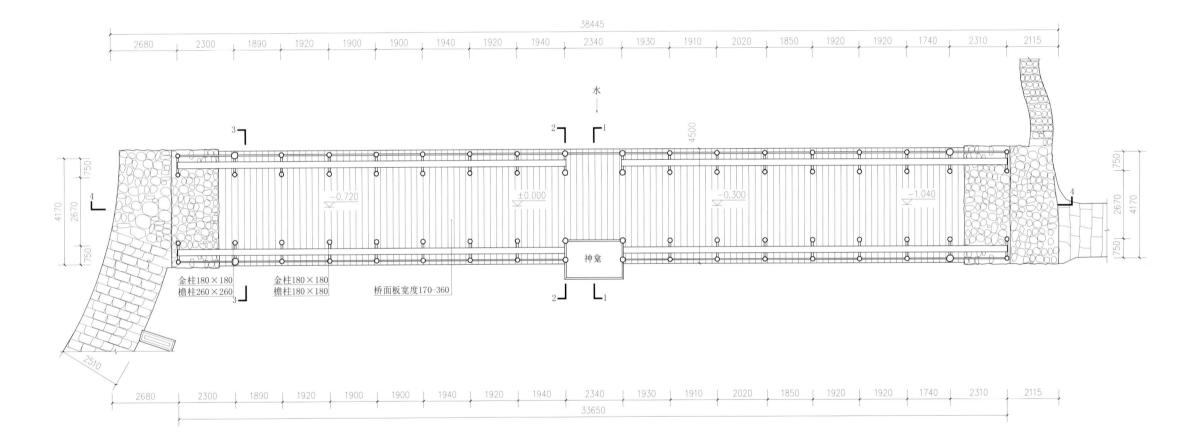

登云桥平面图
Surface floor plan of Dengyun Bridge

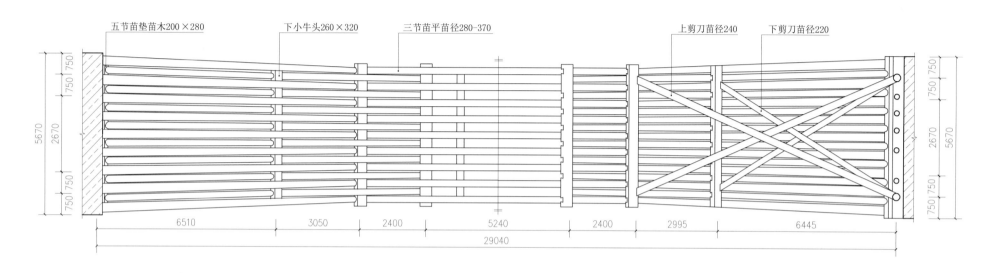

登云桥桥体拱架系统仰视（左）与俯视（右）图
Plan of timber arch system of Dengyun Bridge as seen from below (left) and above (right)

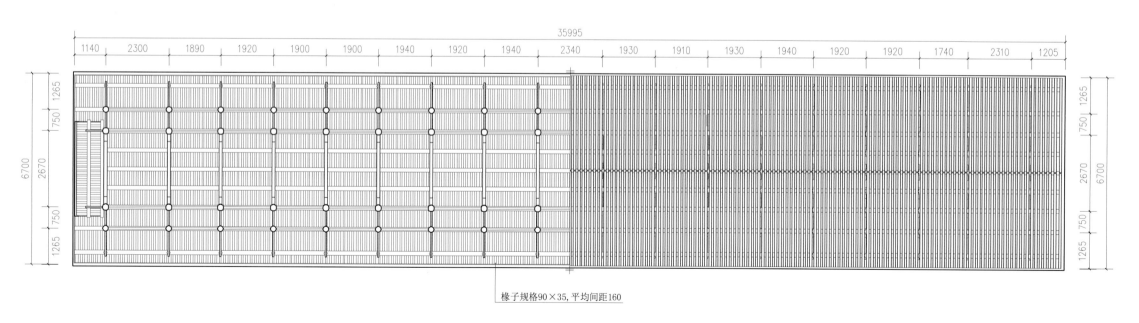

登云桥廊屋梁架仰视（左）与俯视（右）图
Plan of corridor beam framework of Dengyun Bridge as seen from below (left) and above (right)

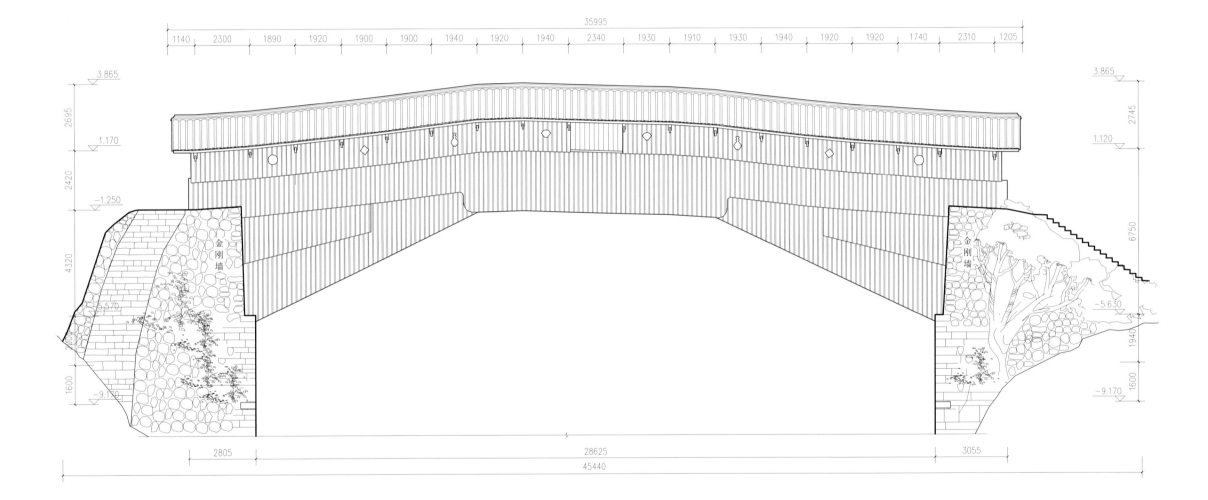

登云桥东立面图
East elevation of Dengyun Bridge

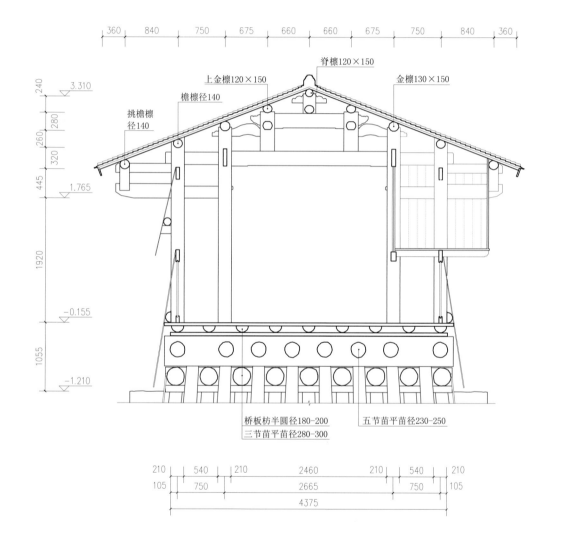
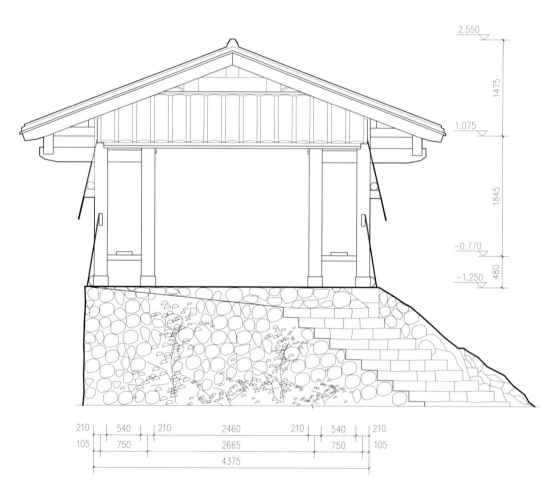

登云桥 1-1 剖面图

Section 1-1 of Dengyun Bridge

登云桥南立面图

South elevation of Dengyun Bridge

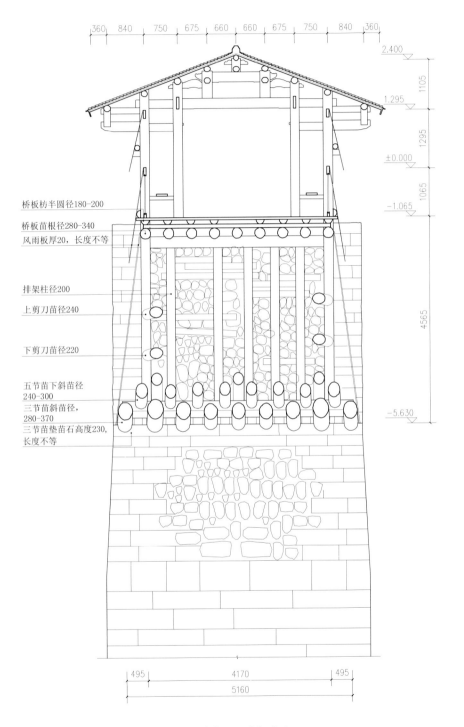
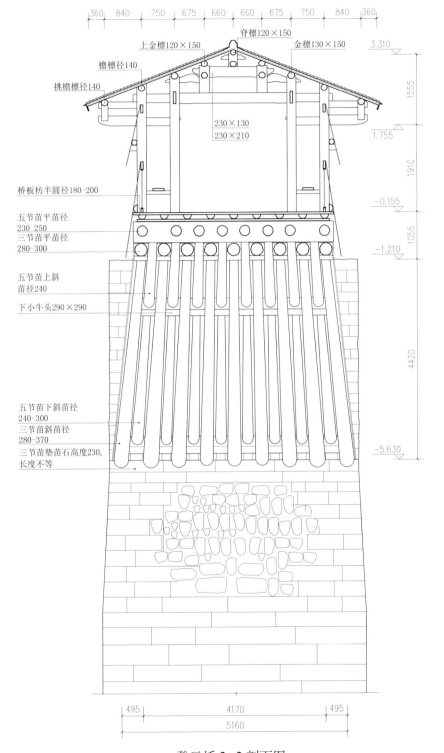

登云桥 3-3 剖面图
Section 3-3 of Dengyun Bridge

登云桥 2-2 剖面图
Section 2-2 of Dengyun Bridge

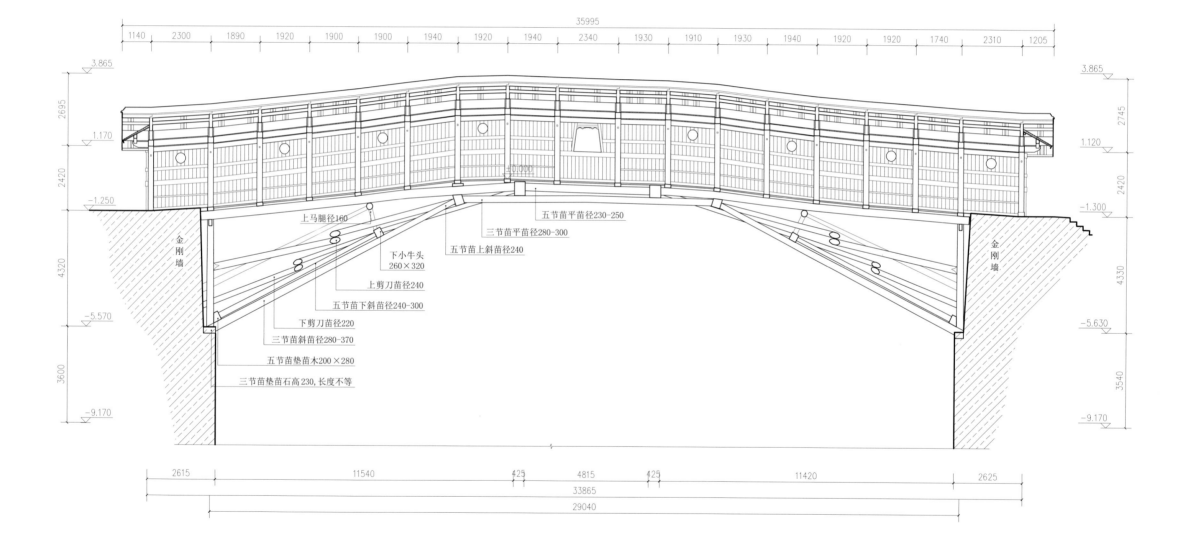

登云桥 4-4 剖面图
Section 4-4 of Dengyun Bridge

仙宫桥

Xiangong Bridge

Xiangong Bridge, also known as Yudai Bridge, was first built in the Ming Dynasty but rebuilt in 1767, the thirty-second year of the Qing-Dynasty emperor Qianlong, and reconstructed again in 1778, Qianlong's forty-third reign year. Located outside the south gate of Old Aoyang Township, the bridge crosses east to west across Chanxi River in a single span. The covered corridor had three octagonal caisson ceilings placed in the center and at both ends of the overhanging gable (*xuanshan*) roof, a structure crowned with an octagonal pyramidal (*cuanjian*) roof. Wooden boards form the bridge deck. First moved from Yizheng temple, the shrine installed in the middle of the corridor is dedicated to Maxian (a female immortal also known as Lady Ma). The temple originally stood to the left of the bridge, but was torn down to build new factories sometime between 1950s and 1960s. Today the column couplets, screens depicting Chinese poetry, and wall paintings of the bridge corridor are dedicated to Maxian, making the bridge a new temple for the female immortal.

仙宫桥，又称「玉带桥」，始建于明代，清代乾隆三十二年（1767年）重建，乾隆四十三年（1778年）再重建，位于鳌阳镇旧城南门外，单孔跨越蟾溪，东西走向。悬山廊屋顶部设3个八角藻井，上部均升起八角攒尖顶。桥体拱架系统上铺木板为桥面，廊屋中部设神龛，祀马仙。原在桥右有祀马仙的懿政祠，在20世纪五六十年代因建工厂被拆后，便把马仙神龛移入廊屋；现桥中楹联、诗屏、壁画均与马仙有关，俨然成为马仙的宫庙。

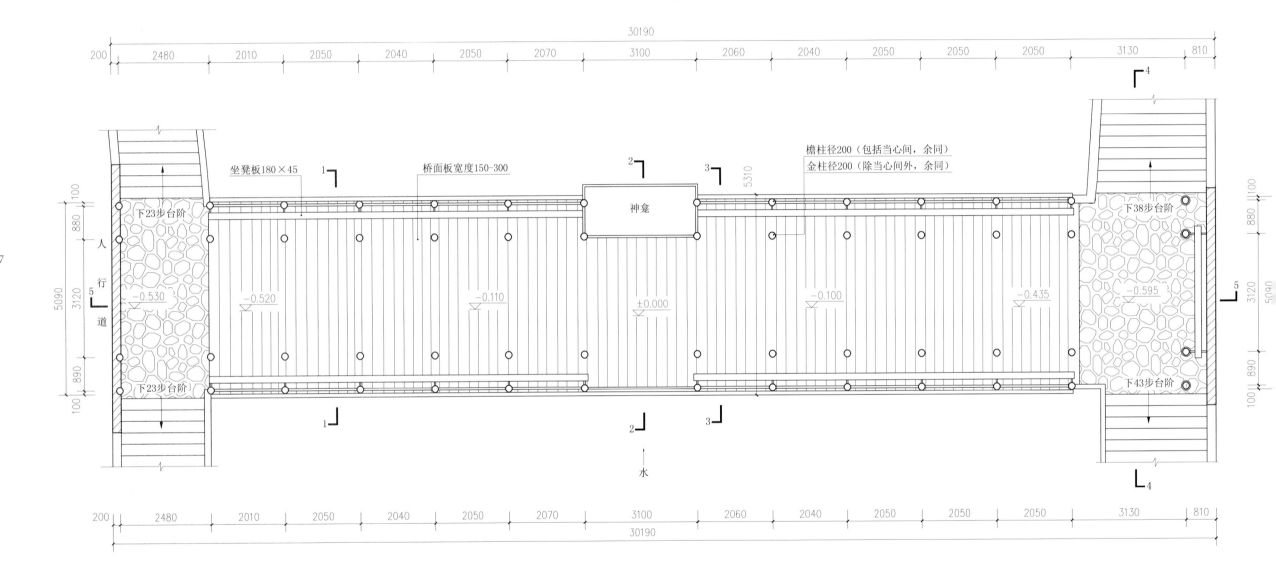

仙宫桥平面图
Surface floor plan of Xiangong Bridge

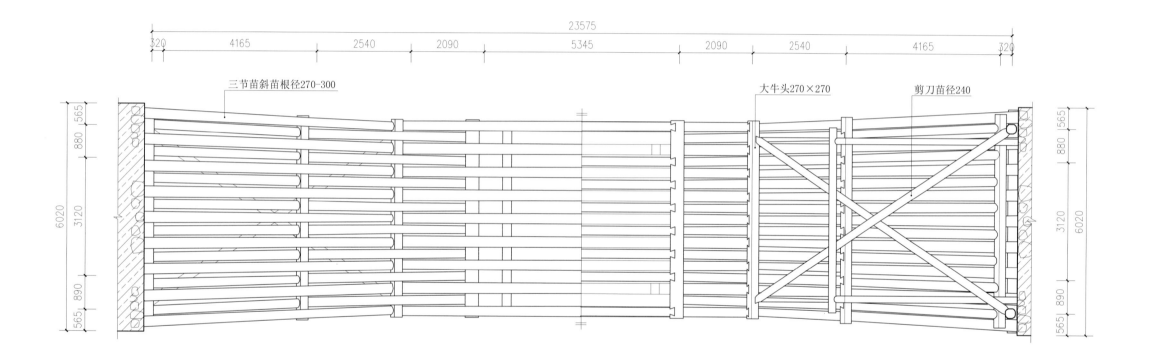

仙宫桥桥体拱架系统仰视（左）与俯视（右）图
Plan of timber arch system of Xiangong Bridge as seen from below (left) and above (right)

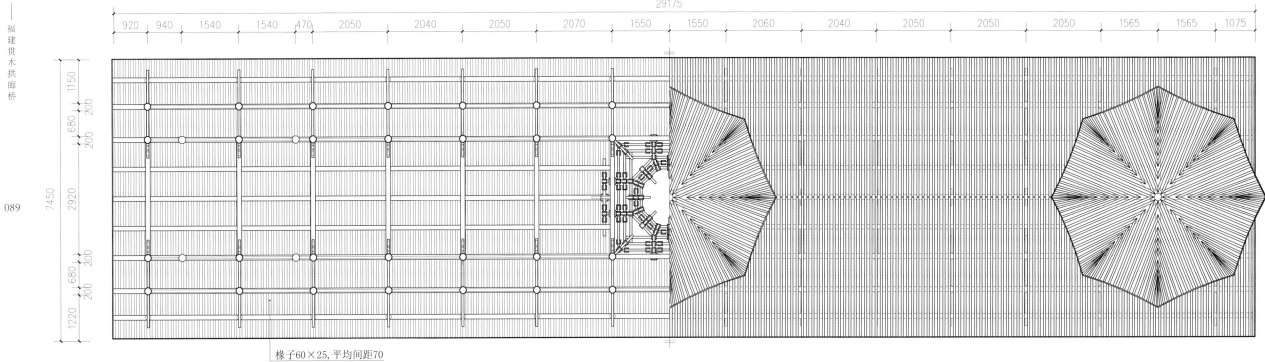

仙宫桥廊屋梁架仰视（左）与俯视（右）图
Plan of corridor beam framework of Xiangong Bridge as seen from below (left) and above (right)

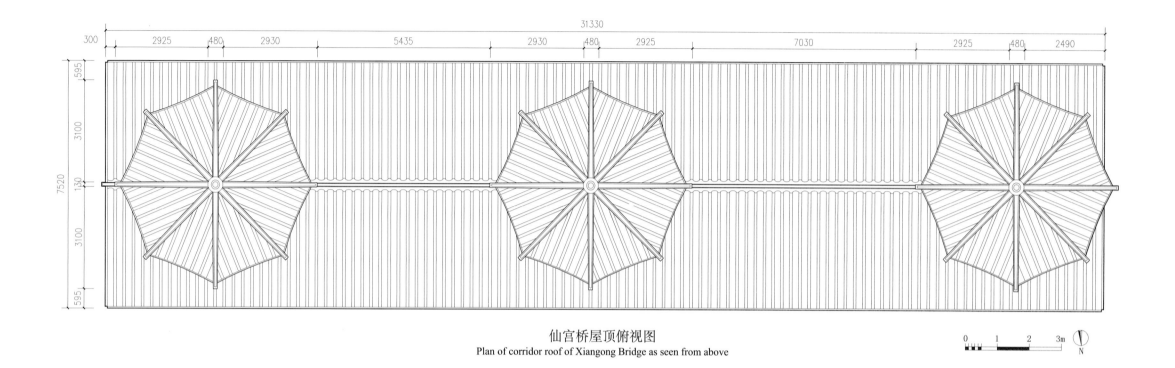

仙宫桥屋顶俯视图
Plan of corridor roof of Xiangong Bridge as seen from above

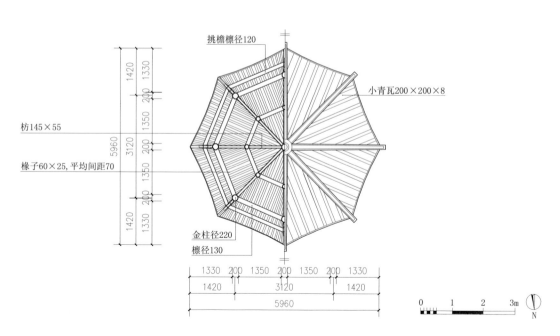

仙宫桥八角攒尖顶仰视（左）与俯视（右）图
Plan of octagonal pyramidal roof of Xiangong Bridge as seen from below (left) and above (right)

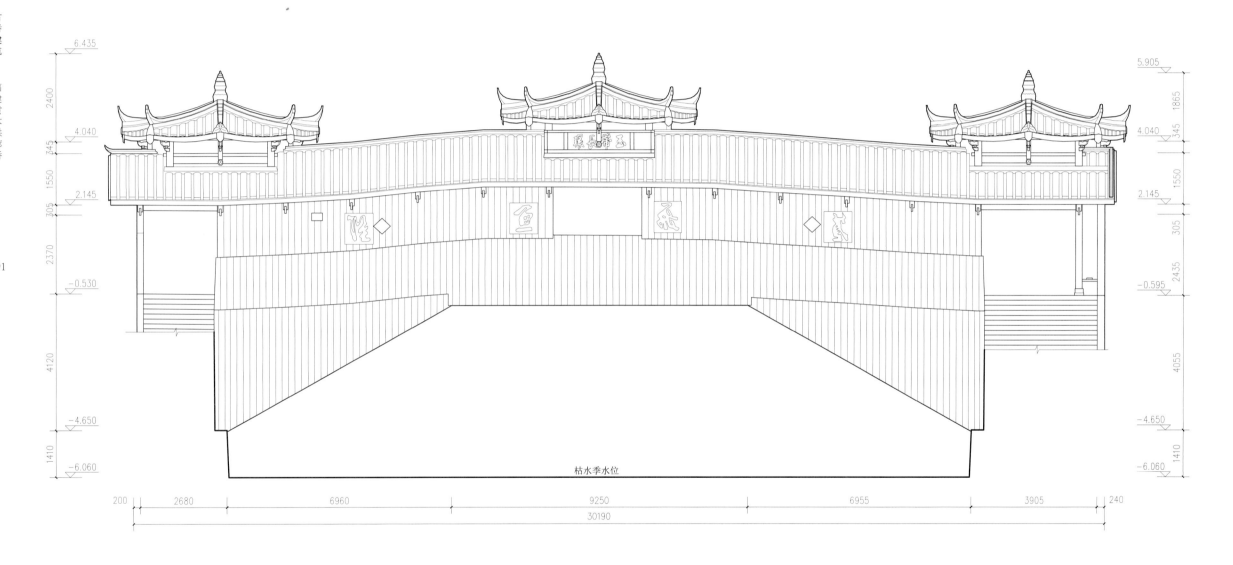

仙宫桥北立面图
North elevation of Xiangong Bridge

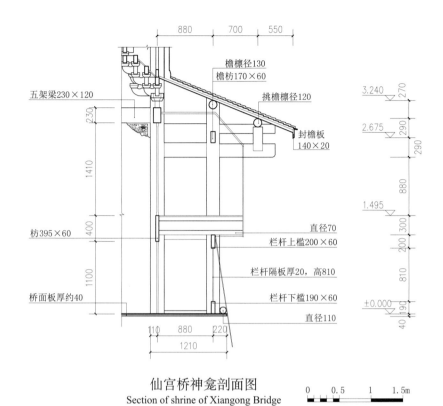

仙宫桥神龛剖面图
Section of shrine of Xiangong Bridge

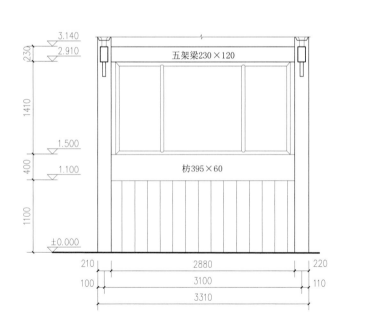

仙宫桥神龛立面图
Elevation of shrine of Xiangong Bridge

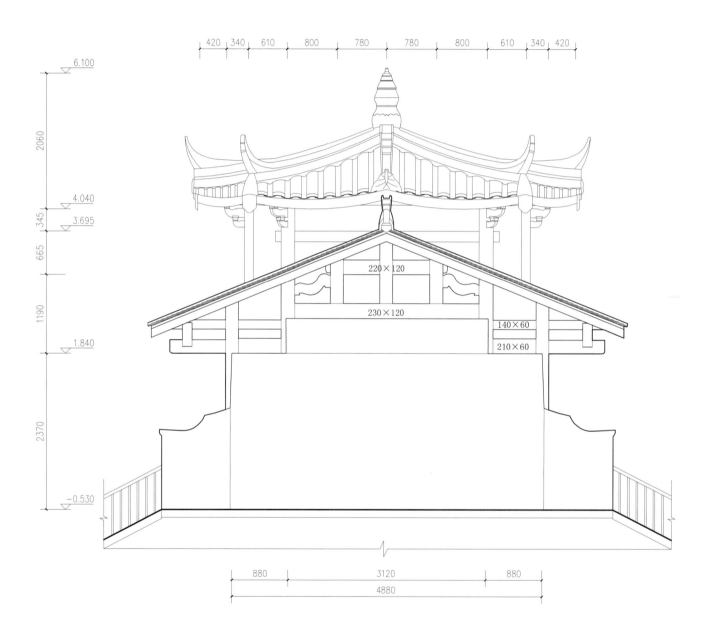

仙宫桥东立面图
East elevation of Xiangong Bridge

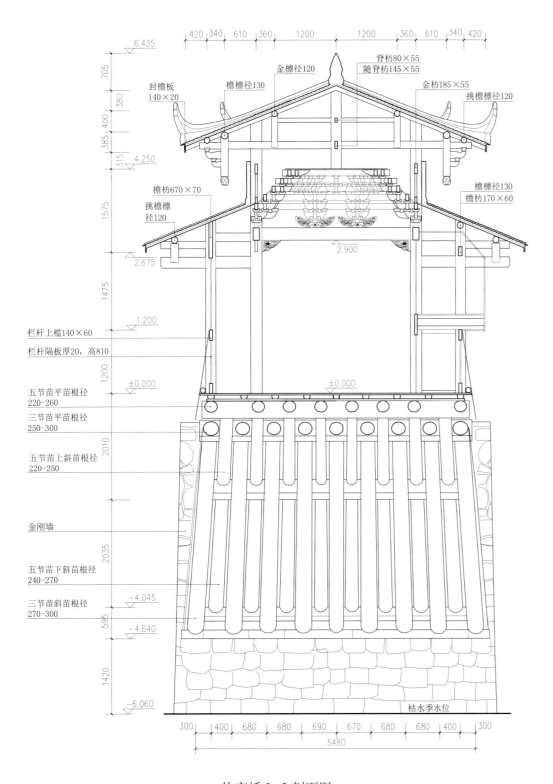

仙宫桥 2-2 剖面图
Section 2-2 of Xiangong Bridge

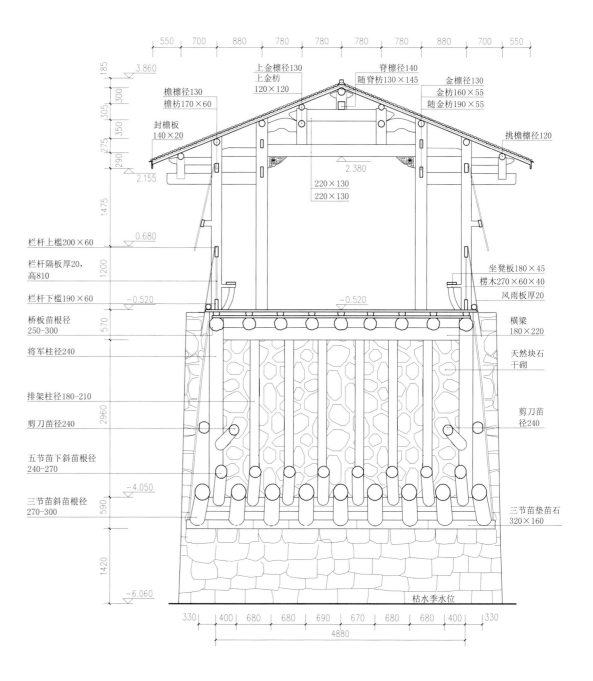

仙宫桥 1-1 剖面图
Section 1-1 of Xiangong Bridge

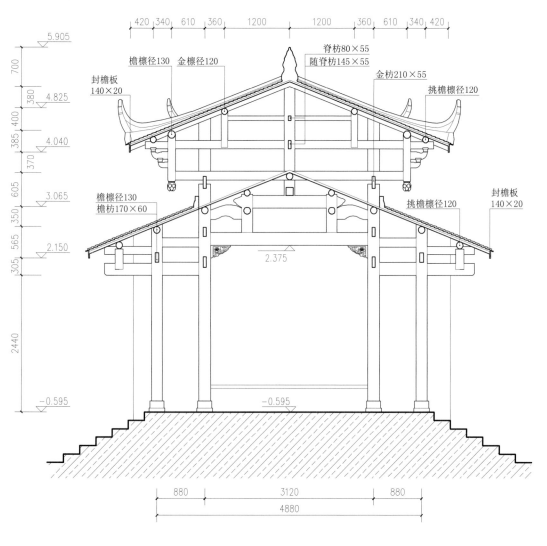

仙宫桥 4-4 剖面图
Section 4-4 of Xiangong Bridge

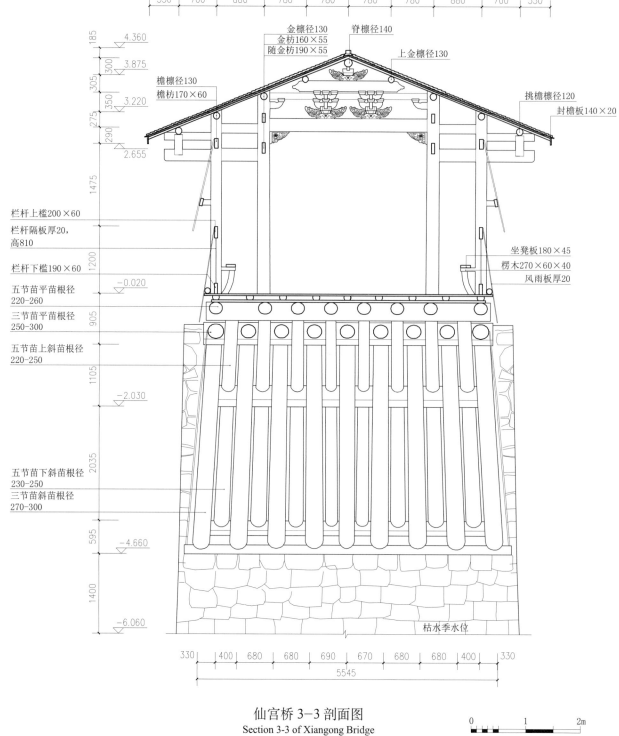

仙宫桥 3-3 剖面图
Section 3-3 of Xiangong Bridge

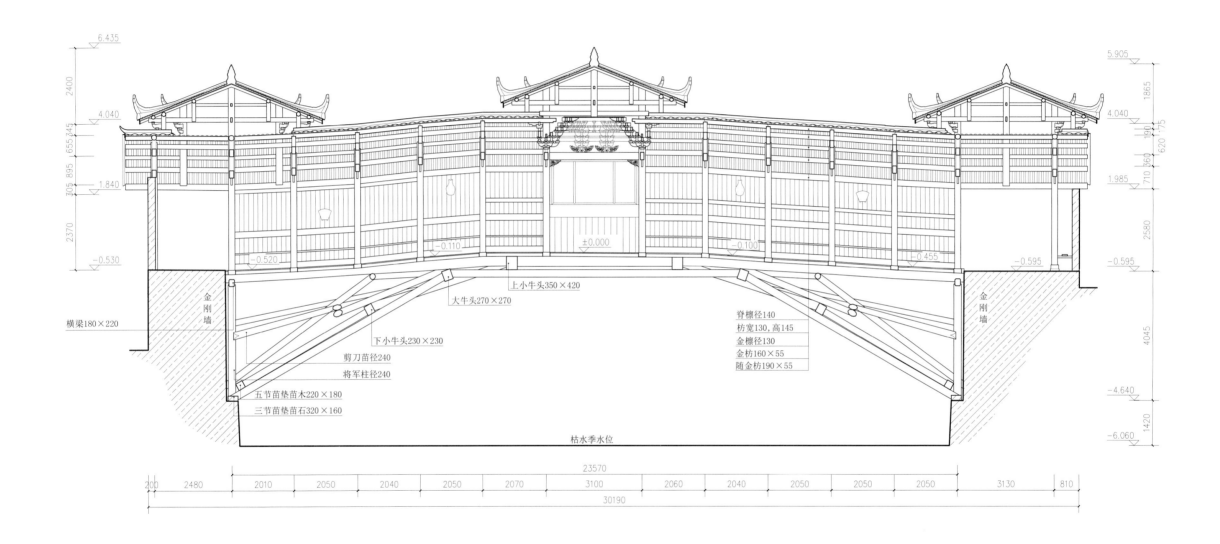

仙宫桥 5-5 剖面图
Section 5-5 of Xiangong Bridge

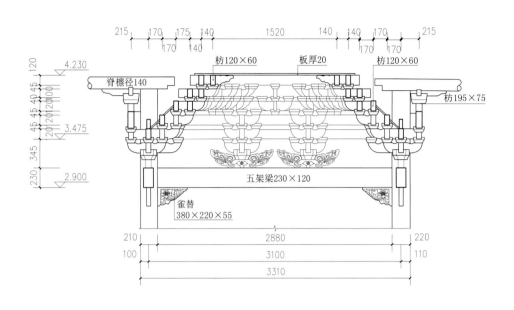

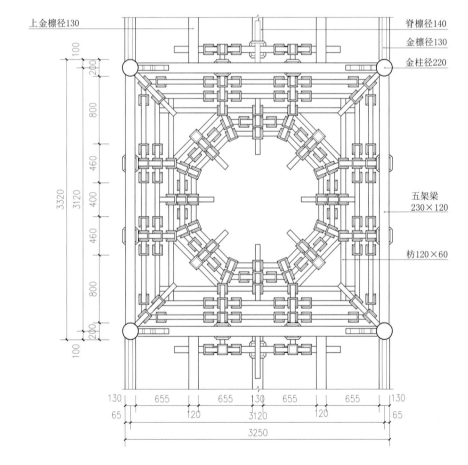

仙宫桥藻井大样图
Caisson ceiling of Xiangong Bridge

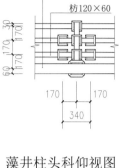

① 藻井柱头科仰视图

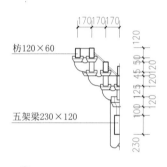

③ 藻井柱头科剖面图

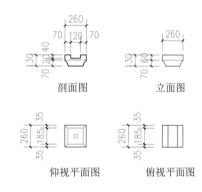

⑤ 三才升详图

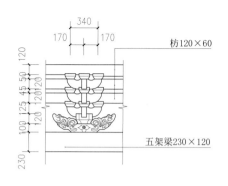

② 藻井柱头科立面图

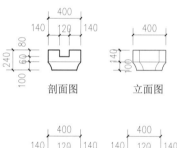

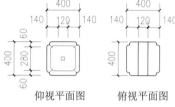

④ 坐斗详图

仙宫桥斗栱大样图
Bracket sets of Xiangong Bridge

升平桥

Shengping Bridge

Shengping Bridge is also known as Dongzuo Bridge. As explained in a local gaztteer from the Kangxi reign period of the Qing dynasty, the name of the bridge, "Dongzuoqiao", means that a day's work begins at sunrise. More commonly known as Hengxi Bridge, the bridge was first built in 1457, the first year of the Tianshun reign period of the Ming dynasty, but rebuilt in 1571, the fifth year of the Longqing reign period of the Ming Dynasty. In 1749, the fourteenth year of the Qianlong reign period of the Qing Dynasty, the bridge was destroyed by a flood, but rebuilt again in 1778, the forty-third year of the Qianlong reign dynasty. The bridge is located in Aoyang township near the Risheng Gate in the Old Town of Shouning. It spans northeast to southwest across Chanxi River in a single span. Atop the middle of the hip-gable (*xieshan*) roof of the covered corridor rises a second hip-gable roof, which corresponds to the octagonal caisson ceiling (*zaojing*) inside. The main ridge is decorated with two Chinese dragons playing with a pearl. Wooden boards are mounted to form a deck, and a shrine is installed in the middle of the corridor for the worship of Guanyin.

升平桥，又称「东作桥」，康熙版县志：匾曰「东作桥」，似寓日出而作之意，俗称「横溪桥」。始建于明代天顺元年（1457年），隆庆五年（1571年）重建，清代乾隆十四年（1749年）毁于洪水，乾隆四十三年（1778年）再重建。位于城关鳌阳镇，紧靠寿宁古城的日升门，单孔跨越蟾溪，东北—西南走向。歇山廊屋顶中部升起歇山式屋顶，内做八角藻井，正脊塑二龙戏珠。桥体拱架系统上铺木板以为桥面，廊屋中部设神龛，祀观音。

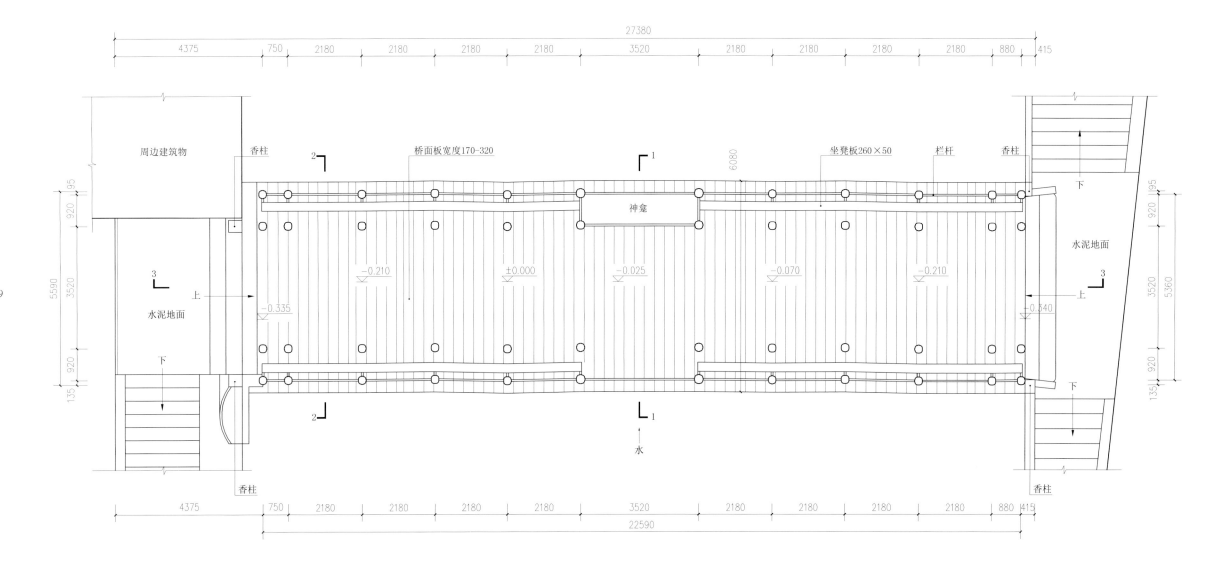

升平桥平面图
Surface floor plan of Shengping Bridge

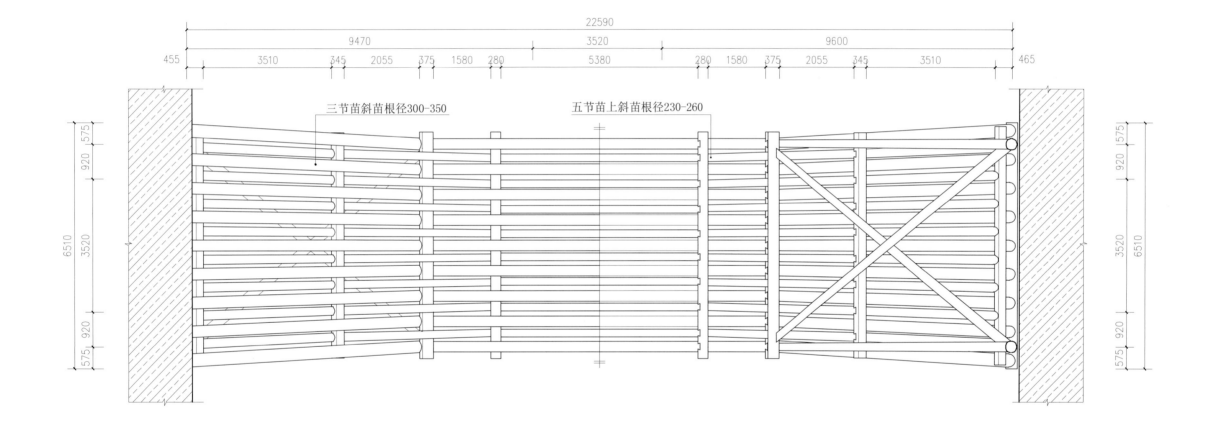

升平桥桥体拱架系统仰视（左）与俯视（右）图

Plan of timber arch system of Shengping Bridge as seen from below (left) and above (right)

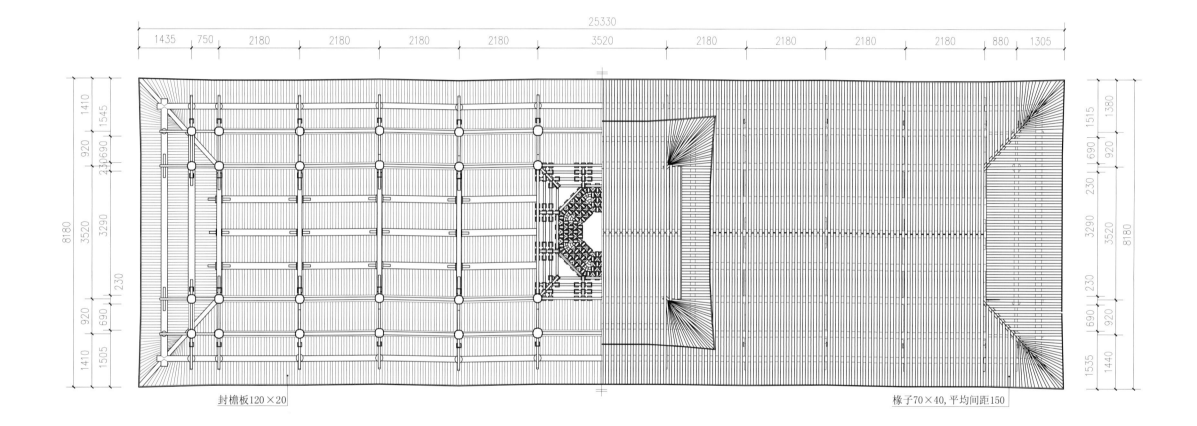

升平桥廊屋梁架仰视（左）与俯视（右）图
Plan of corridor beam framework of Shengping Bridge as seen from below (left) and above (right)

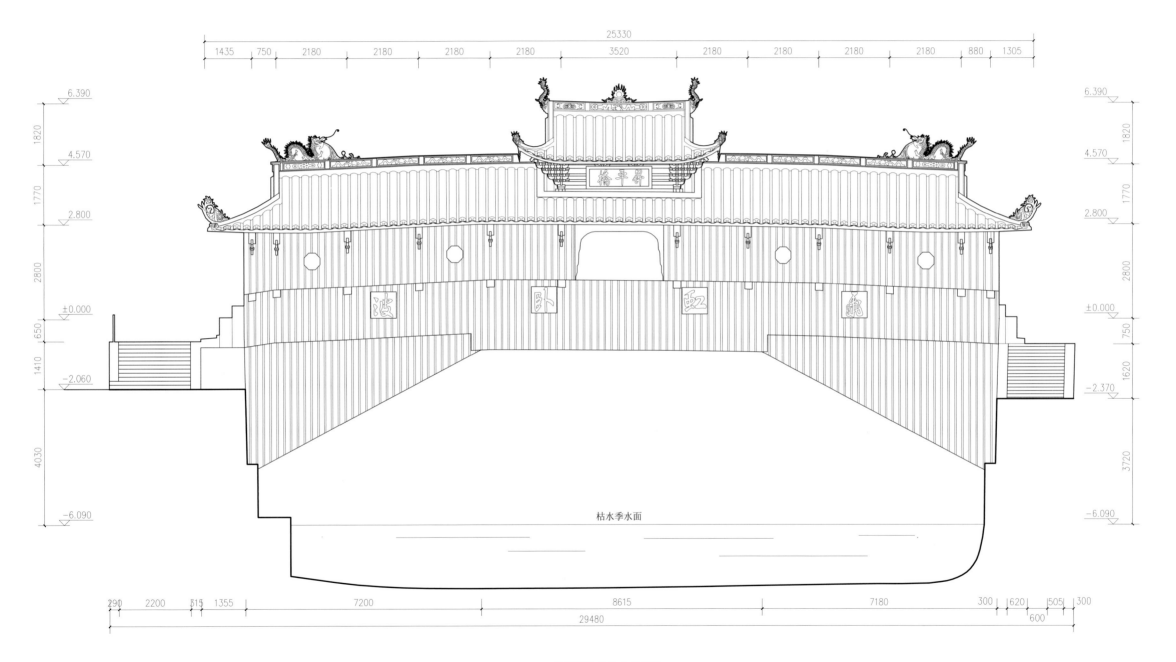

升平桥西北立面图
Northwest elevation of Shengping Bridge

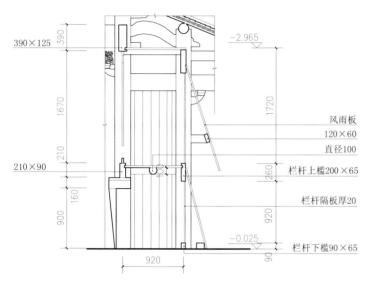

升平桥神龛剖面图
Section of shrine of Shengping Bridge

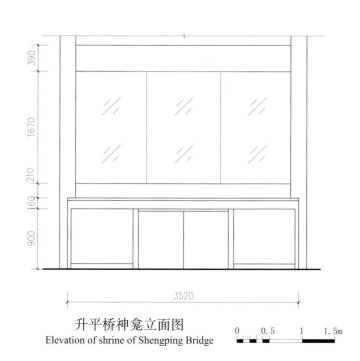

升平桥神龛立面图
Elevation of shrine of Shengping Bridge

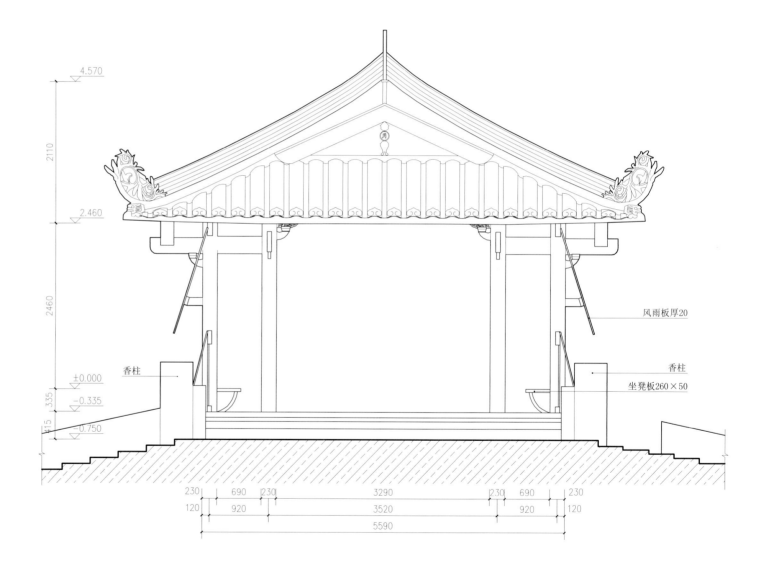

升平桥西南立面图
Southwest elevation of Shengping Bridge

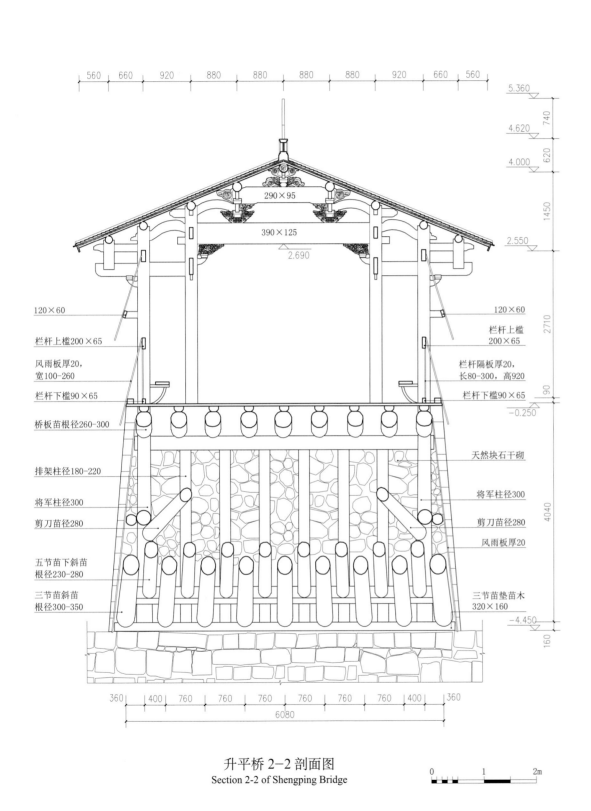

升平桥 2-2 剖面图

Section 2-2 of Shengping Bridge

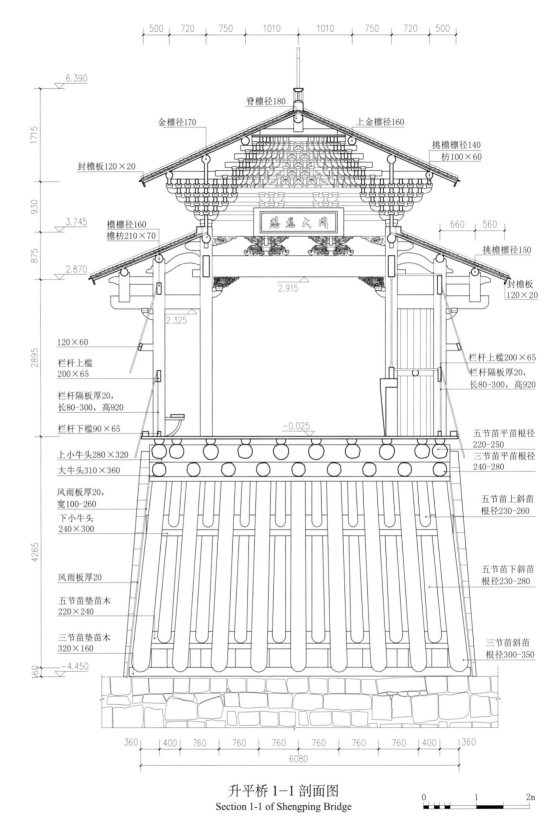

升平桥 1-1 剖面图

Section 1-1 of Shengping Bridge

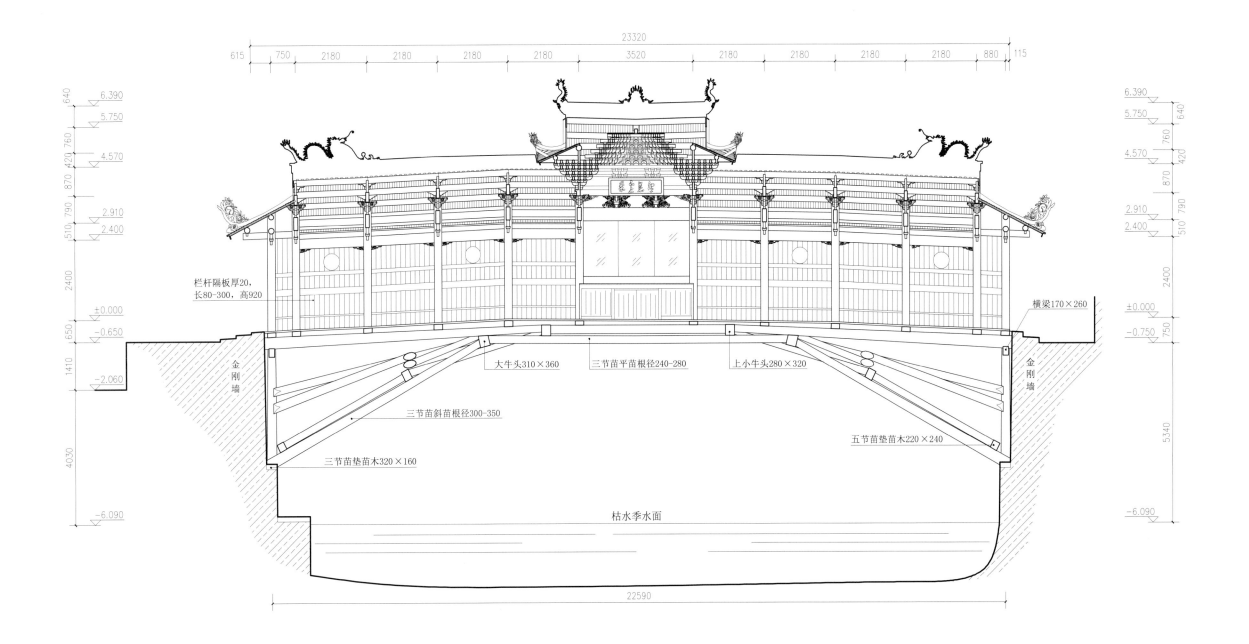

升平桥 3-3 剖面图

Section 3-3 of Shengping Bridge

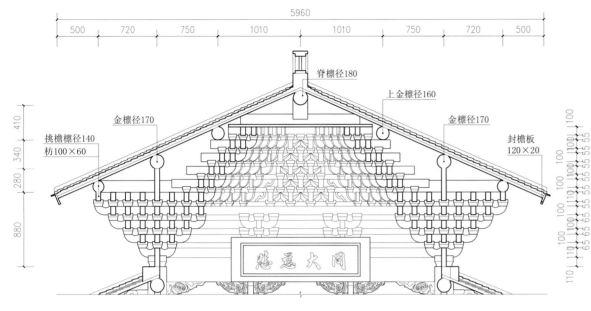

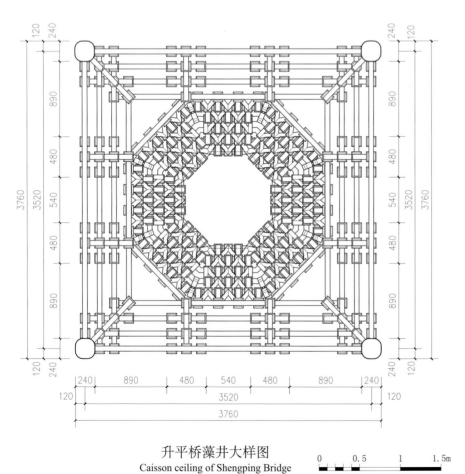

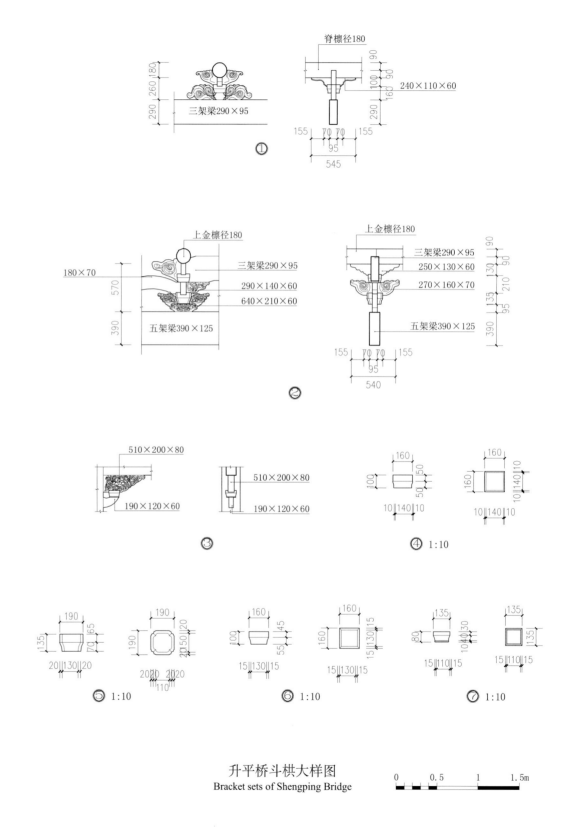

升平桥藻井大样图
Caisson ceiling of Shengping Bridge

升平桥斗栱大样图
Bracket sets of Shengping Bridge

里仁桥

Liren Bridge

Liren Bridge, also known as Youxixia Bridge, was first built in 1832, the twelfth year of the Daoguang reign period of the Qing Dynasty. Located at the end of Youxi village in Qinyang township, the bridge extends from north to south across the Youxi River in a single span. Wooden boards form the bridge deck, and a shrine is installed in the middle of the covered corridor to worship Guanyin. The bridge beams and joists bear many inscriptions that give clues about the site's construction history. At the north end of the bridge stands a furnace to burn paper, and on a nearby hill stands a temple.

里仁桥，又称「尤溪下桥」，始建于清代道光十二年（1832年），位于芹洋乡尤溪村东侧水尾，单孔跨越尤溪，南北走向。桥体拱架系统上铺木板为桥面，廊屋中部设神龛，祀观音。桥内梁枋所书文字较多，建桥资料丰富。北面桥头有焚纸炉，附近小山头建有神庙。

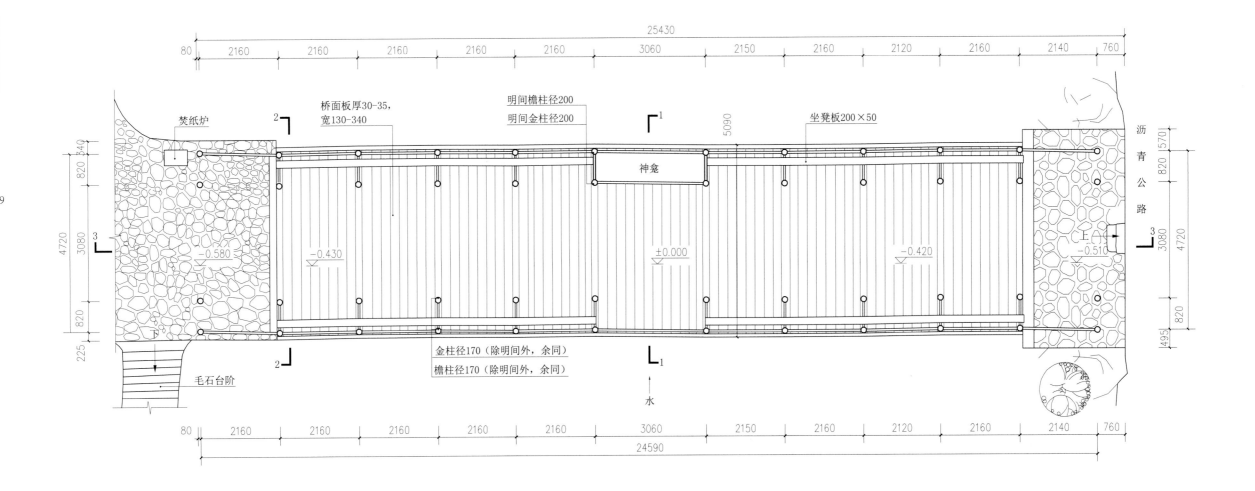

里仁桥平面图
Surface floor plan of Liren Bridge

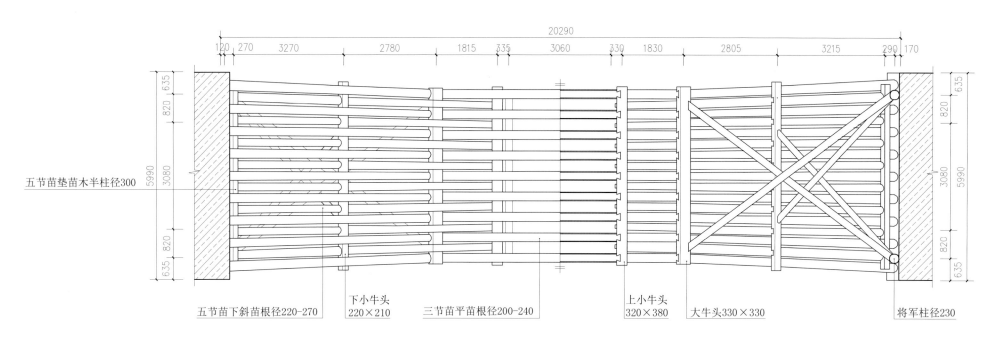

里仁桥桥体拱架系统仰视（左）与俯视（右）图
Plan of timber arch system of Liren Bridge as seen from below (left) and above (right)

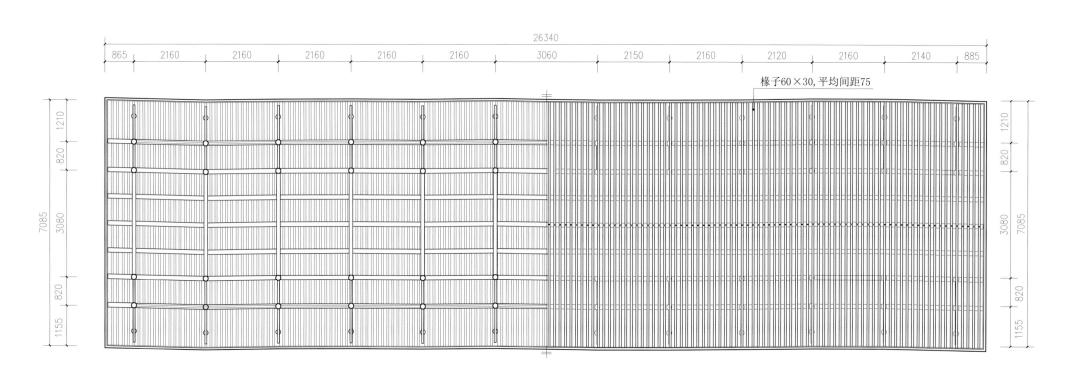

里仁桥廊屋梁架仰视（左）与俯视（右）图
Plan of corridor beam framework of Liren Bridge as seen from below (left) and above (right)

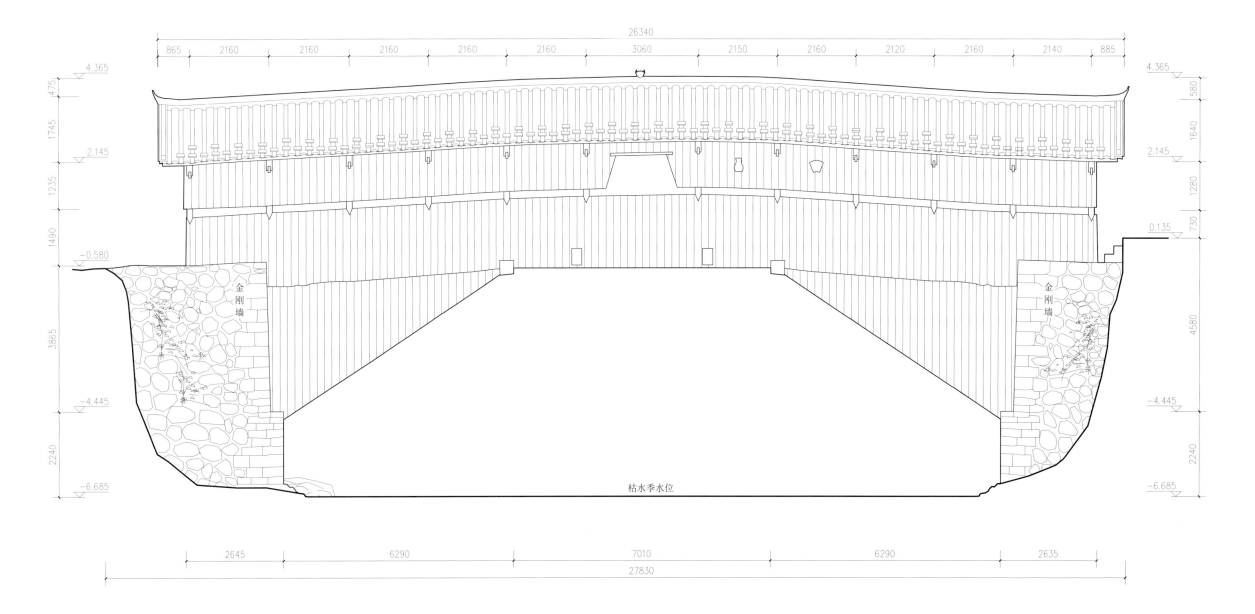

里仁桥西立面图
West elevation of Liren Bridge

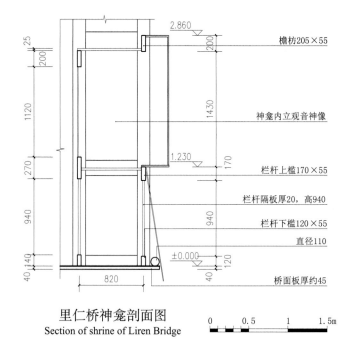

里仁桥神龛剖面图
Section of shrine of Liren Bridge

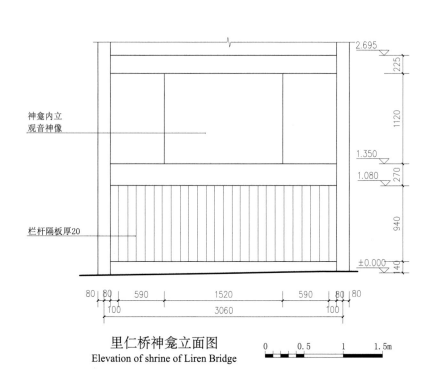

里仁桥神龛立面图
Elevation of shrine of Liren Bridge

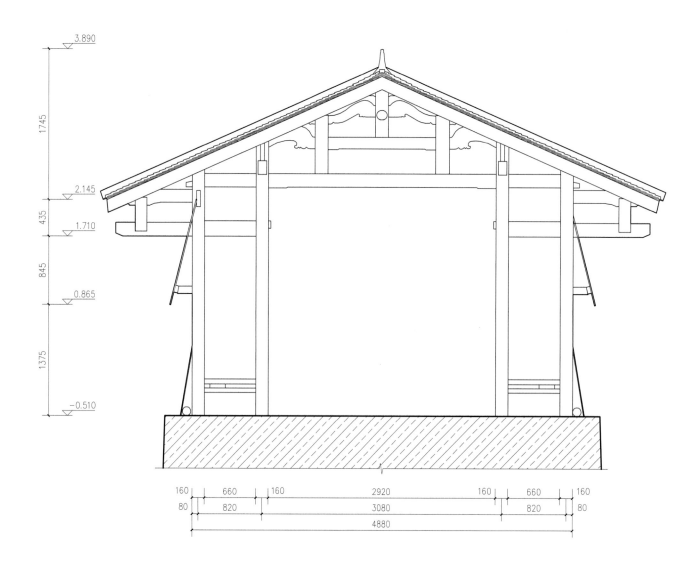

里仁桥南立面图
South elevation of Liren Bridge

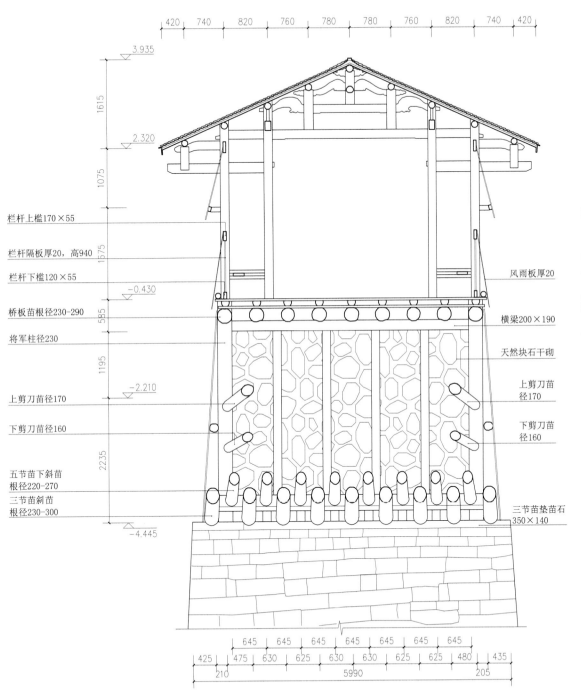

里仁桥 2-2 剖面图　　　里仁桥 1-1 剖面图

Section 2-2 of Liren Bridge　　　Section 1-1 of Liren Bridge

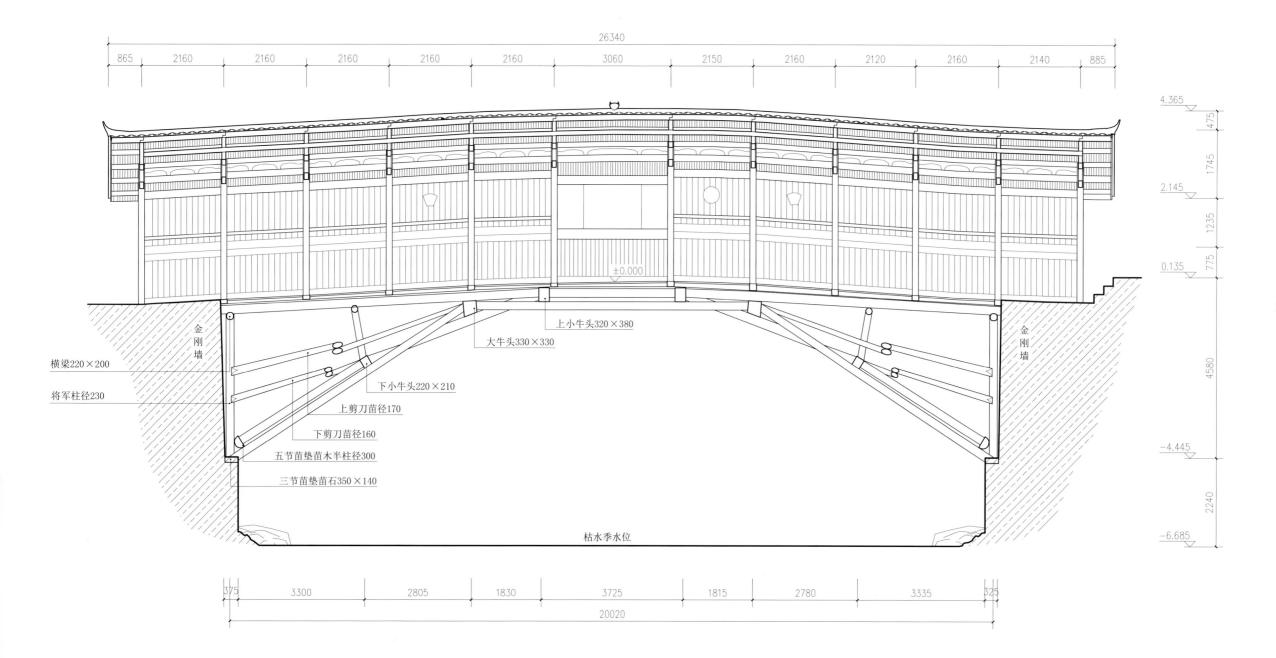

里仁桥 3-3 剖面图
Section 3-3 of Liren Bridge

飞云桥

Feiyun Bridge

Feiyun Bridge, also known as Buyun Bridge or more commonly, as Houdun Bridge, was first built in 1463, the seventh year of the Tianshun reign period of the Ming Dynasty, but rebuilt in 1818, the twenty-third year of the Jiaqing reign period of the Qing Dynasty. Located in Houdun village of Aoyang township, the bridge spans north to south across Chanxi Stream in a single span. Three octagonal caisson ceilings are installed inside the covered corridor. A hip-gable (*xieshan*) roof with two sets of eaves crowns the outside of the roof. The steep upwards turn of the eaves evokes the feeling that the bridge is poised to rise up into the air and fly, a feeling from which the bridge derives its name—Feiyun (Flying clouds) Bridge. Wooden boards form a deck, and a shrine is installed in the middle of the corridor dedicated to Lady Linshui and Huangsangong. At the bridge head stands a Guanyin Pavilion rebuilt during the Republican era (1912-1949).

The bridge is believed to be the ancestral temple of Lady Linshui, with complementary poetic lines written on red paper and mounted on paired columns, and these column couplets eulogize the beauty of the local landscape and its indigenous culture. Some couplets offer the prayers of local villagers for peace and happiness.

Originally, there were likely six interlocked timber-arched covered bridges spanning across Chanxi Stream located within a less than 2 km distance from the Shouning country seat, but only four of them have survived—Feiyun Bridge, Shengping Bridge, Xiangong Bridge, and Dengyun Bridge.

飞云桥，又称『步云桥』，俗称『后墩桥』，始建于明代天顺七年（1463年），清代嘉庆二十三年（1818年）重建。位于鳌阳镇后墩村，南北走向，单孔跨越蟾溪。悬山廊屋顶部设3个八角藻井，中部升起重檐歇山顶楼阁，使整座廊桥呈飘然欲飞形态，『飞云桥』之桥名或许由此而来。桥体拱架系统上铺木板为桥面，廊屋中部设神龛，祀临水夫人和黄三公。桥头有一座中华民国时期重建的观音阁。

此桥被远近民众认为是临水夫人的祖殿，桥上每楹均有对联，每联都与赞此地山水秀美、民间信仰、祈福平安有关。

据称在流贯寿宁县城的蟾溪不到2km的河段上，曾有6座贯木拱廊桥跨越，现留下4座。飞云桥是第1座，升平桥是第2座，仙宫桥是第3座，登云桥是第4座。

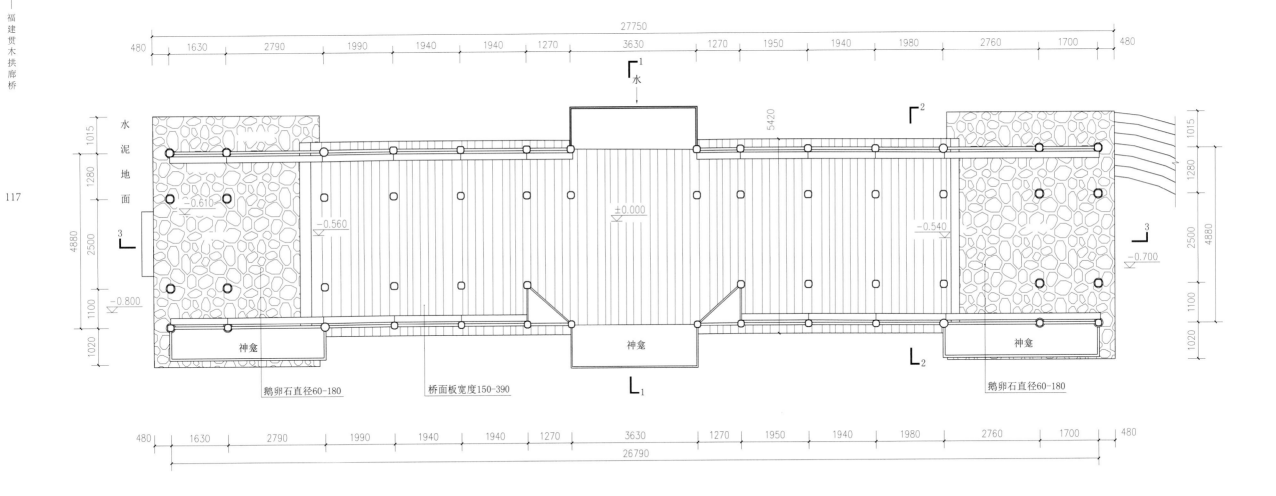

飞云桥平面图
Surface floor plan of Feiyun Bridge

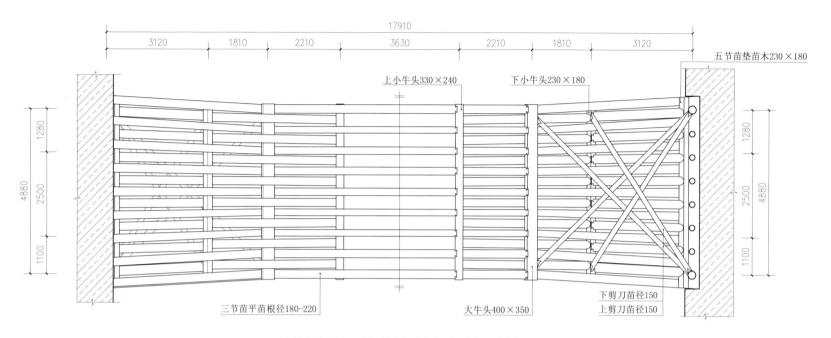

飞云桥桥体拱架系统仰视（左）与俯视（右）图
Plan of timber arch system of Feiyun Bridge as seen from below (left) and above (right)

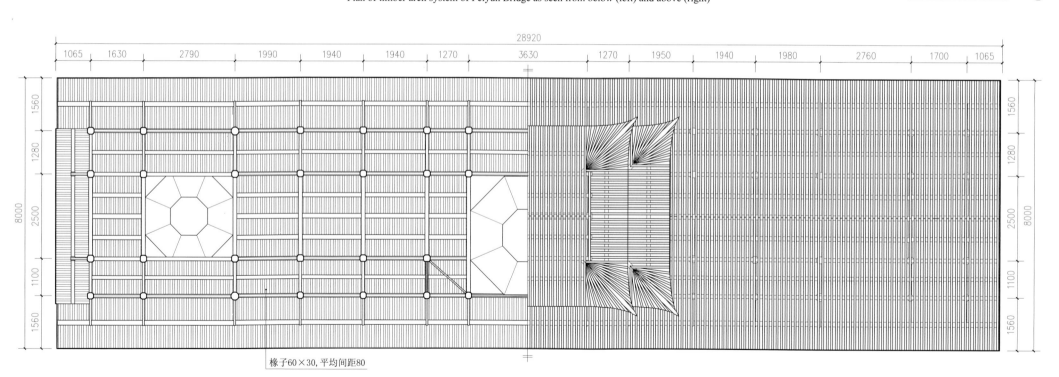

飞云桥廊屋梁架仰视（左）与俯视（右）图
Plan of corridor beam framework of Feiyun Bridge as seen from below (left) and above (right)

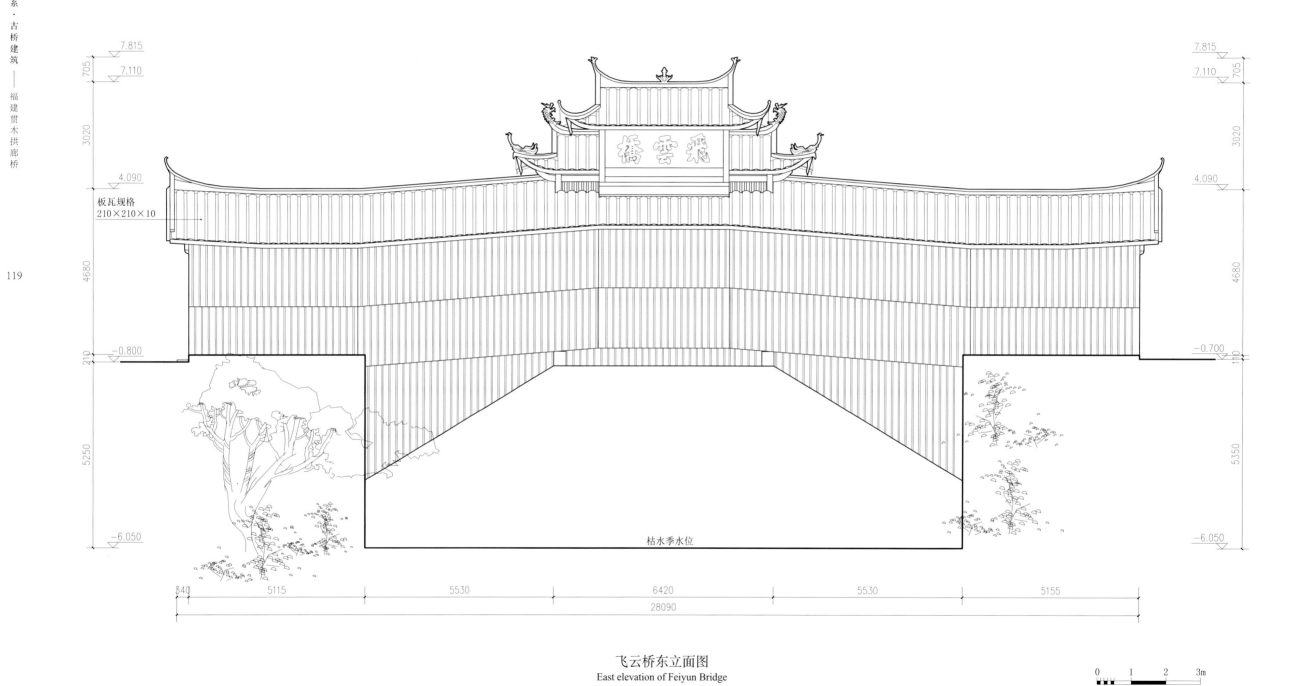

飞云桥东立面图
East elevation of Feiyun Bridge

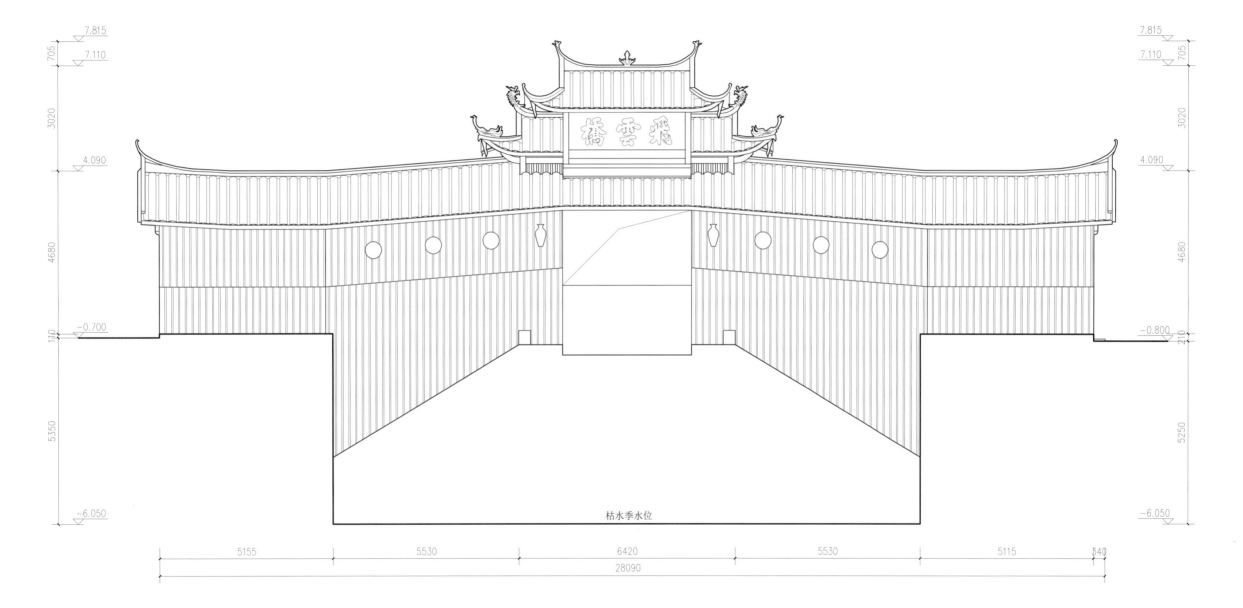

飞云桥西立面图
West elevation of Feiyun Bridge

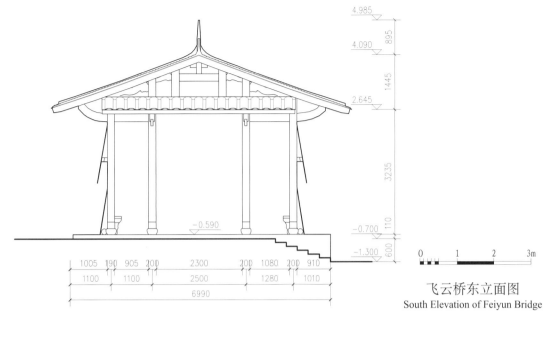

飞云桥东立面图
South Elevation of Feiyun Bridge

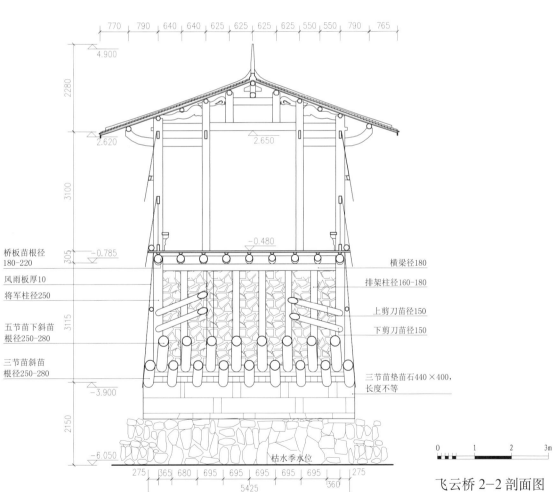

飞云桥 2-2 剖面图
Section 2-2 of Feiyun Bridge

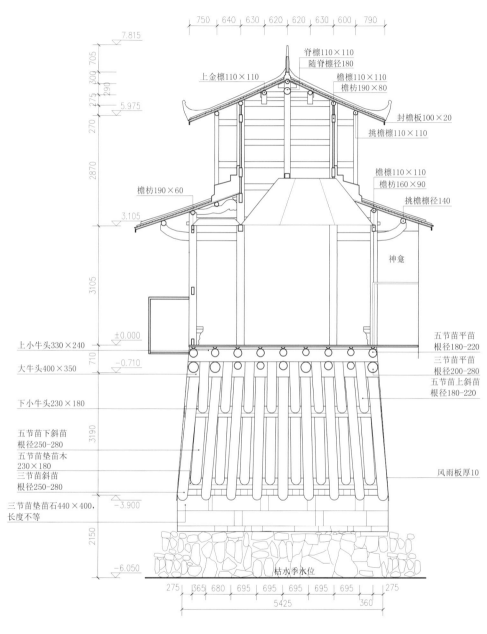

飞云桥 1-1 剖面图
Section 1-1 of Feiyun Bridge

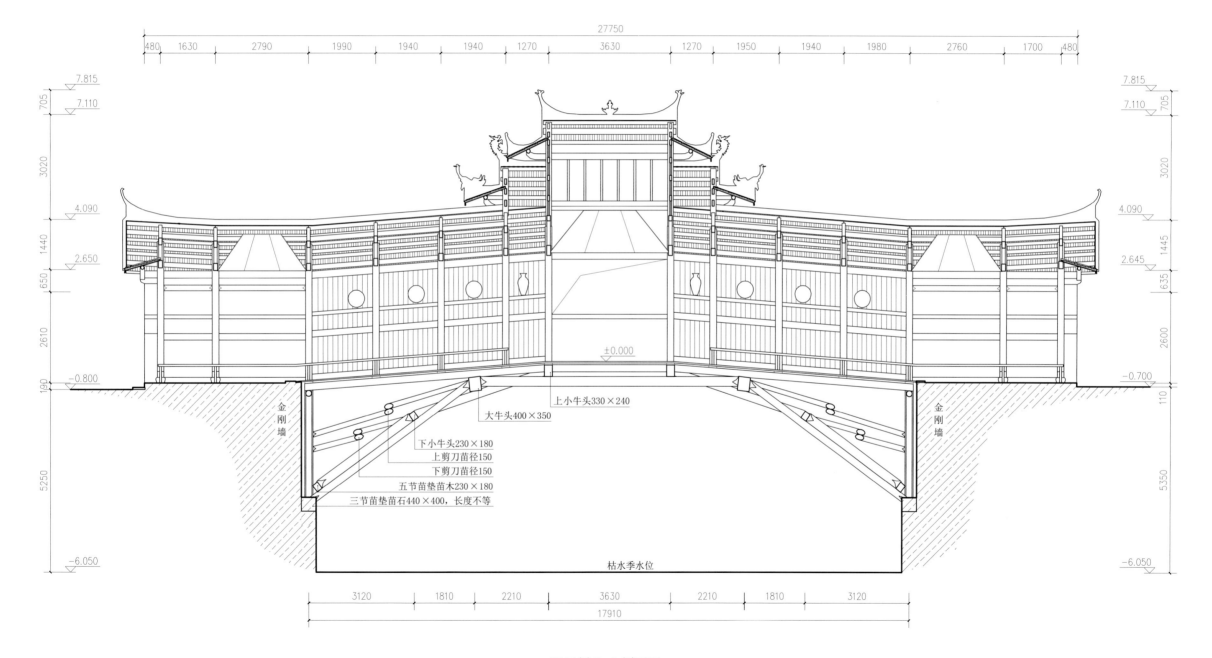

飞云桥 3-3 剖面图
Section 3-3 of Feiyun Bridge

回澜桥

Huilan Bridge

Huilan Bridge, also known as Botan Bridge, was first built in 1893, the nineteenth year of the Guangxu reign period of the Qing Dynasty. In 1959, the bridge was torn down to make space for a livestock farm but was subsequently rebuilt again in 1964. Located at the southern end of Nanyang village in Nanyang township, the bridge extends from east to west across a Nanyang Stream tributary in a single span. Wooden boards are mounted to form a deck, and a shrine is installed in the covered corridor dedicated to Lady Linshui, which is now gone. The eastern bridge end extends into a room called a 'pavilion.' To the east of the bridge stands Guanyin (Avalokiteśvara) Pavilion and Yuanshuai (Marshal/Supreme Commander) Palace. Couplets decorate the corridor columns.

回澜桥，又称「渤潭桥」，始建于清代光绪十九年（1893年），1959年建畜牧场时被拆，1964年重建。位于南阳镇南阳村南，单孔跨越南阳溪支流上，东西走向。桥体拱架系统上铺木板为桥面，廊屋中部设神龛，祀临水夫人，现无存。东侧伸出一间为路亭，桥东有观音阁、元帅宫，廊桥中有诸多楹联。

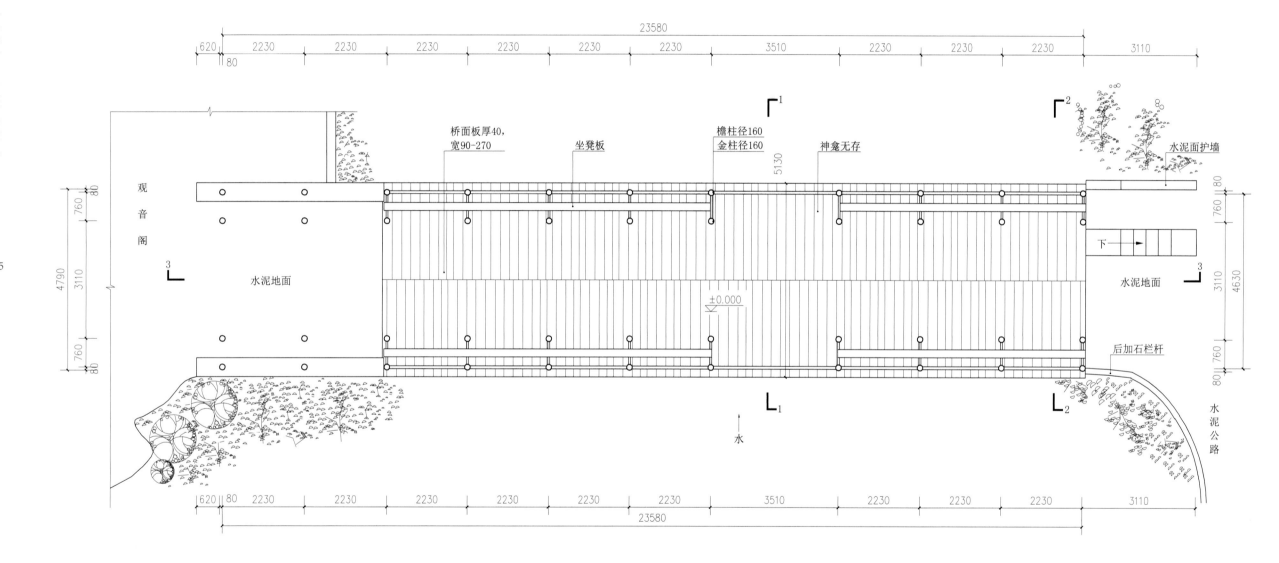

回澜桥平面图
Surface floor plan of Huilan Bridge

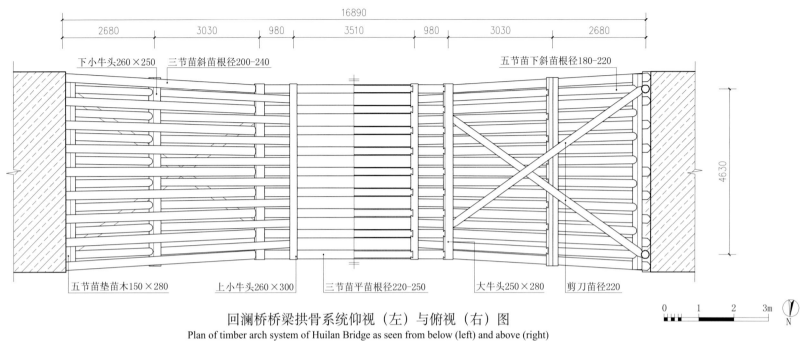

回澜桥桥梁拱骨系统仰视（左）与俯视（右）图
Plan of timber arch system of Huilan Bridge as seen from below (left) and above (right)

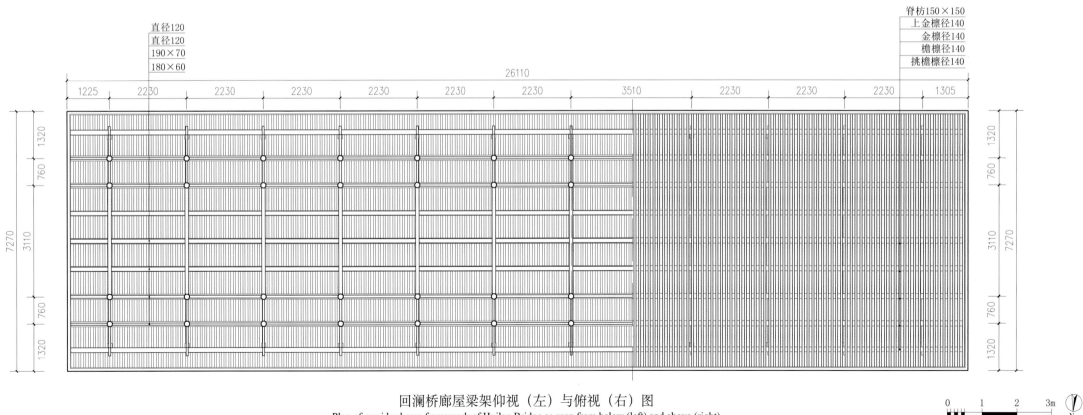

回澜桥廊屋梁架仰视（左）与俯视（右）图
Plan of corridor beam framework of Huilan Bridge as seen from below (left) and above (right)

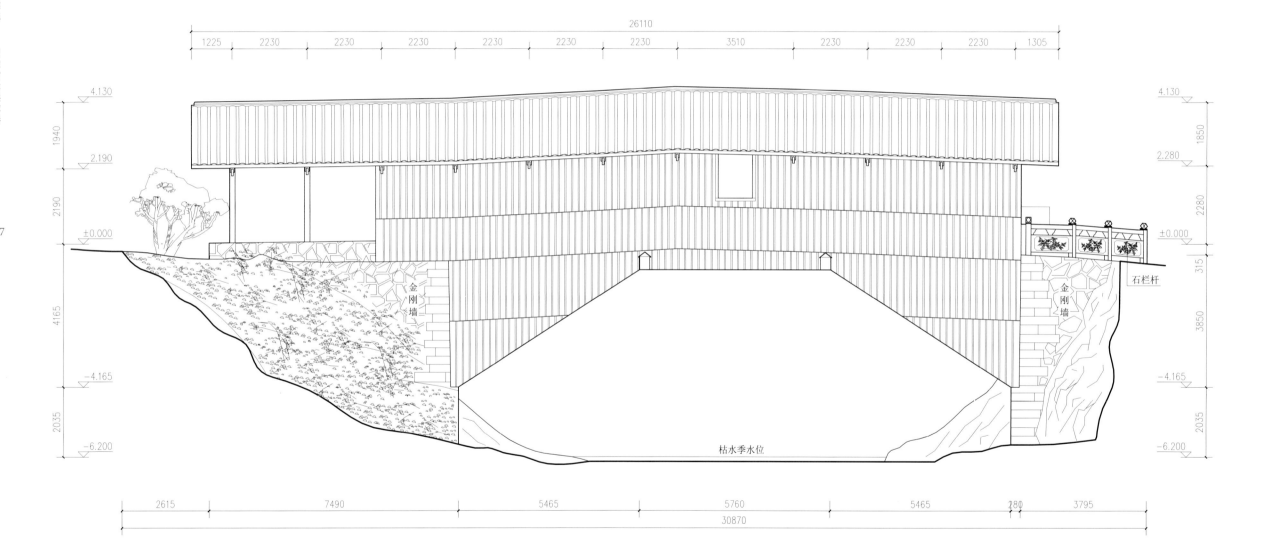

回澜桥北立面图
North elevation of Huilan Bridge

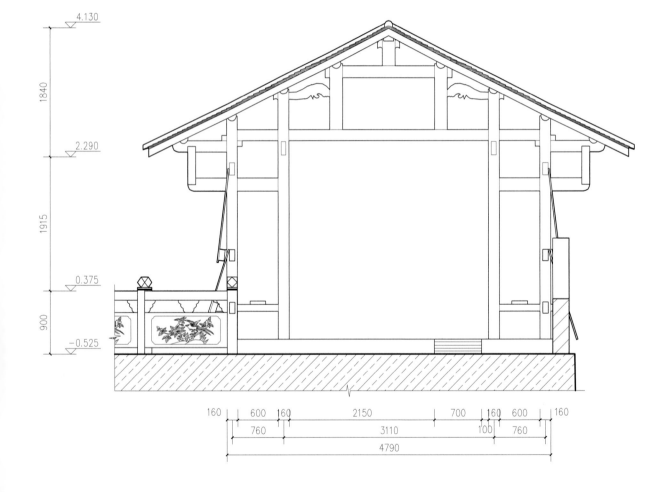
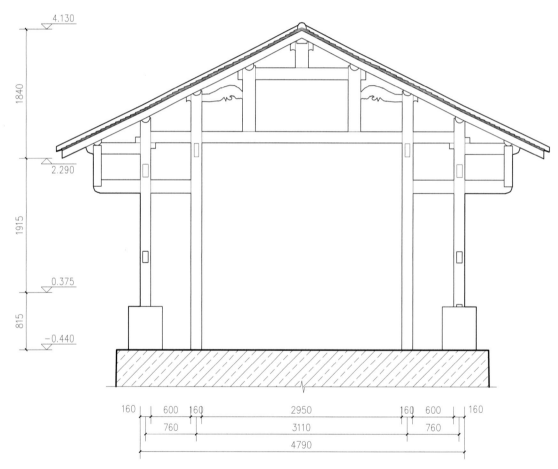

回澜桥西立面图
West elevation of Huilan Bridge

回澜桥东立面图
East elevation of Huilan Bridge

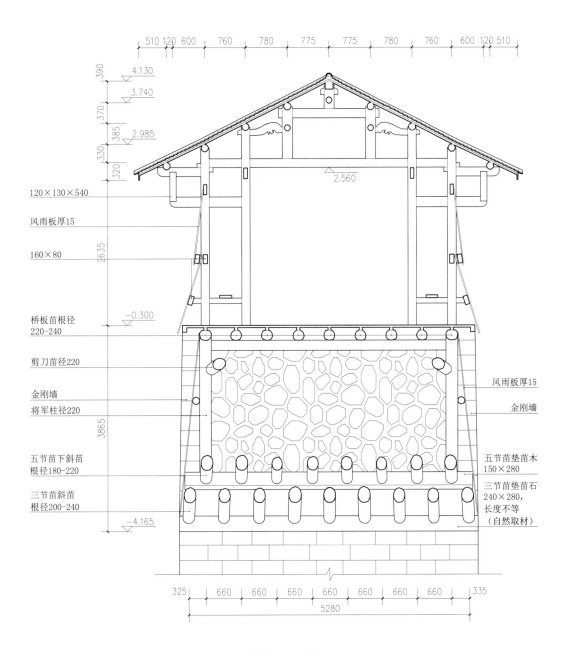

回澜桥 2-2 剖面图
Section 2-2 of Huilan Bridge

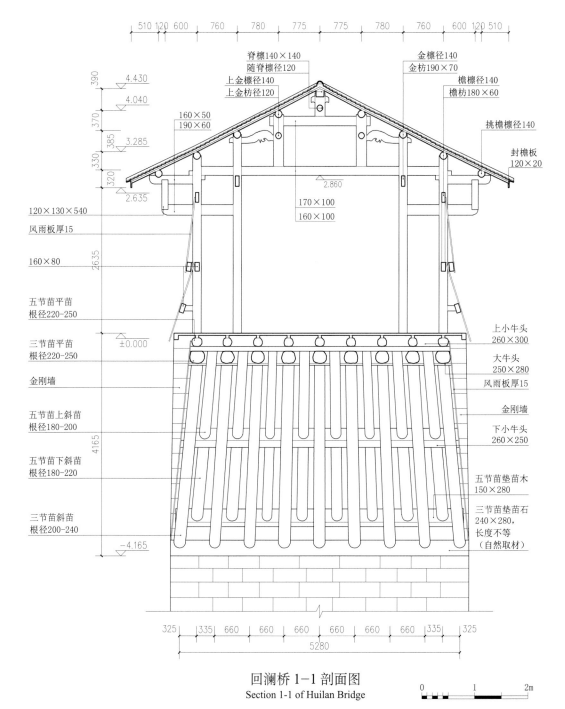

回澜桥 1-1 剖面图
Section 1-1 of Huilan Bridge

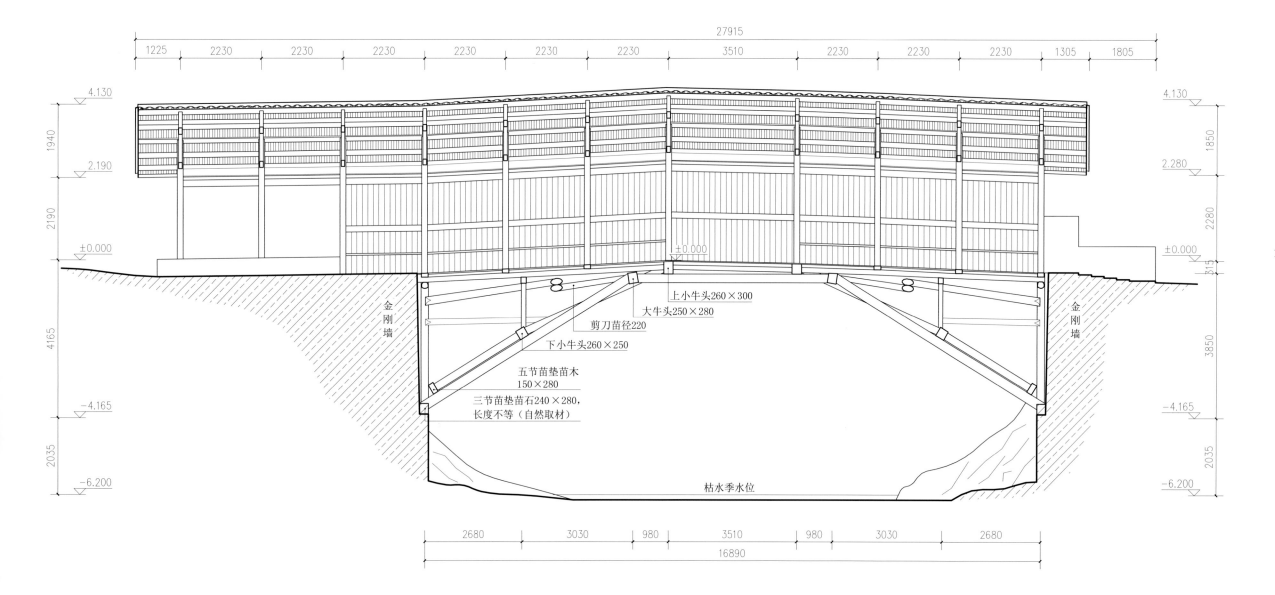

回澜桥 3-3 剖面图
Section 3-3 of Huilan Bridge

尤溪上桥

Youxishang Bridge

Youxishang Bridge, also known as Wenming Bridge or Zhongcun Bridge, was built in 1832, the twelfth year of the Daoguang reign period of the Qing Dynasty. Located at the head of Youxi village in Qinyang township, the bridge spans north to south across a tributary of the Changlai Stream in a single span. Wooden boards form a deck, and a shrine is ensconced in the middle of the covered corridor for the worship of Guanyin. Another shrine is nestled into the sloping hillside adjacent to the road to the south of the bridge.

尤溪上桥，又称『文明桥』、『中村桥』，建于清代道光十二年（1832年），位于芹洋乡尤溪村西侧水头，单孔跨越长濑溪的支流上，南北走向。桥体拱架系统上铺木板为桥面，廊屋中部设神龛，祀观音。桥南路旁利用山岩建一神龛，祀土地神。

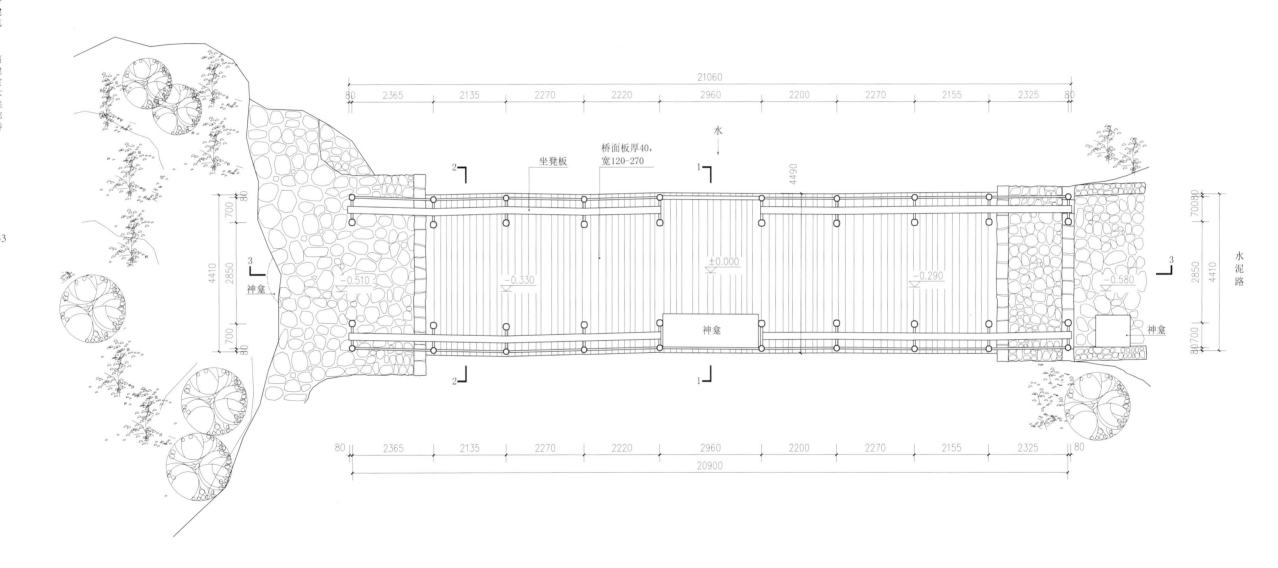

尤溪上桥平面图
Surface floor plan of Youxishang Bridge

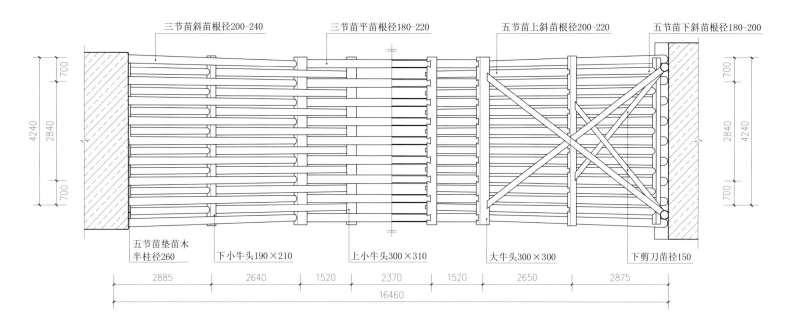

尤溪上桥桥体拱架系统仰视（左）与俯视（右）图
Plan of timber arch system of Youxishang Bridge as seen from below (left) and above (right)

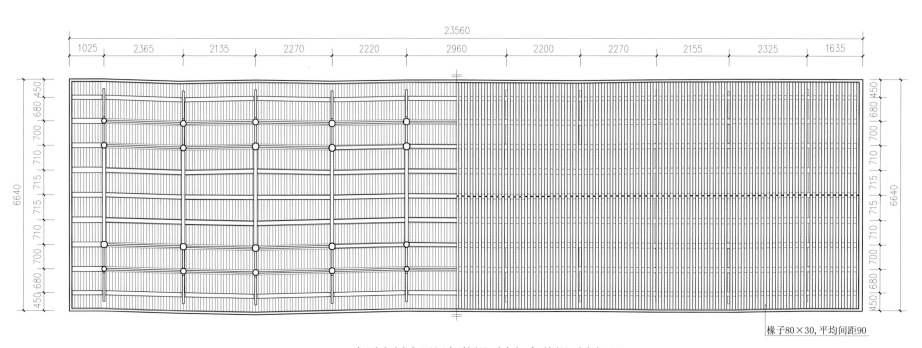

尤溪上桥廊屋梁架仰视（左）与俯视（右）图
Plan of corridor beam framework of Youxishang Bridge as seen from below (left) and above (right)

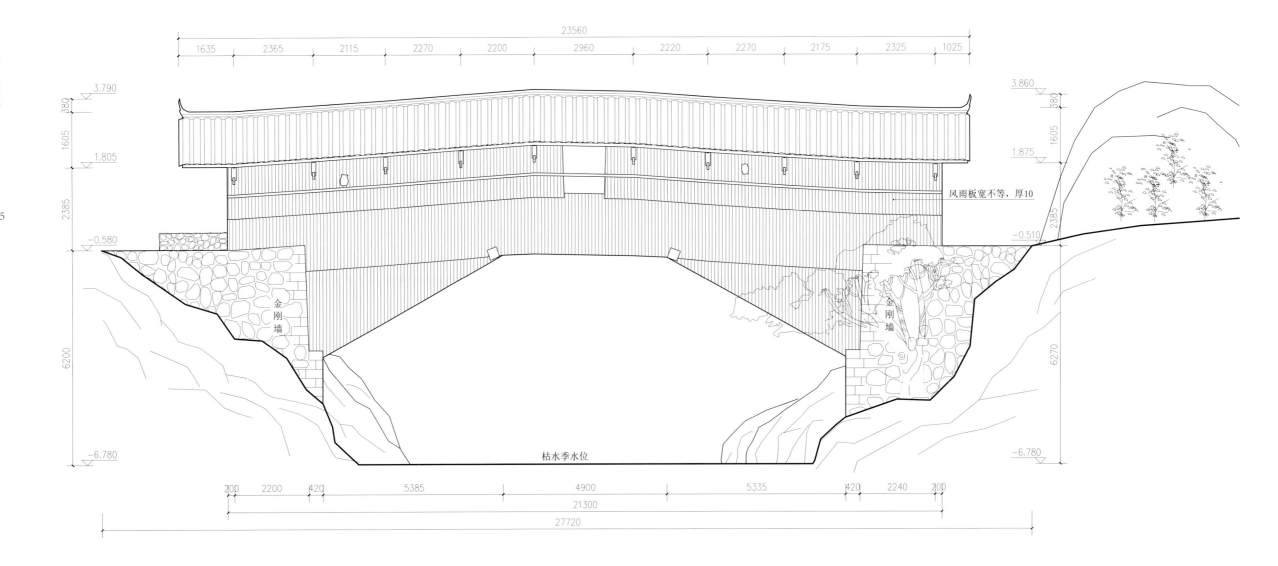

尤溪上桥东立面图
East elevation of Youxishang Bridge

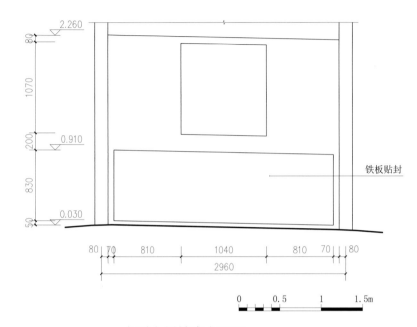

尤溪上桥神龛立面图
Elevation of shrine of Youxishang Bridge

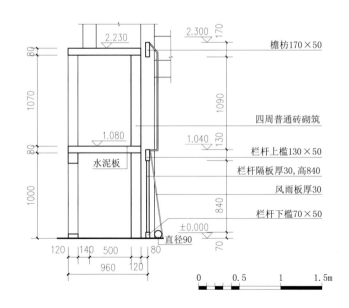

尤溪上桥神龛剖面图
Section of shrine of Youxishang Bridge

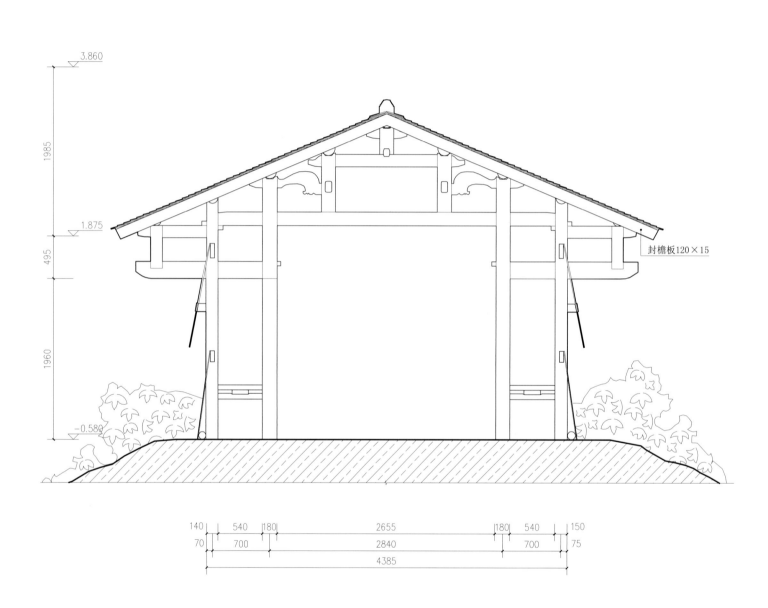

尤溪上桥北立面图
North elevation of Youxishang Bridge

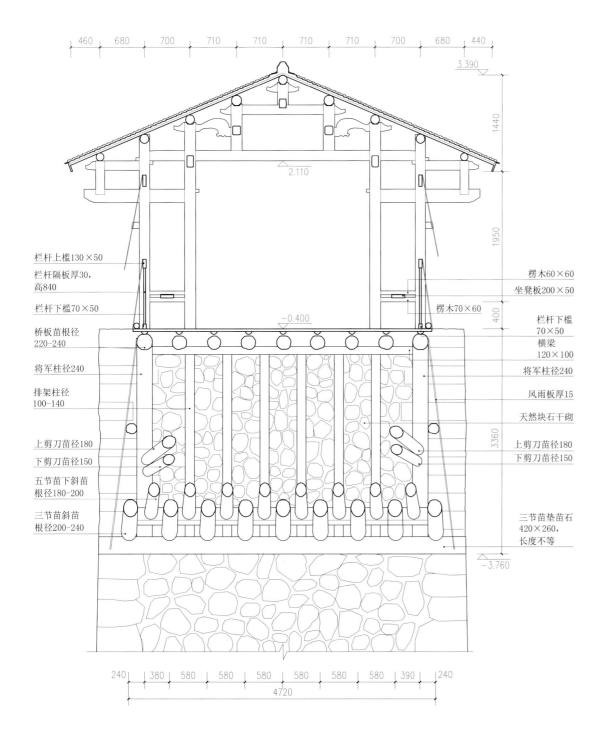
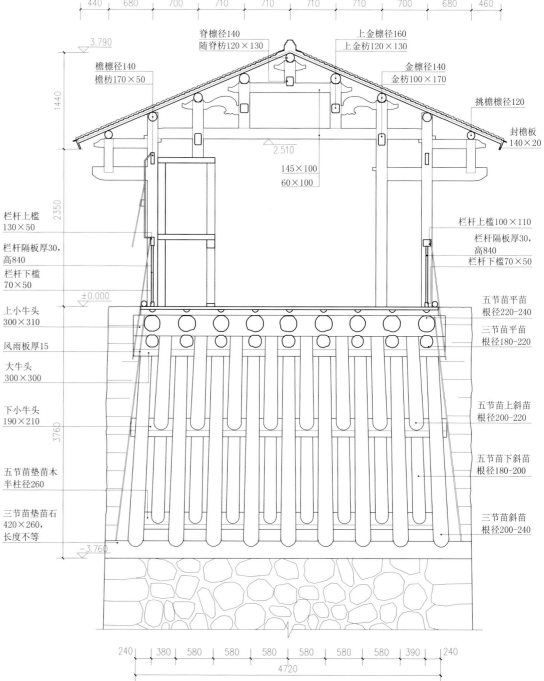

尤溪上桥 2-2 剖面图
Section 2-2 of Youxishang Bridge

尤溪上桥 1-1 剖面图
Section 1-1 of Youxishang Bridge

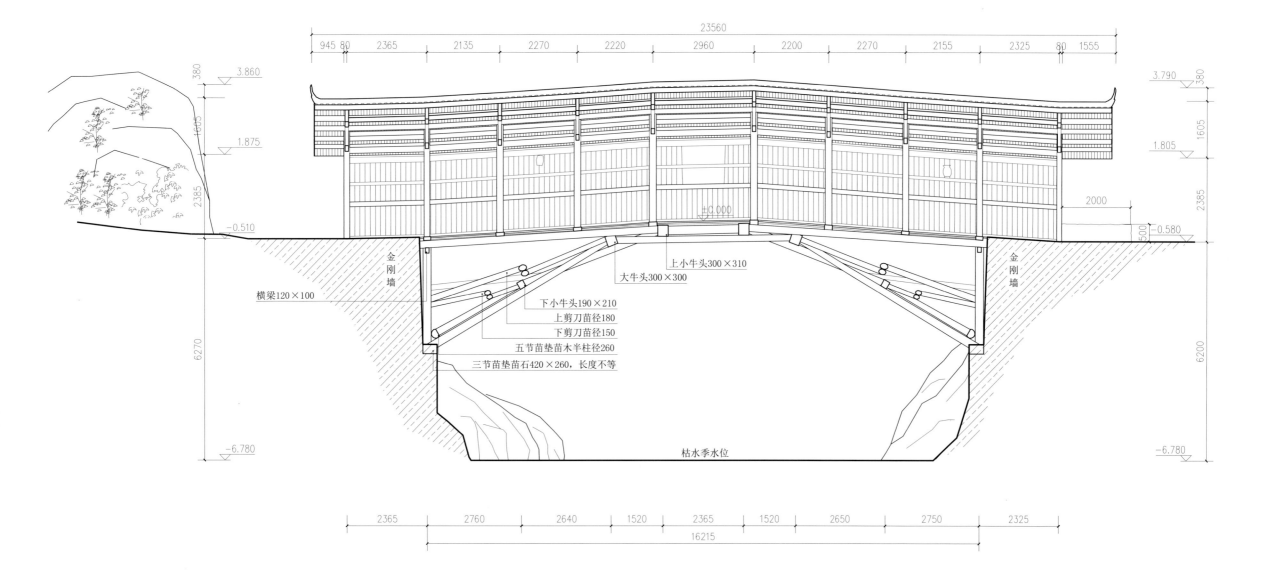

尤溪上桥 3-3 剖面图
Section 3-3 of Youxishang Bridge

小东上桥

Xiaodongshang Bridge

Xiaodongshang Bridge, first built in the Ming Dynasty, was rebuilt in 1801, the sixth year of the Jiaqing reign period of the Qing Dynasty. Located in Xiaodong village of Kengdi township, the bridge crosses the stream that flows south out of Menghu village in a single span from east to west. Wooden boards are mounted as the bridge deck, and a shrine has been built in the middle of the covered corridor to worship Guanyin. Wooden benches are built to the opposite of the shrine to store the passengers' belongings or to allow for rest. Another shrine dedicated to Tudi, the Lord of the Soil and the Ground, stands beside the road to the west of the bridge on a sloping hillside.

小东上桥，明代始建，清代嘉庆六年（1801年）重建，位于坑底乡小东村，单孔跨越由猛虎村南来的溪流，东西走向。桥体拱架系统上铺木板为桥面，廊屋中部设神龛，祀观音，与神龛相对一侧左右两间设榻，供人放物和躺卧歇息。桥西公路边山岩上凿有神龛，祀土地神。

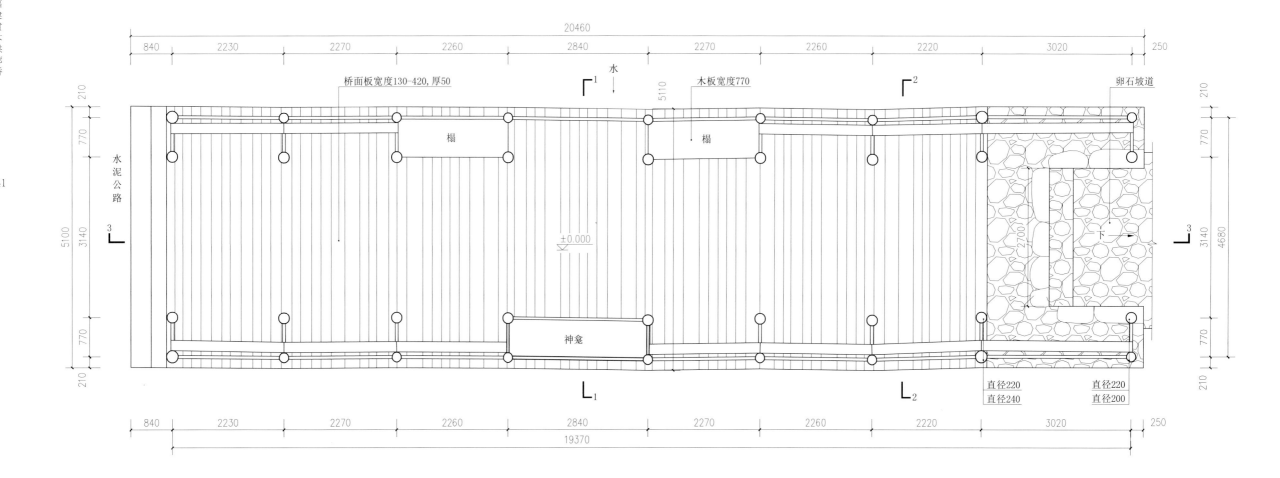

小东上桥平面图
Surface floor plan of Xiaodongshang Bridge

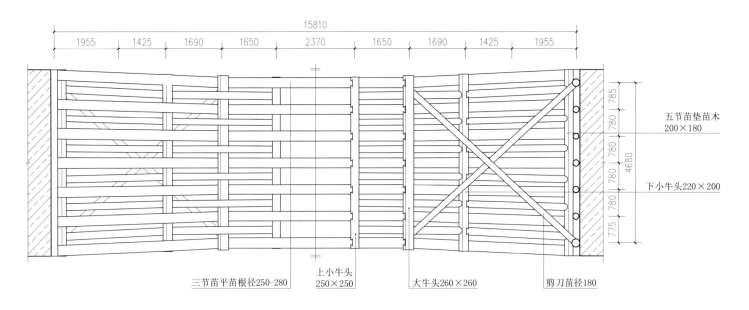

小东上桥桥体拱架系统仰视（左）与俯视（右）图

Plan of timber arch system of Xiaodongshang Bridge as seen from above (left) and below (right)

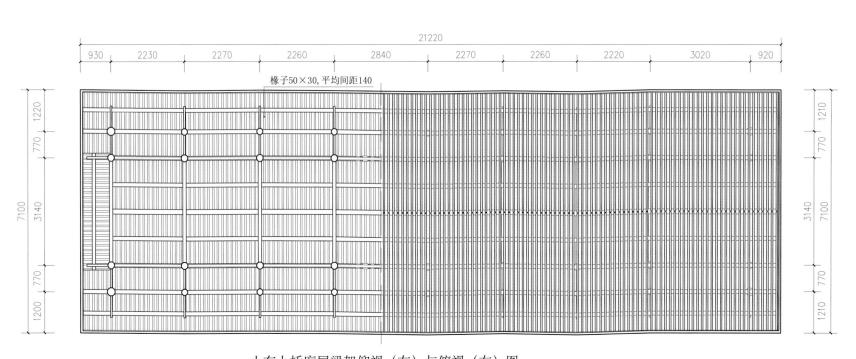

小东上桥廊屋梁架仰视（左）与俯视（右）图

Plan of corridor beam framework of Xiaodongshang Bridge as seen from below (left) and above (right)

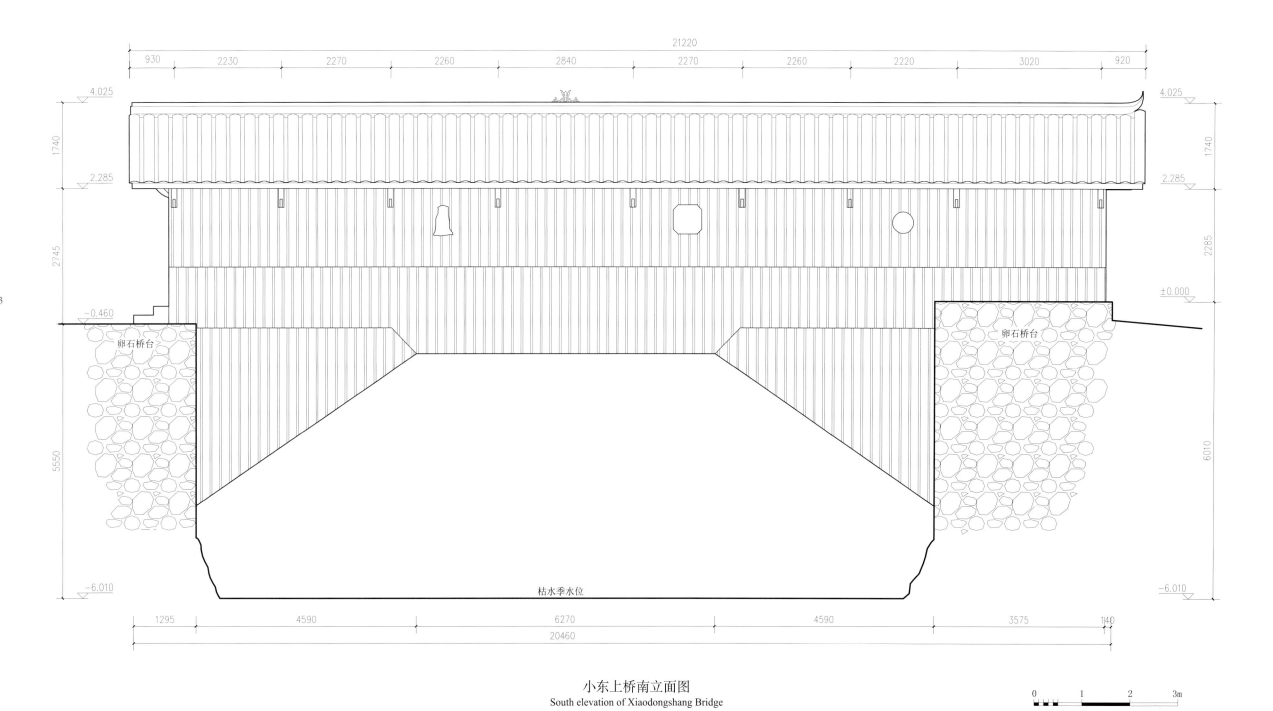

小东上桥南立面图
South elevation of Xiaodongshang Bridge

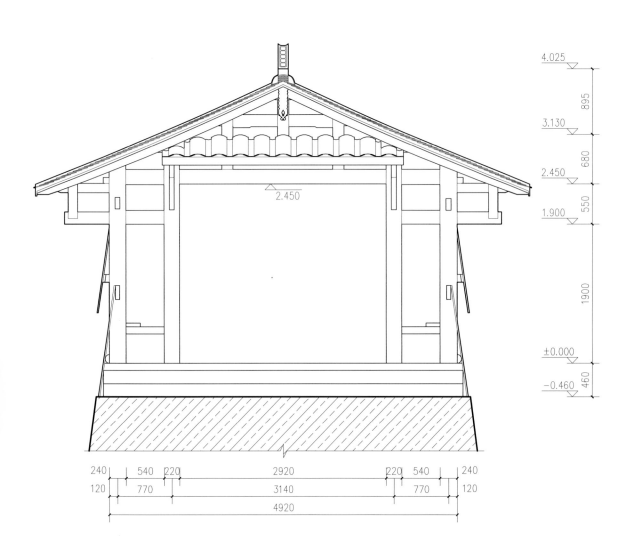
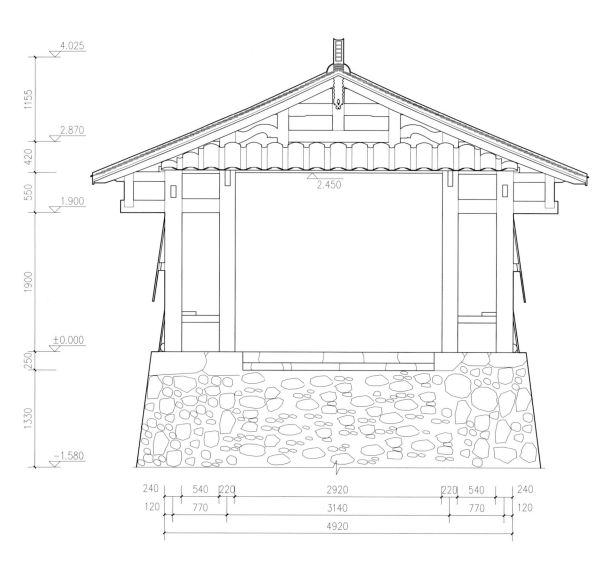

小东上桥西立面图
West elevation of Xiaodongshang Bridge

小东上桥东立面图
East elevation of Xiaodongshang Bridge

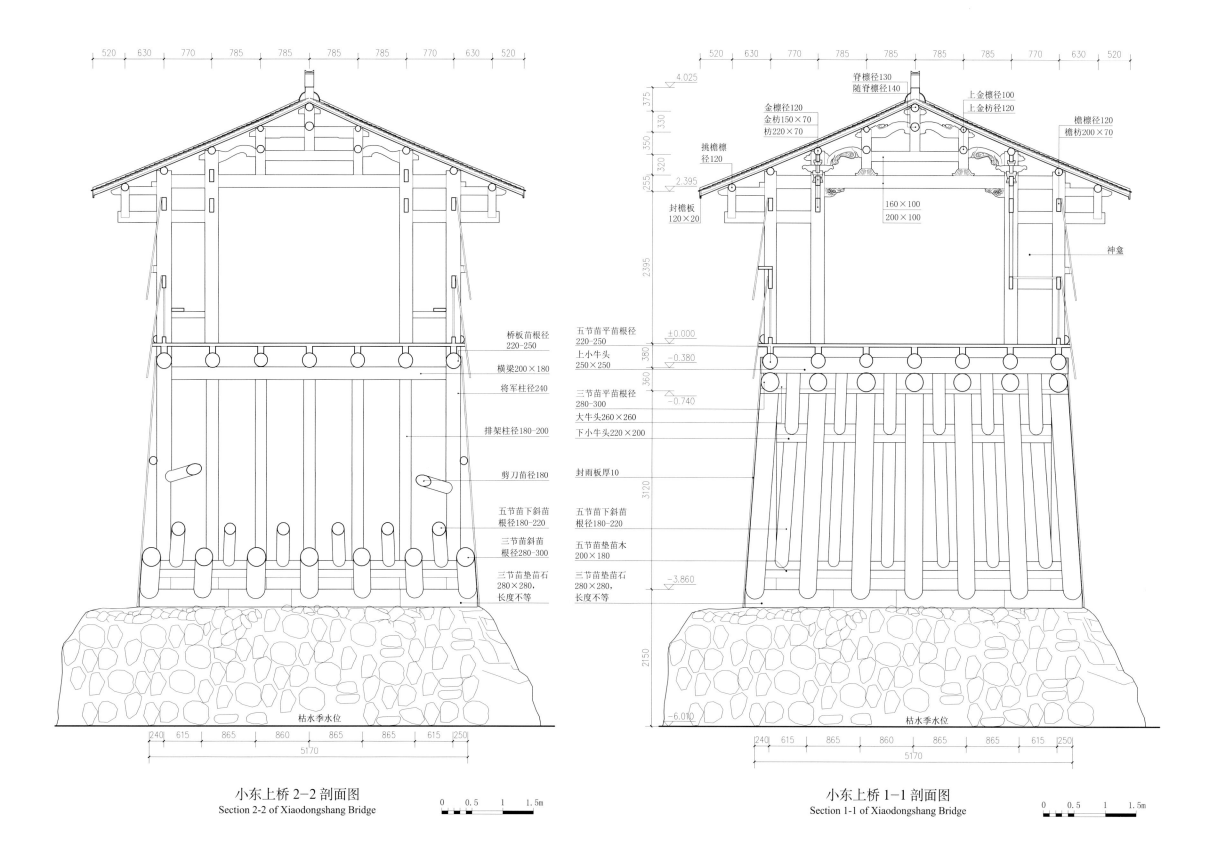

小东上桥 2-2 剖面图
Section 2-2 of Xiaodongshang Bridge

小东上桥 1-1 剖面图
Section 1-1 of Xiaodongshang Bridge

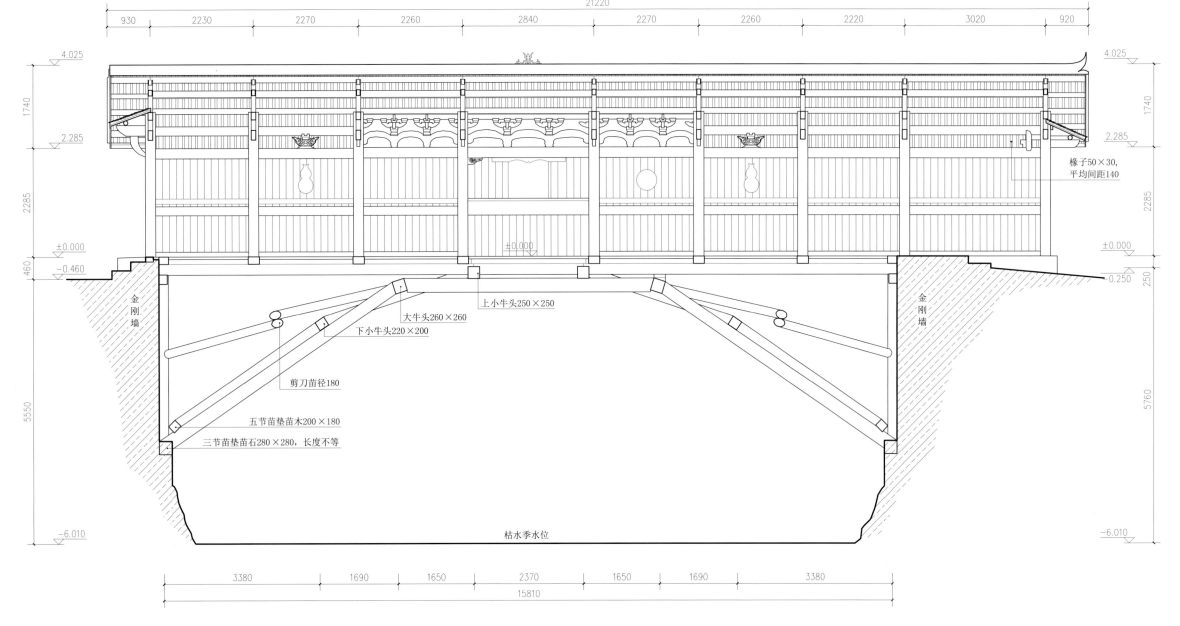

小东上桥 3-3 剖面图
Section 3-3 of Xiaodongshang Bridge

溪南桥

Xi'nan Bridge

Xi'nan Bridge, also known as Puji Bridge, first built in the Ming Dynasty but rebuilt and destroyed on several occasions over the past centuries. The current bridge was built in 1965. Located in Xi'nan village of Nanyang township, the bridge spans northwest to southeast across a tributary of Nanyang Stream. Wooden boards form a bridge deck, and a shrine is installed in the covered corridor dedicated to worship Lady Linshui. In the small nearby garden northwestern of the bridge and fenced in by short walls stands another shrine on the hilly terrain that is dedicated to Tudi, the Lord of the Soil and the Ground.

溪南桥，又称『普济桥』，明代始建，屡废，1965年重建，位于南阳镇溪南村中，单孔跨越南阳溪支流，西北—东南走向。桥体拱架系统上铺木板为桥面，廊屋中部设神龛，祀临水夫人。在桥西北不远处用一堵短墙围成的小园林中，依山设一神龛，祀本地土地神。

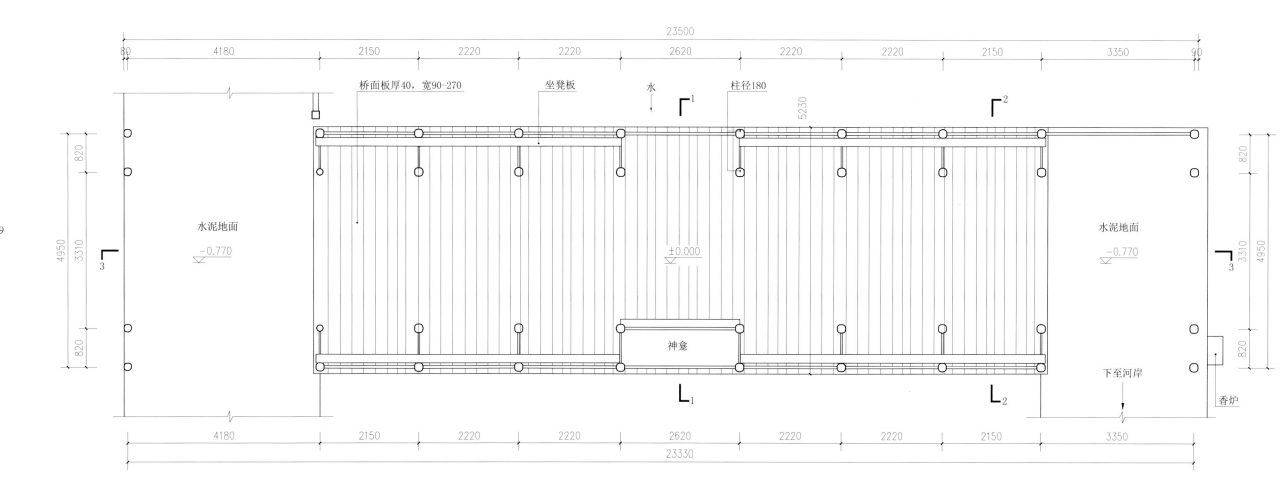

溪南桥平面图
Surface floor plan of Xi'nan Bridge

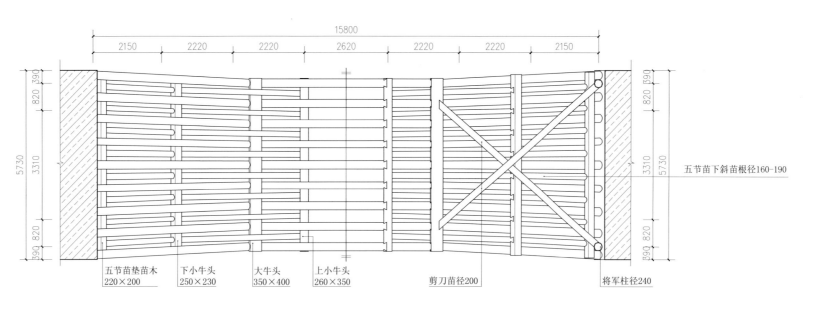

溪南桥桥梁拱骨系统仰视（左）与俯视（右）图
Plan of timber arch system of Xi'nan Bridge as seen from below (left) and above (right)

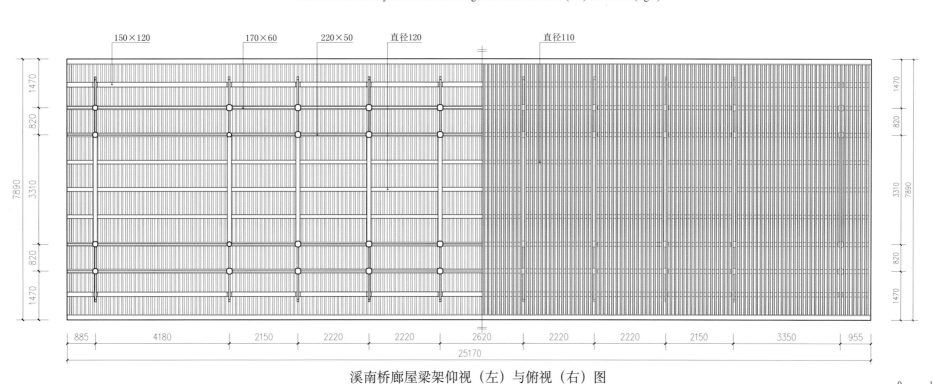

溪南桥廊屋梁架仰视（左）与俯视（右）图
Plan of corridor beam framework of Xi'nan Bridge as seen from below (left) and above (right)

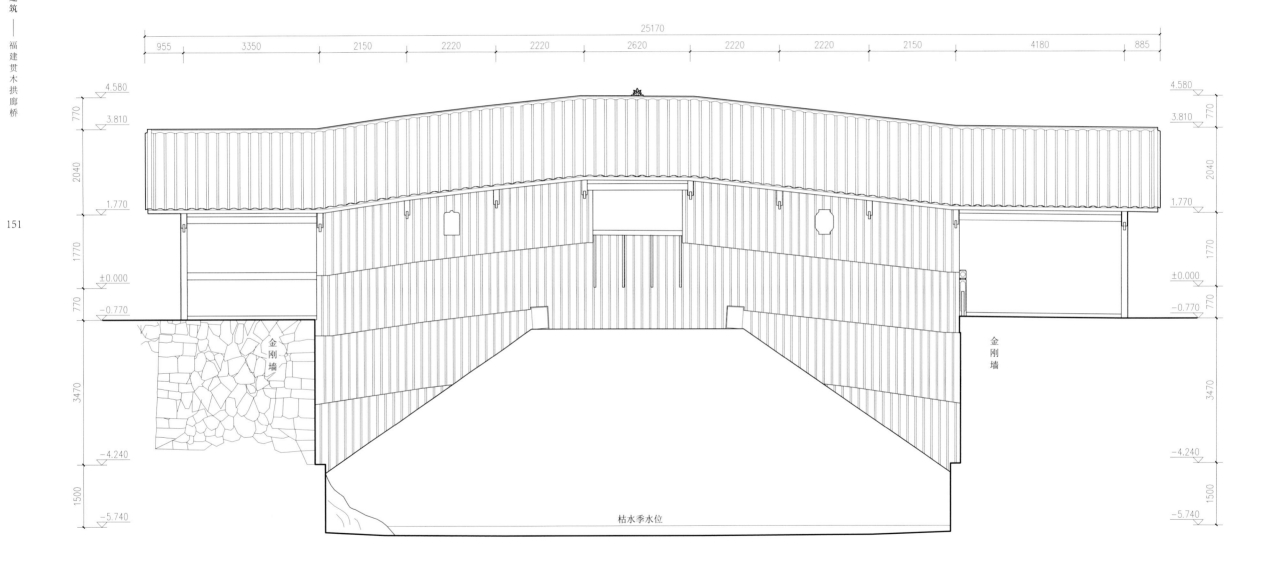

溪南桥东北立面图
Northeast elevation of Xi'nan Bridge

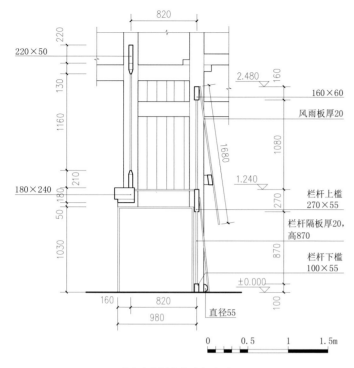

溪南桥神龛剖面图
Section of shrine of Xi'nan Bridge

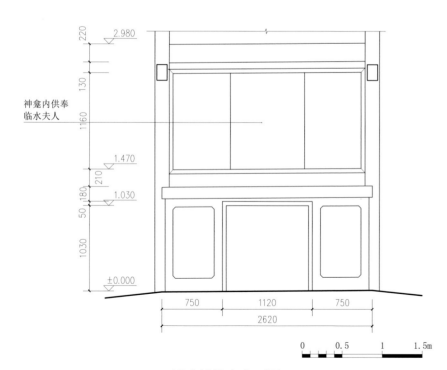

溪南桥神龛立面图
Elevation of shrine of Xi'nan Bridge

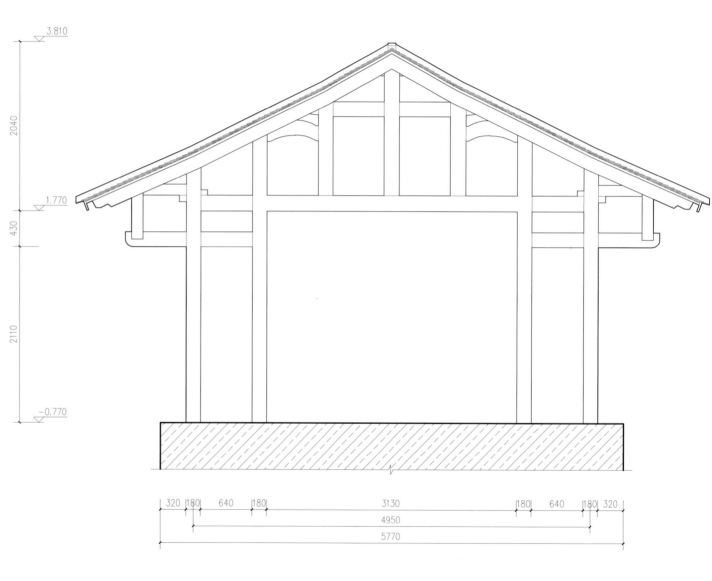

溪南桥东南立面图
Southeast elevation of Xi'nan Bridge

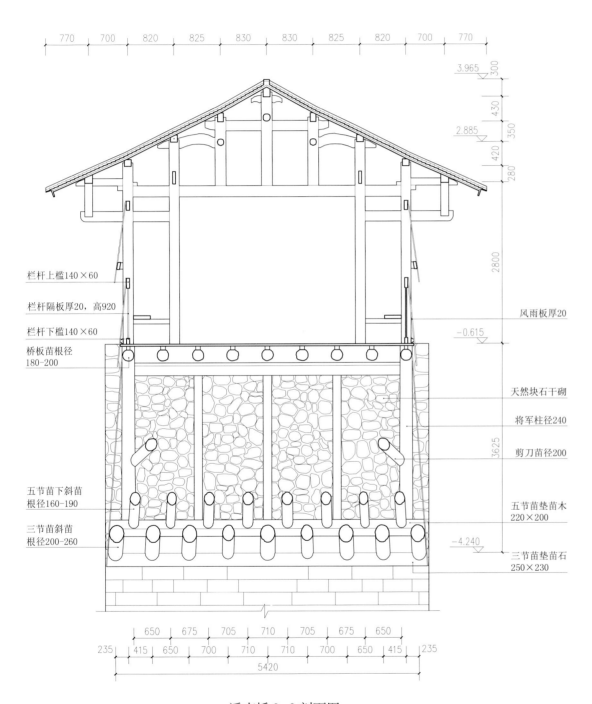

溪南桥 2-2 剖面图
Section 2-2 of Xi'nan Bridge

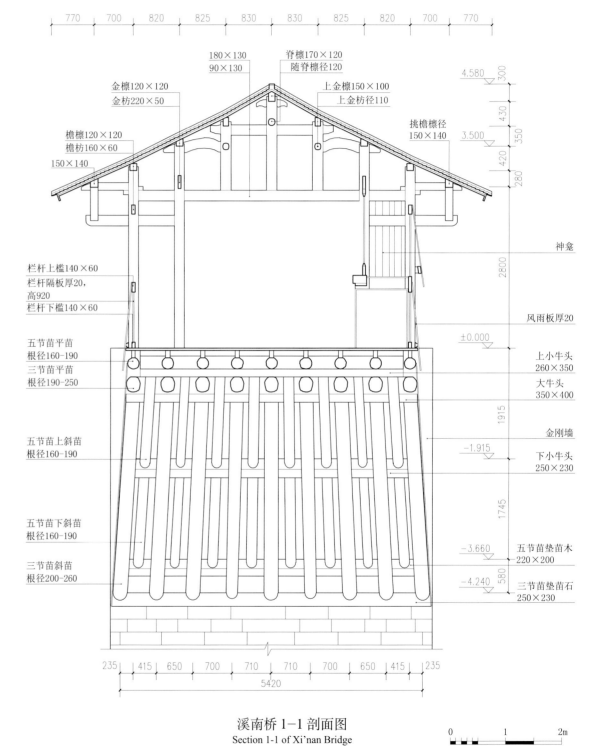

溪南桥 1-1 剖面图
Section 1-1 of Xi'nan Bridge

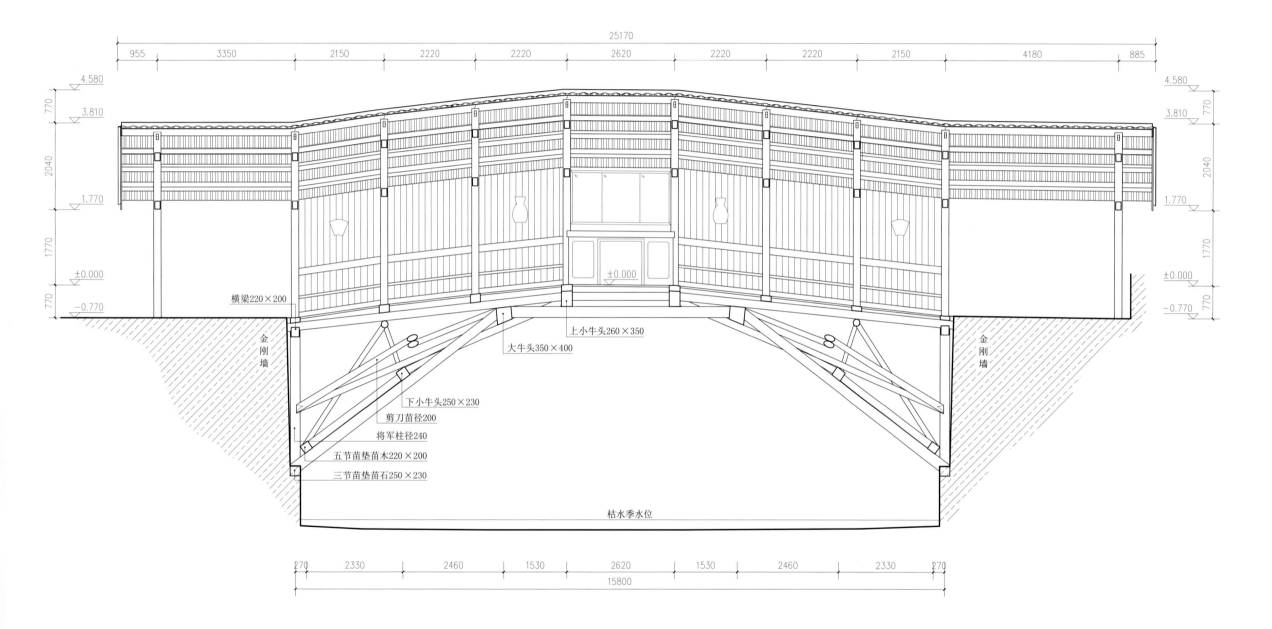

溪南桥 3-3 剖面图
Section 3-3 of Xi'nan Bridge

单桥

Dan Bridge

Dan Bridge was first built in 1792, the fifty-seventh year of the Qianlong reign period of the Qing dynasty, but rebuilt in 1939, the twenty-eighth year of the Republican era. Located in the south of Menghulin village, Kengdi township, the bridge spans northeast to southwest across a tributary of the Houxi Stream in a single span. Wooden boards form a bridge deck, and a shrine is installed in the covered corridor dedicated to Lady Linshui.

单桥，始建于清代乾隆五十七年（1792年），现桥为中华民国28年（1939年）重建，位于坑底乡猛虎林村村南，单孔跨越后溪上游的支流，东北—西南走向。桥体拱架系统上铺木板为桥面，廊屋中部设神龛，祀临水夫人。

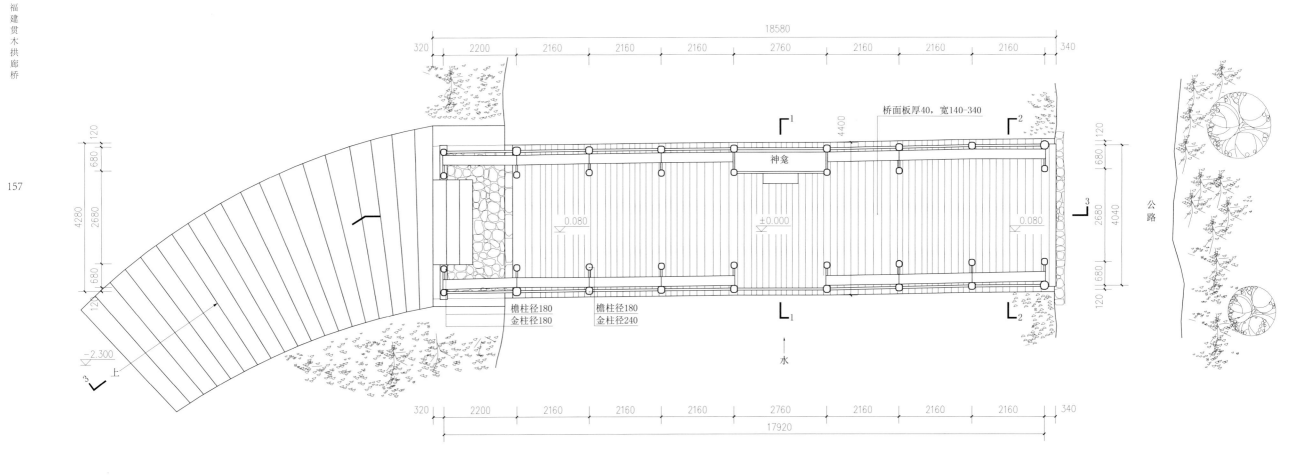

单桥平面图
Surface floor plan of Dan Bridge

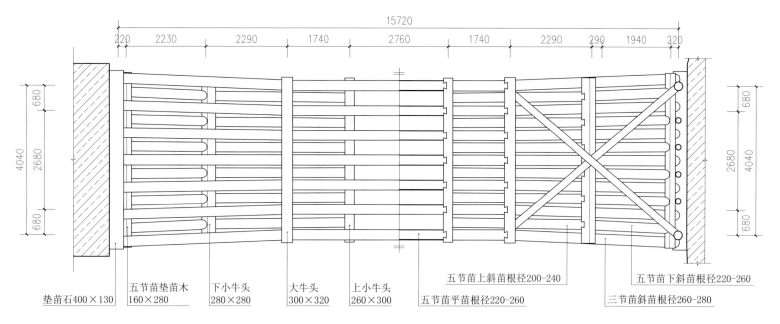

单桥桥梁拱骨系统仰视（左）与俯视（右）图
Plan of timber arch system of Dan Bridge as seen from below (left) and above (right)

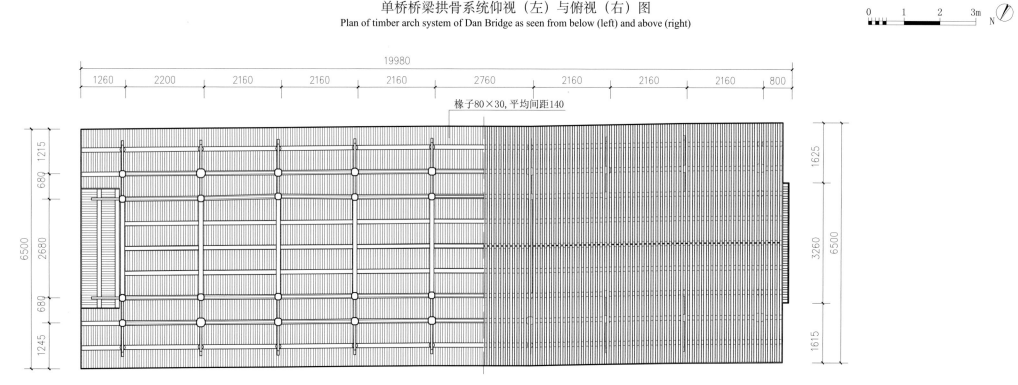

单桥廊屋梁架仰视（左）与俯视（右）图
Plan of corridor beam framework of Dan Bridge as seen from below (left) and above (right)

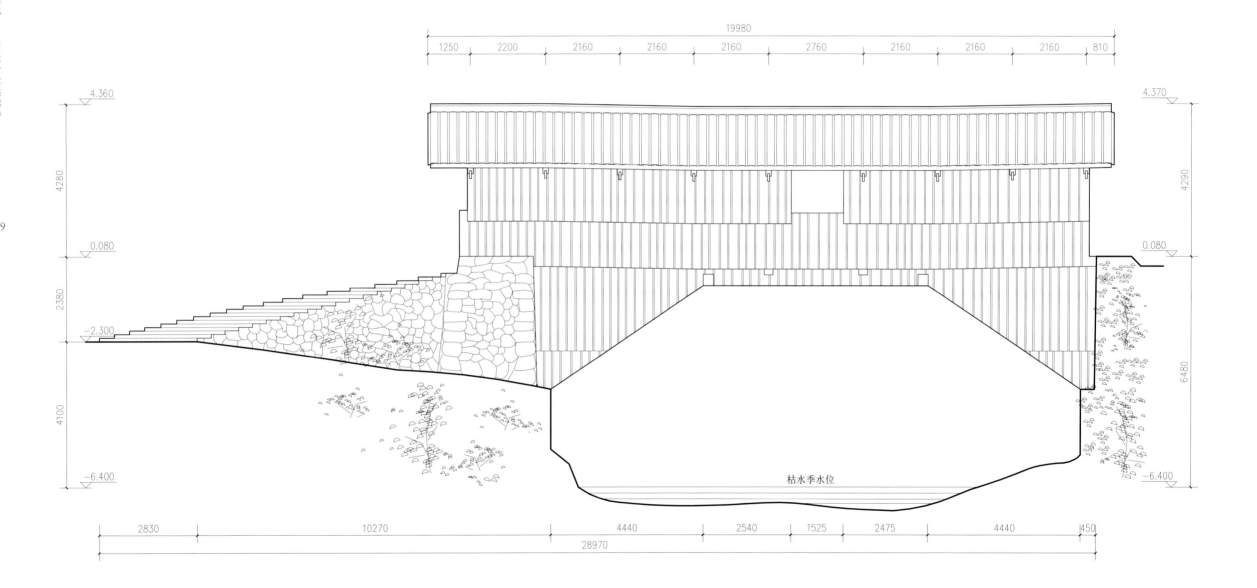

单桥西北立面图
Northwest elevation of Dan Bridge

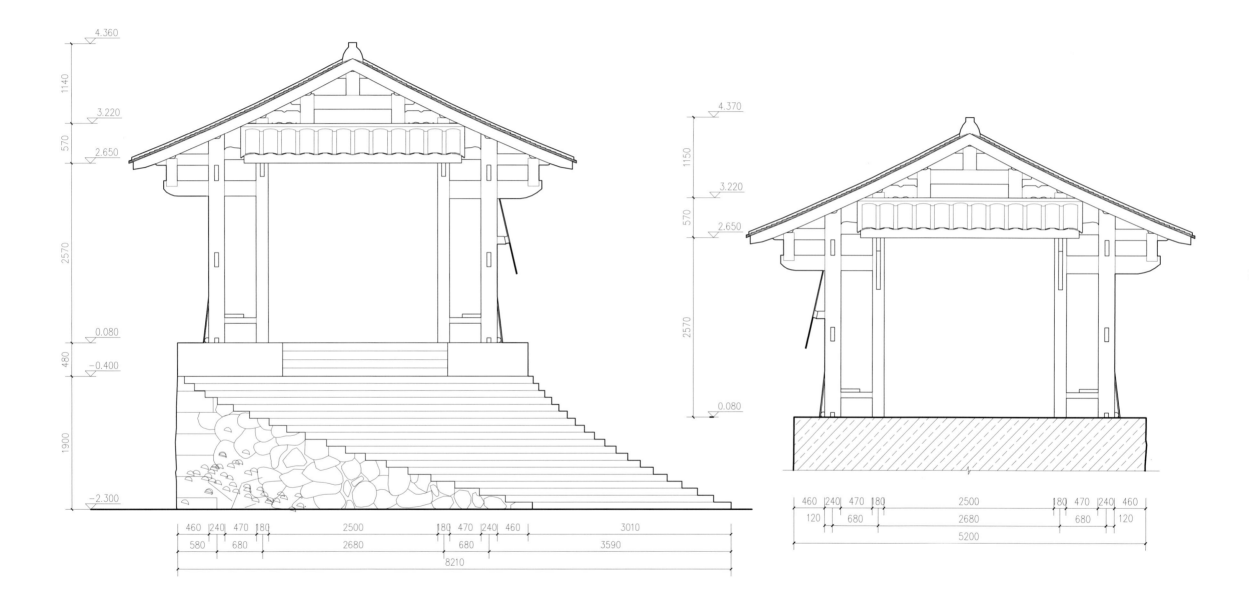

单桥东北立面图
Northeast elevation of Dan Bridge

单桥西南立面图
Southwest elevation of Dan Bridge

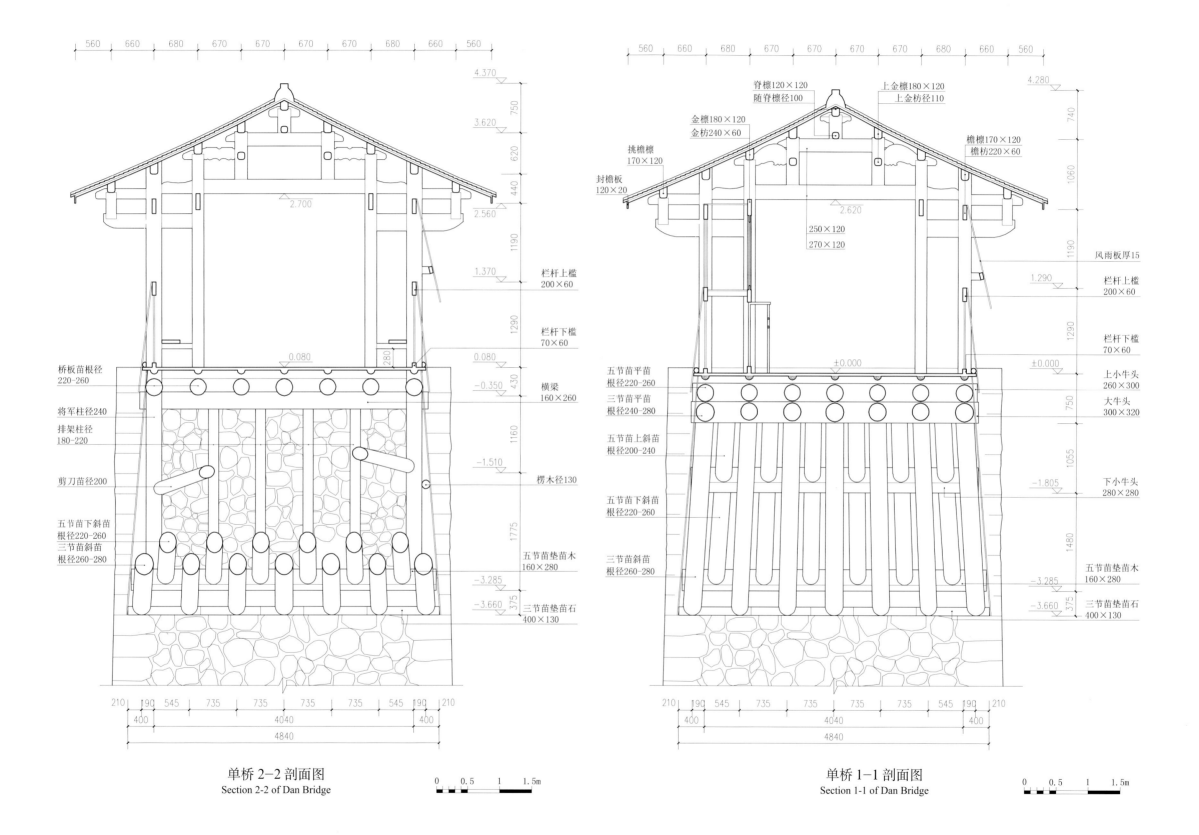

单桥 2-2 剖面图　　Section 2-2 of Dan Bridge

单桥 1-1 剖面图　　Section 1-1 of Dan Bridge

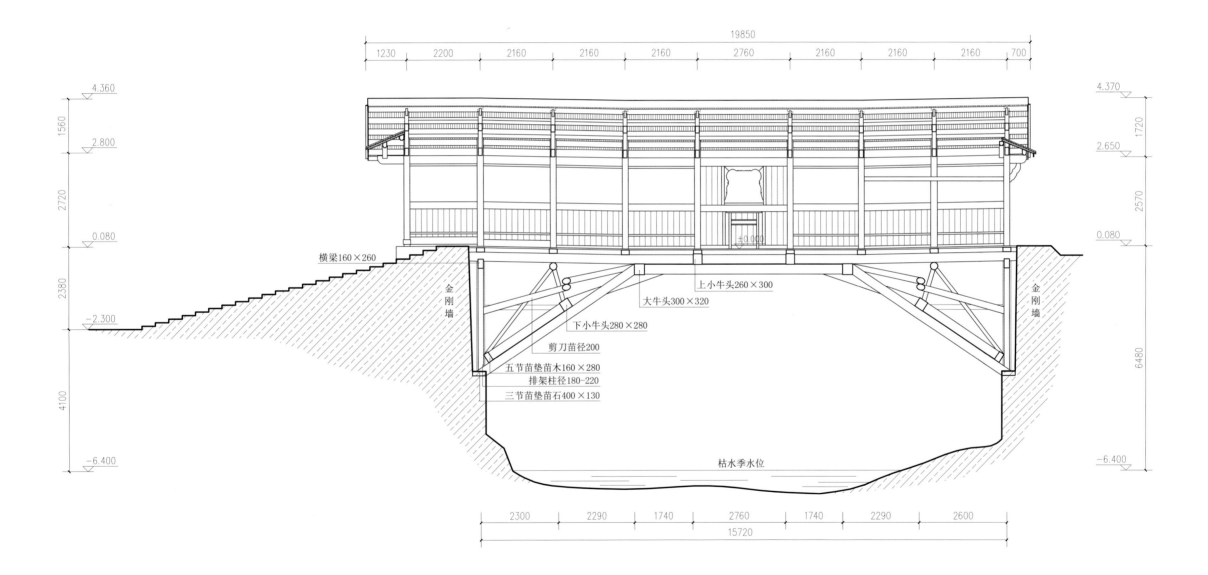

单桥 3-3 剖面图
Section 3-3 of Dan Bridge

寿春桥

Shouchun Bridge

Shouchun Bridge, also known as Wengkeng Bridge, was first built in 1693 (the thirty-second year of the Kangxi reign period of the Qing Dynasty), but destroyed by a fire in 1853, the third year of the Xianfeng reign period of the Qing Dynasty. In 1867, the sixth year of the Tongzhi reign period of the Qing Dynasty, the bridge was rebuilt. Located in Wengkeng village of Xixi township, the bridge crosses north to south across the village creek in a single span. Wooden boards form a deck, and a shrine is put up in the middle of the covered corridor dedicated to the worship Guanyin. Another Taoist shrine was built to the south of the bridge and dedicated to Wuxian Dadi (Emperor Wuxian, also know as Wutong Dadi, Mawangye), Tudi (Lord of the Soil and the Ground), and Wenchangdi (known as God of Culture and Literature). Couplets decorate the corridor columns.

寿春桥，又称『翁坑桥』，始建于清代康熙三十二年（1693年），咸丰三年（1853年）毁于火灾，同治六年（1867年）重建，位于犀溪乡翁坑村，单孔跨越流过村边的小溪，南北走向。桥体拱架系统上铺木板为桥面，廊屋中部设神龛，祀观音等菩萨；桥南端也设神龛，祀五显大帝、土地神、文昌帝；桥上有多对楹联。

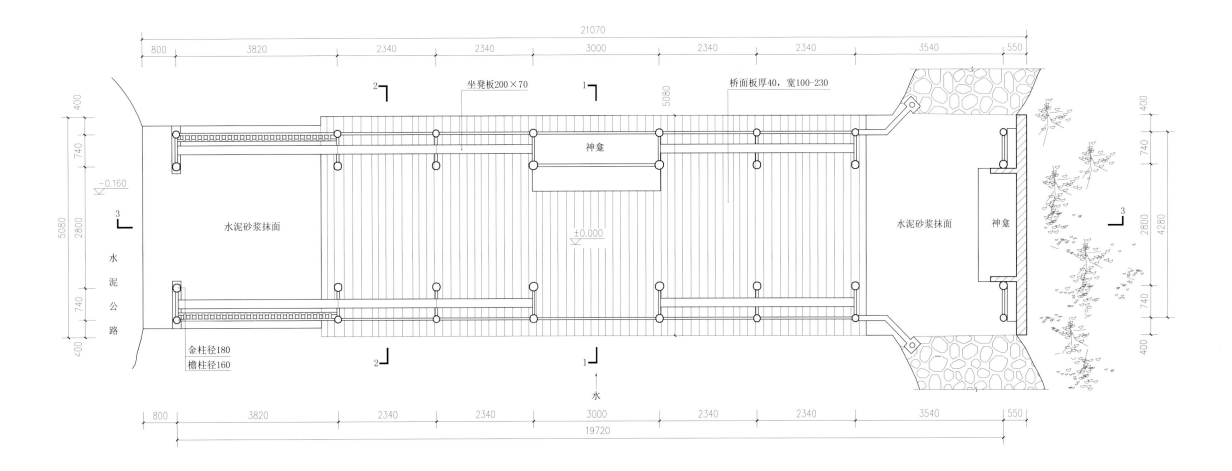

寿春桥平面图
Surface floor plan of Shouchun Bridge

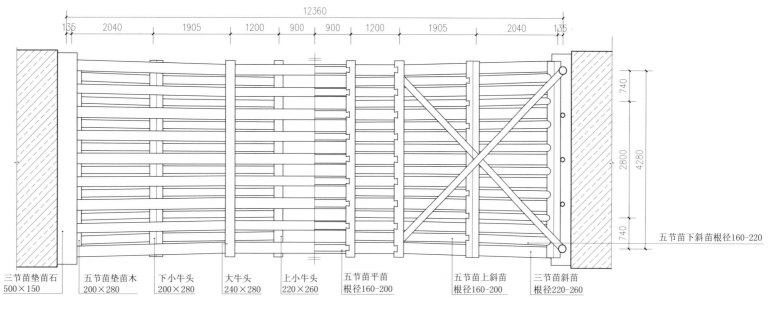

寿春桥桥梁拱骨系统仰视（左）与俯视（右）图
Plan of timber arch system of Shouchun Bridge as seen from below (left) and above (right)

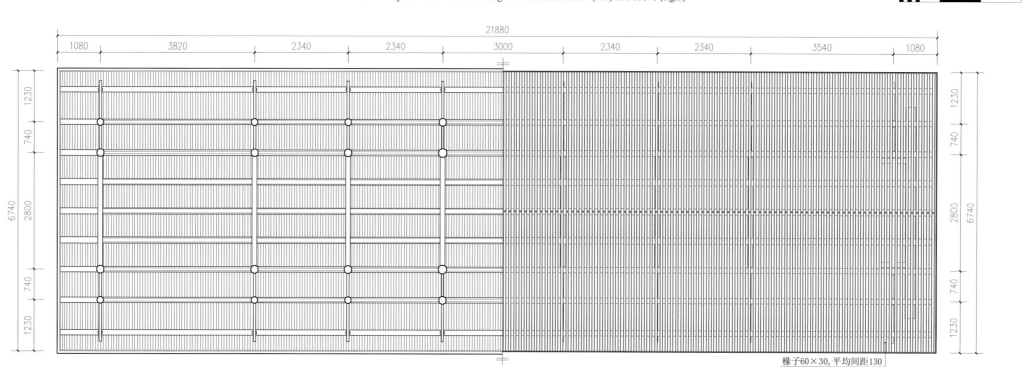

寿春桥廊屋梁架仰视（左）与俯视（右）图
Plan of corridor beam framework of Shouchun Bridge as seen from below (left) and above (right)

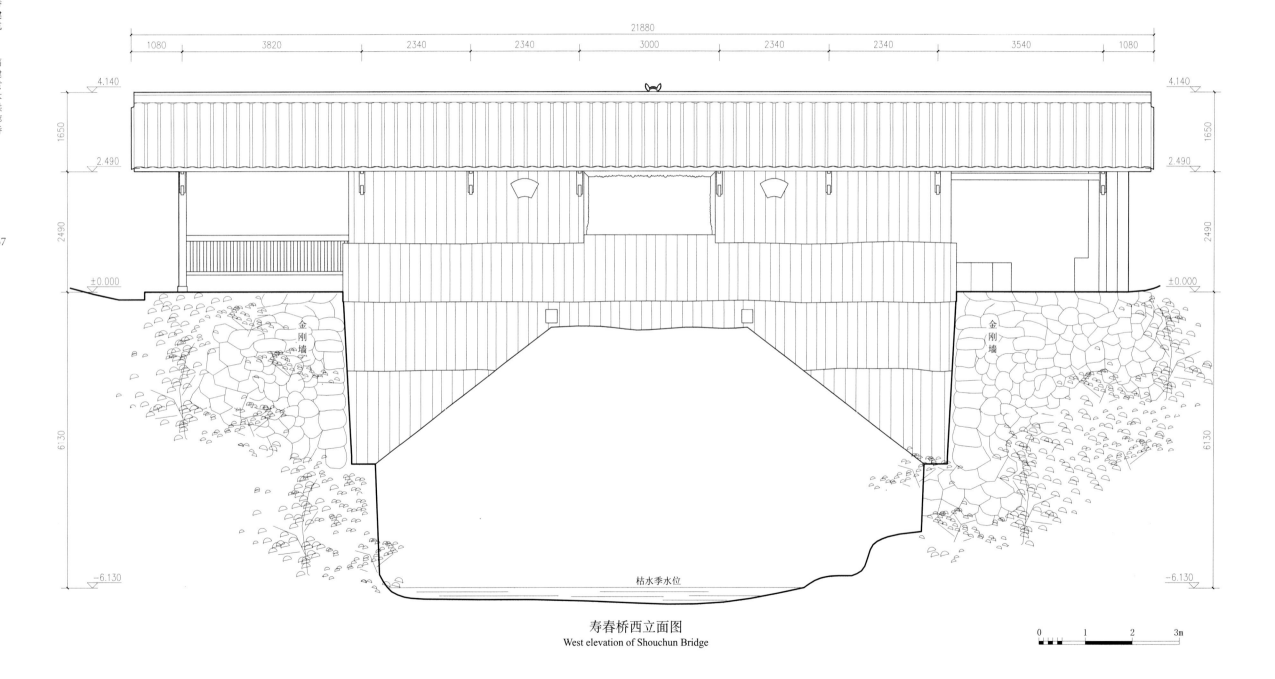

寿春桥西立面图
West elevation of Shouchun Bridge

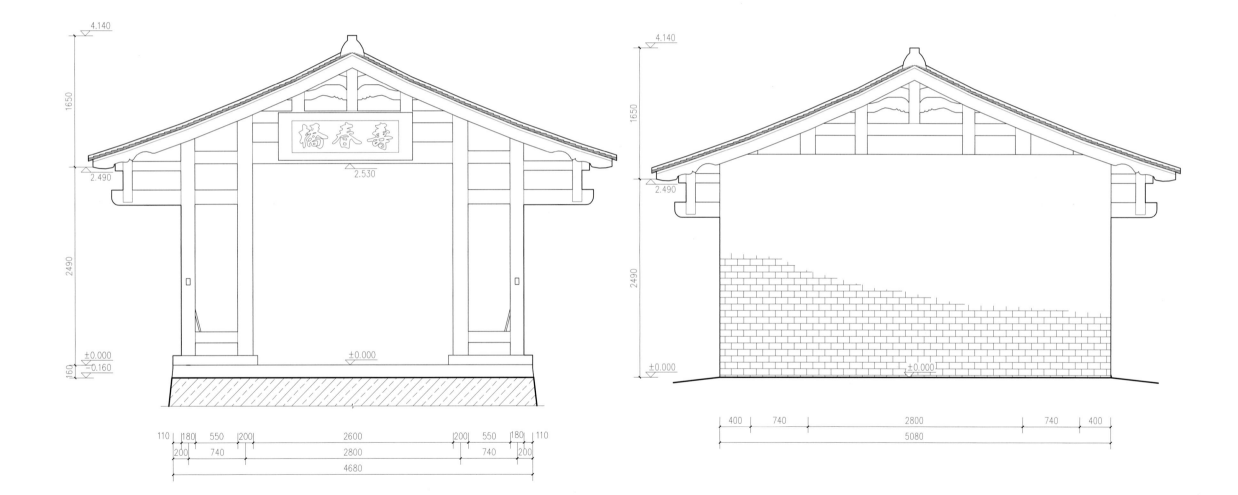

寿春桥北立面图
North elevation of Shouchun Bridge

寿春桥南立面图
South elevation of Shouchun Bridge

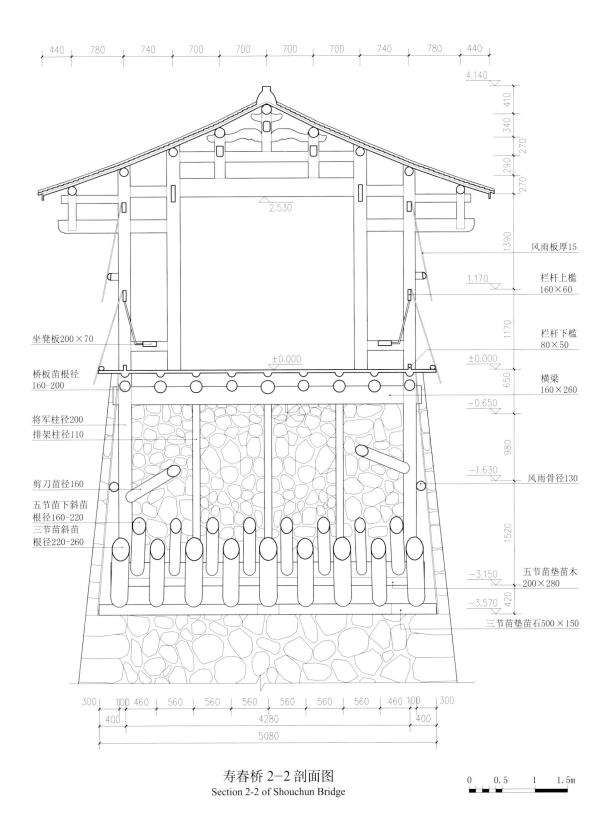
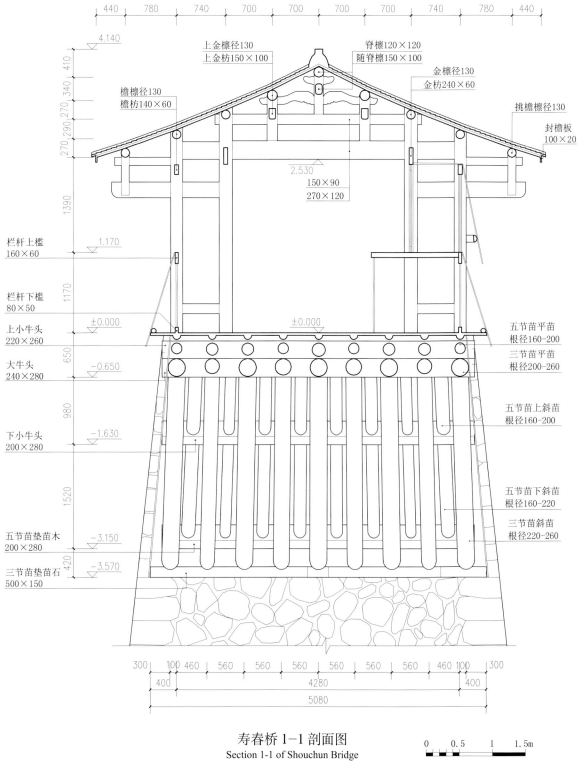

寿春桥 2-2 剖面图　　寿春桥 1-1 剖面图

Section 2-2 of Shouchun Bridge　　Section 1-1 of Shouchun Bridge

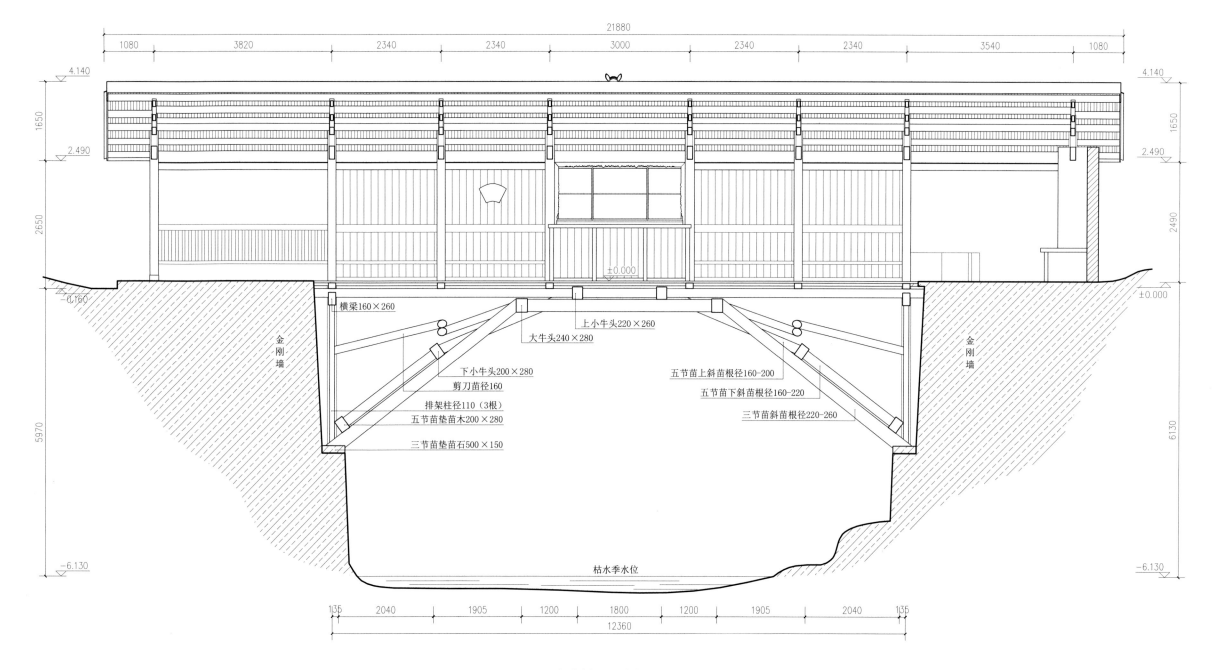

寿春桥 3-3 剖面图
Section 3-3 of Shouchun Bridge

屏南贯木拱廊桥

The Interlocked
Timber-Arched
Covered Bridges
in Pingnan County

百祥桥

Baixiang Bridge

Baixiang Bridge, also known as Baiyang Bridge or Baisong Bridge, was first built in the Duzong reign period of the Southern Song Dynasty (1265-1274). Located nearby Baiyang village at the border between Tangkou township and Shoushan township, Baixiang Bridge spans east to west across Tangkou River in a single span. Wooden boards are mounted to form a deck. To worship Zhenwudi (Emperor Zhenwu; True Warrior also known as Xuanwu, Xuandi), a shrine was built in the middle of the covered corridor. Five stone steles stand east of the bridge. In 1852, the second year of the Xianfeng reign period of the Qing Dynasty, the villagers raised the funds necessary for the purchase of the piece of land located west of the bridge. Later they planted firs there to ensure a continuous supply of the timber for repair of the bridge, from which the name of the land derives—Bridge Mountain. A stone stele standing west of the bridge confirms that said plot of land has been protected and used (for the preservation of the bridge) ever since.

百祥桥，又称『白洋桥』『柏松桥』，始建于南宋度宗年间（1265—1274年），位于棠口镇与寿山乡交界处的白洋村附近，单孔跨越棠口溪，东西走向。桥体拱架系统上铺木板为桥面，廊屋中部设神龛，祀真武帝。桥东立五方石碑。村民于清代咸丰二年（1852年）集资买下桥西一片山坡，植杉树并称为『桥山』，以作永久修桥专用林，现仍被保护和利用，有立于桥西的石碑为证。

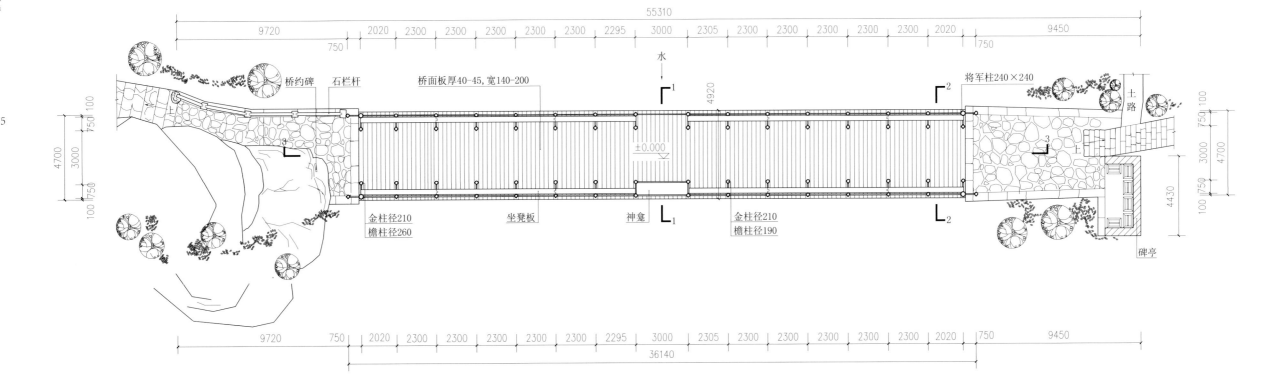

百祥桥平面图
Surface floor plan of Baixiang Bridge

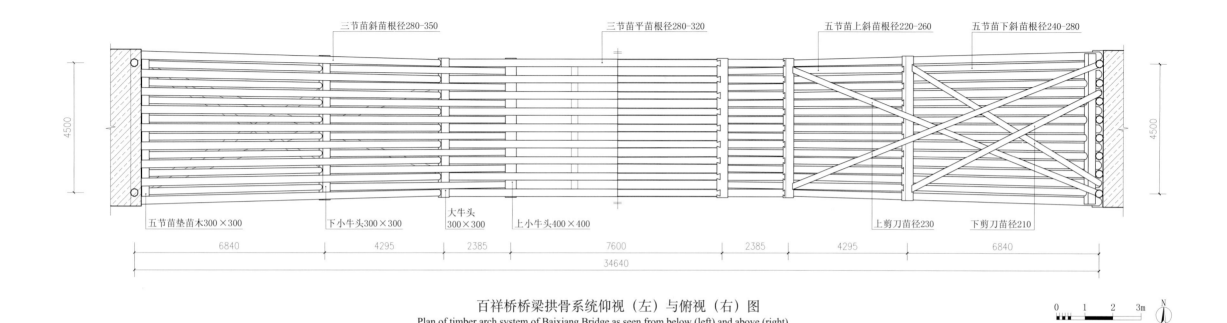

百祥桥桥梁拱骨系统仰视（左）与俯视（右）图
Plan of timber arch system of Baixiang Bridge as seen from below (left) and above (right)

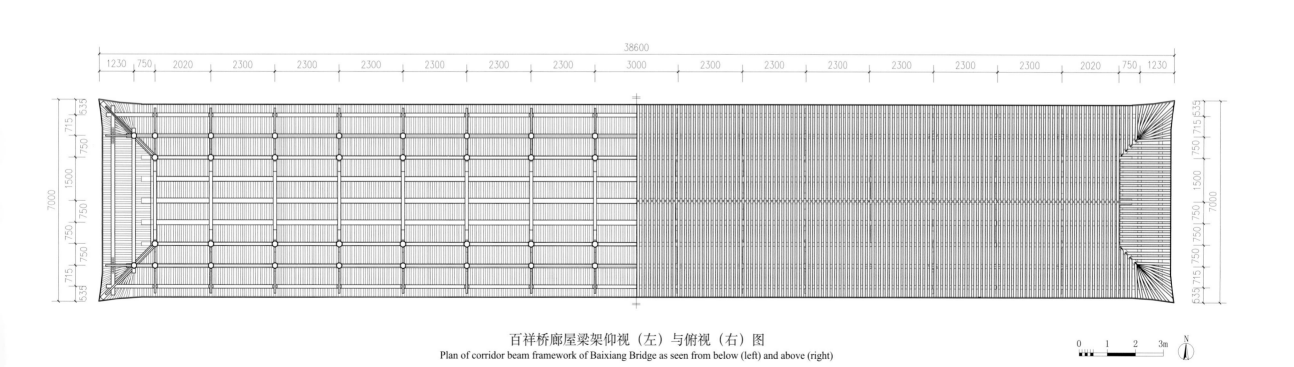

百祥桥廊屋梁架仰视（左）与俯视（右）图
Plan of corridor beam framework of Baixiang Bridge as seen from below (left) and above (right)

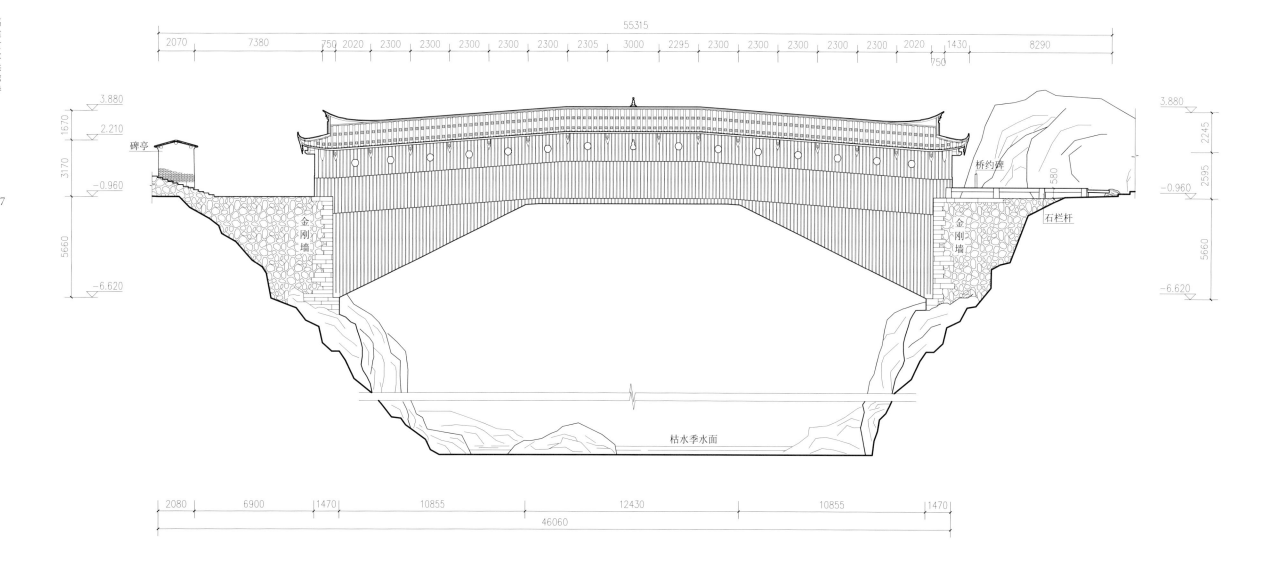

百祥桥北立面图
North elevation of Baixiang Bridge

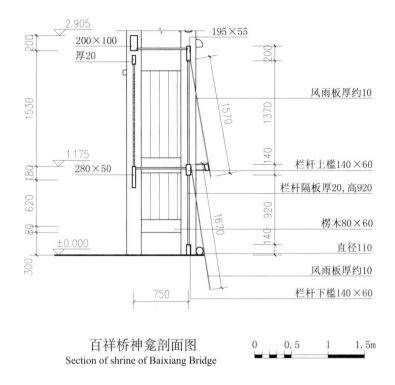

百祥桥神龛剖面图
Section of shrine of Baixiang Bridge

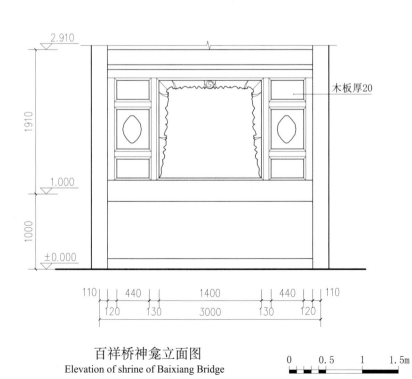

百祥桥神龛立面图
Elevation of shrine of Baixiang Bridge

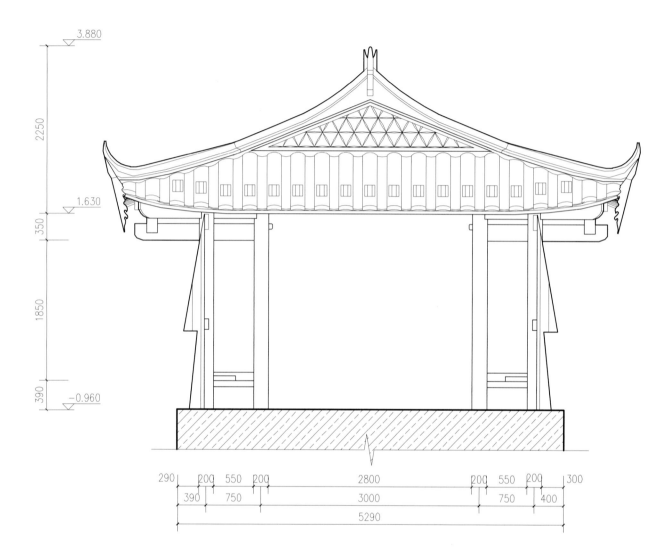

百祥桥东立面图
East elevation of Baixiang Bridge

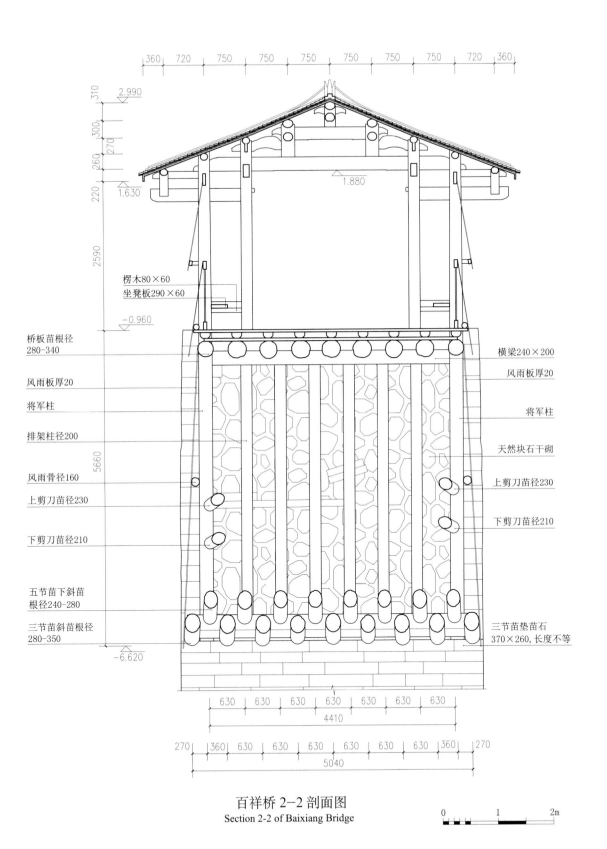

百祥桥 2-2 剖面图
Section 2-2 of Baixiang Bridge

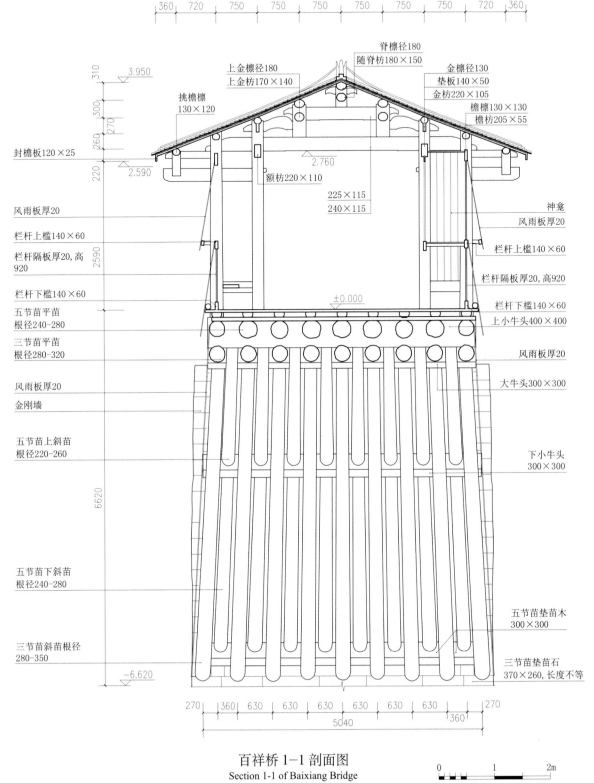

百祥桥 1-1 剖面图
Section 1-1 of Baixiang Bridge

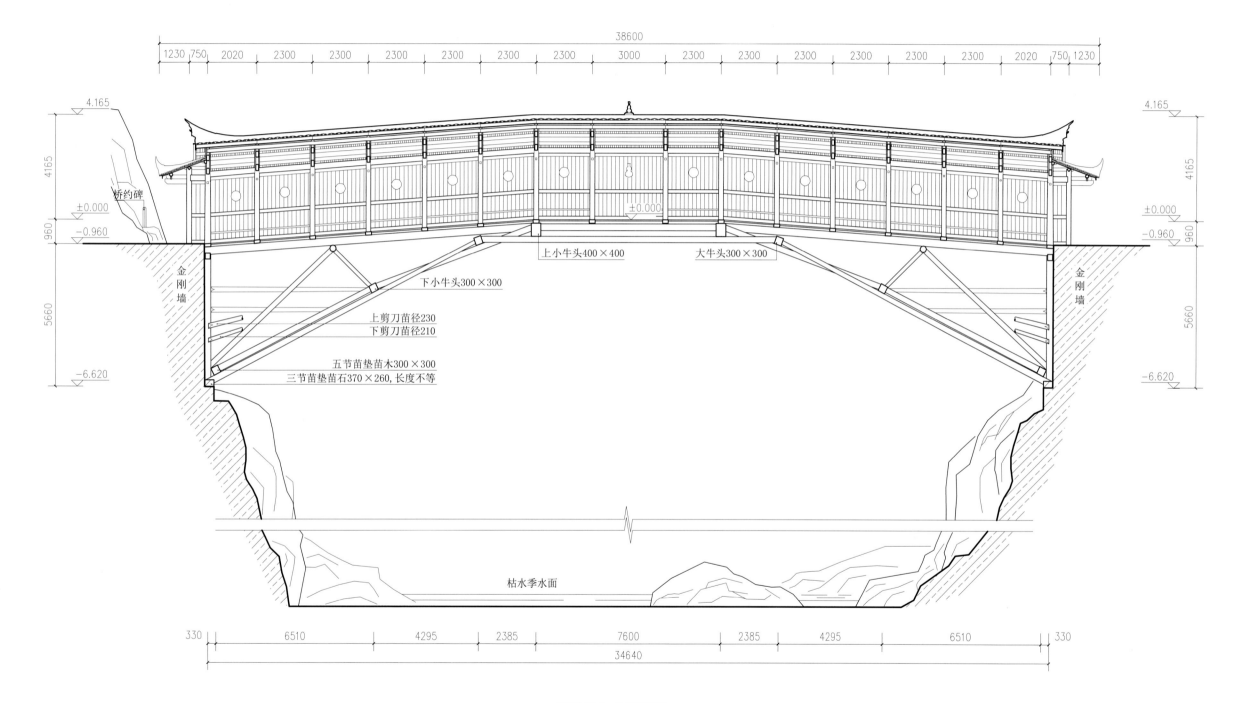

百祥桥 3-3 剖面图
Section 3-3 of Baixiang Bridge

金造桥

Jinzao Bridge

Jinzao Bridge, first built in the Ming Dynasty, was originally located in Jinzao village (a part of Jitou village) in Tangkou township. Because of the construction of the Jinzaoqiao Hydropower Station, the Jinzao bridge was relocated to the side of Ningping Highway, as it was in danger of being destroyed by flooding in its original location. It now crosses a valley in a single span through east to west. The bridge is now seldom used. Wooden boards are affixed on top of the arched-system to form a deck. A shrine is installed in the middle of the covered corridor dedicated to Guanyin. Three stone steles stand at the head of the bridge.

金造桥，始建于明代，原位于棠口乡漈头村金造村。因建设金造桥水电站，使得该桥处于水库淹没区内，后被整体搬迁到宁屏公路旁保存，东西走向，单孔跨越山谷，基本不被使用。桥体拱架系统上铺木板为桥面，廊屋中部设神龛，祀观音。桥头立三方石碑。

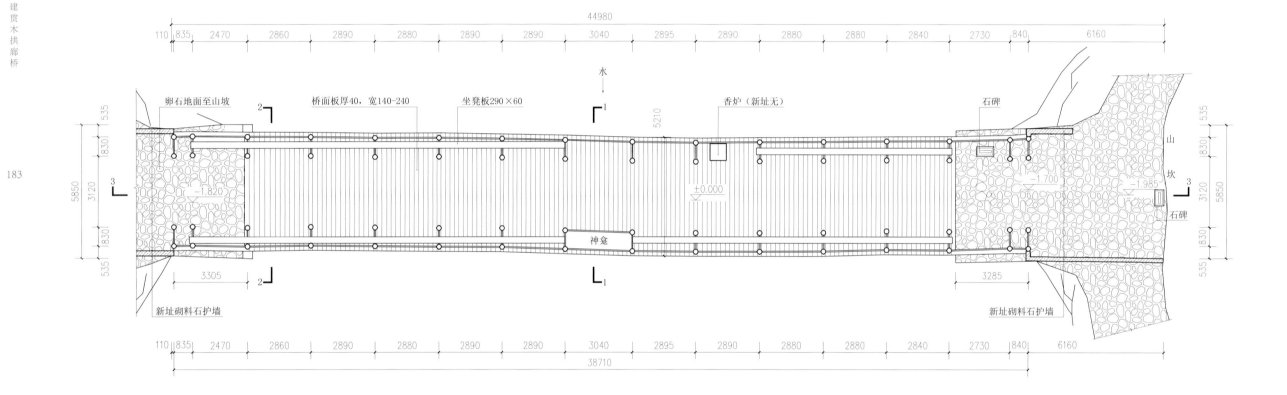

金造桥平面图
Surface floor plan of Jinzao Bridge

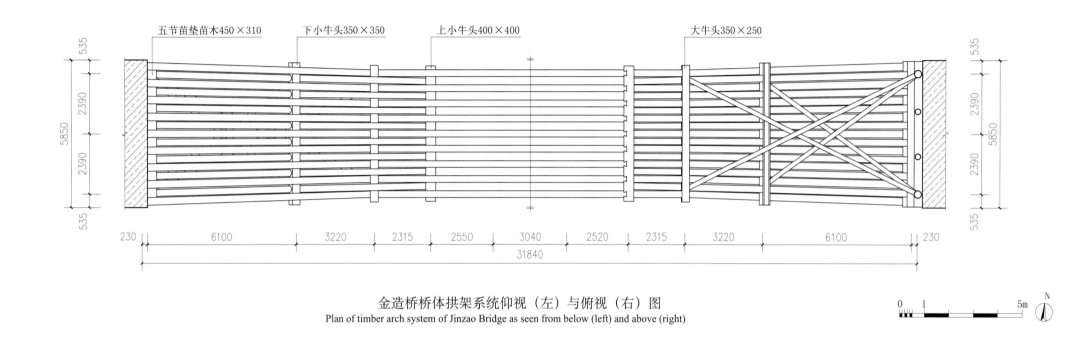

金造桥桥体拱架系统仰视（左）与俯视（右）图

Plan of timber arch system of Jinzao Bridge as seen from below (left) and above (right)

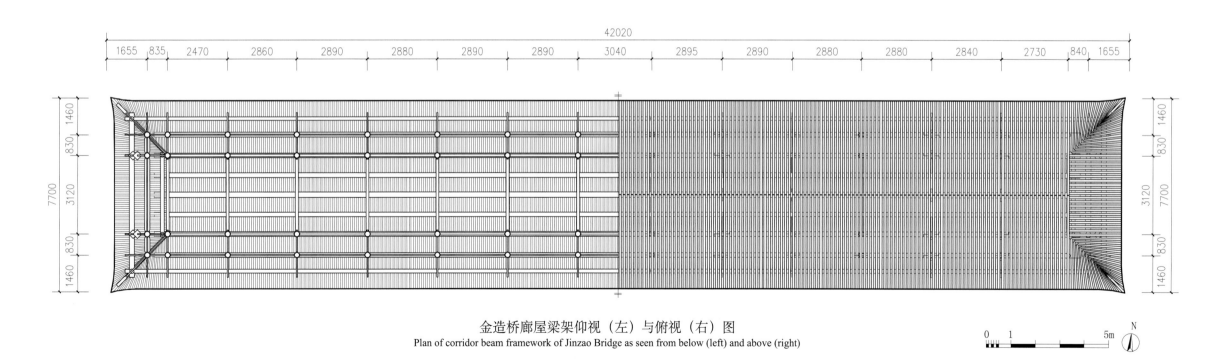

金造桥廊屋梁架仰视（左）与俯视（右）图

Plan of corridor beam framework of Jinzao Bridge as seen from below (left) and above (right)

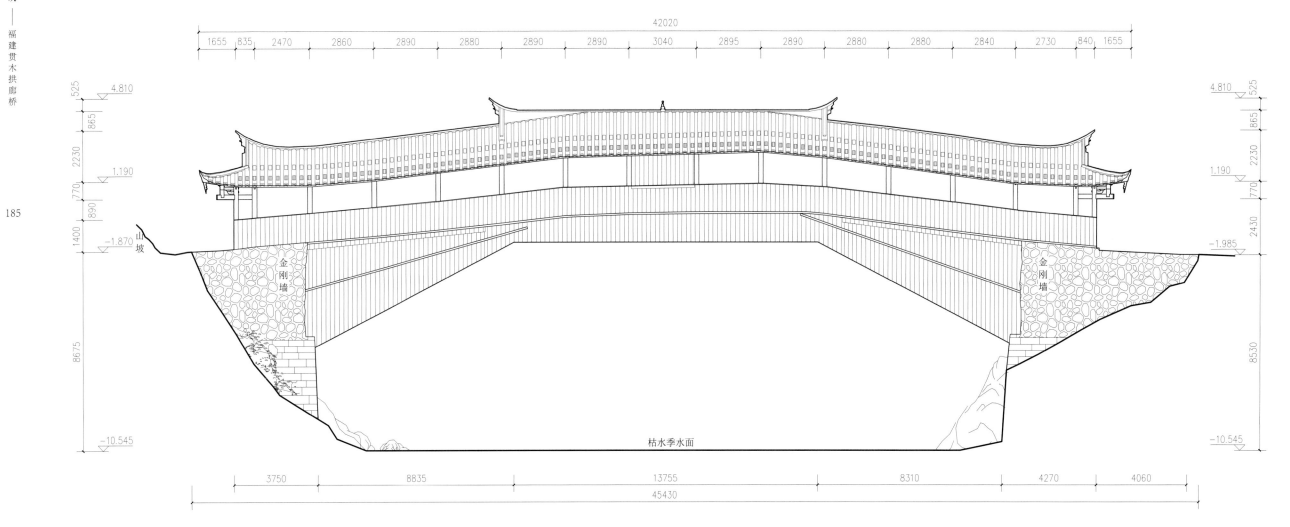

金造桥南立面图
South elevation of Jinzao Bridge

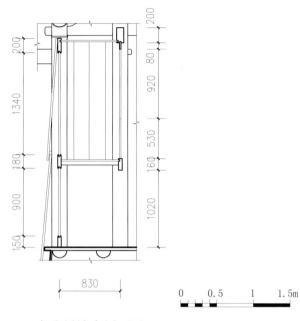

金造桥神龛剖面图
Section of shrine of Jinzao Bridge

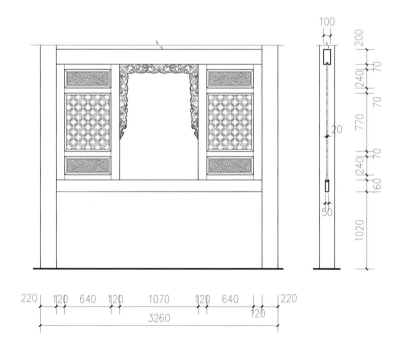

金造桥神龛立面图
Elevation of shrine of Jinzao Bridge

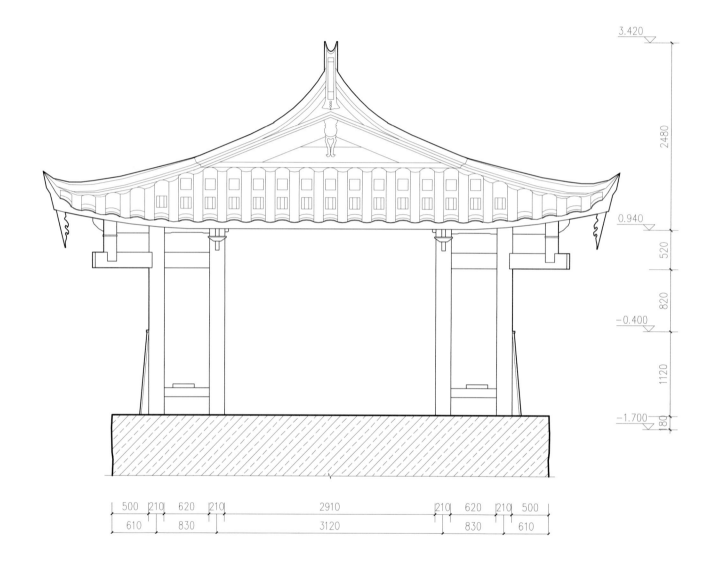

金造桥东立面图
East elevation of Jinzao Bridge

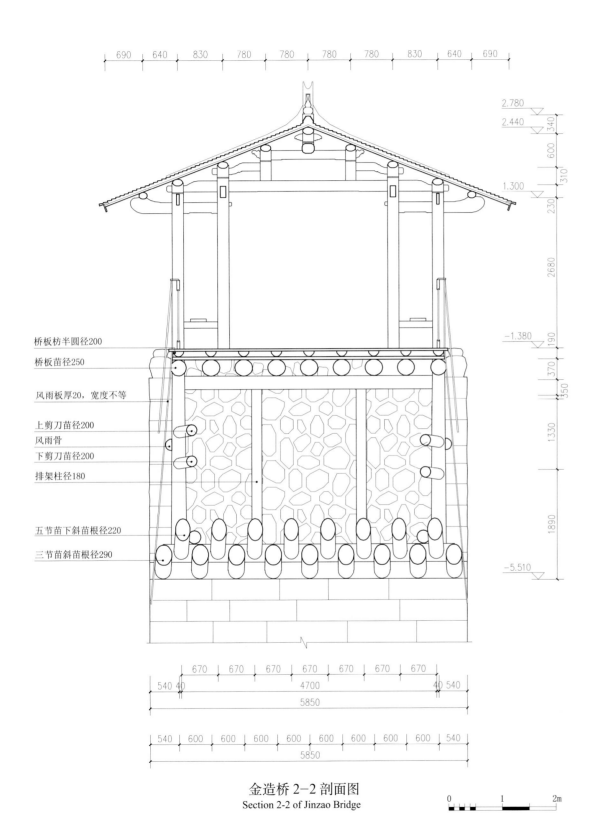

金造桥 2-2 剖面图
Section 2-2 of Jinzao Bridge

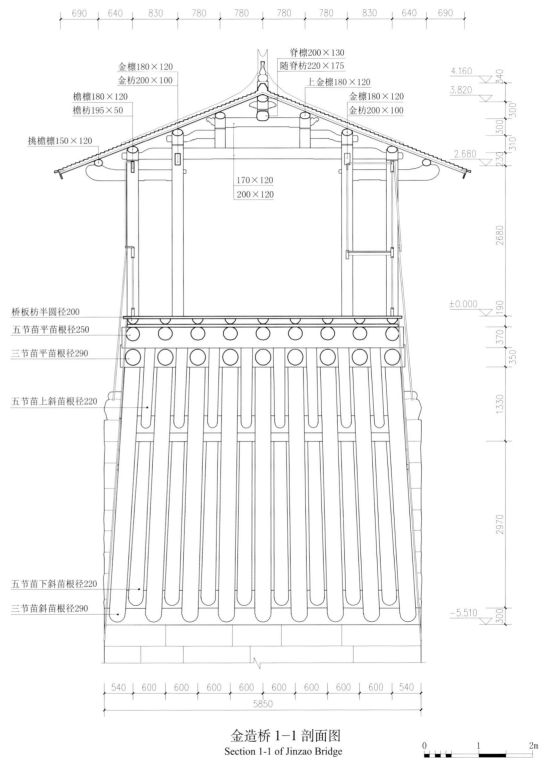

金造桥 1-1 剖面图
Section 1-1 of Jinzao Bridge

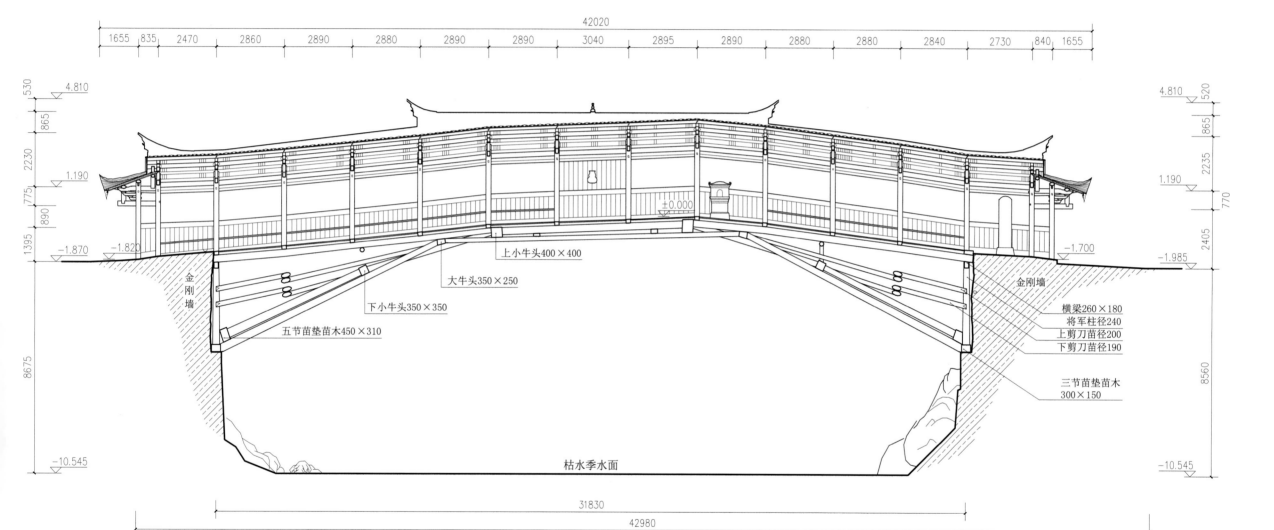

金造桥 3-3 剖面图
Section 3-3 of Jinzao Bridge

千乘桥

Qiansheng Bridge

千乘桥,又称"祥峰桥""棠口桥",始建于南宋理宗年间(1225—1264年),位于棠口乡棠口村,跨越棠口溪,南北走向。桥体拱架系统上铺木板为桥面,廊屋中部设神龛,祀五显大帝。桥一墩二孔,墩尖呈鸡啄形,整座桥梁形似昂首展翅在水面上飞行的公鸡,被载入《中国科学技术史·桥梁卷》。桥东有祥峰寺,桥西有奎光阁、夫人宫、林公殿。

Qiansheng Bridge (local pronunciation), also known as Xiangfeng Bridge or Tangkou Bridge, was first built in the Lizong reign period of the Southern Song Dynasty (1225-1264). Located in Tangkou village of Tangkou township, the bridge spans north to south across Tangkou River. Wooden boards are mounted to form a deck, and a shrine is installed in the middle of the covered corridor to worship Wuxian Dadi (Emperor Wuxian, also know as Wutong Dadi, Mawangye). The (double-span) bridge is supported by a beak-shaped central pier, which makes the bridge look like a rooster flying over the water. The bridge is recorded in *Zhongguo Kexue Jishu Shi* (History of Chinese Science and Technology) volume on bridges. To the east of the bridge stands Xiangfeng Monastery (*si*), and to its west, Kuiguang Pavilion (*ge*), Furen Palace (*gong*), and Lingong Hall (*dian*).

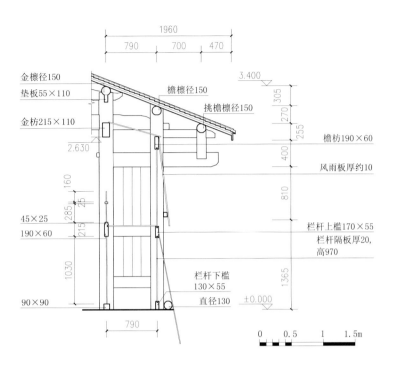

千乘桥神龛剖面图
Section of shrine of Qiansheng Bridge

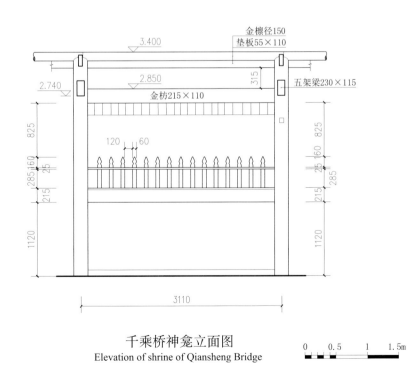

千乘桥神龛立面图
Elevation of shrine of Qiansheng Bridge

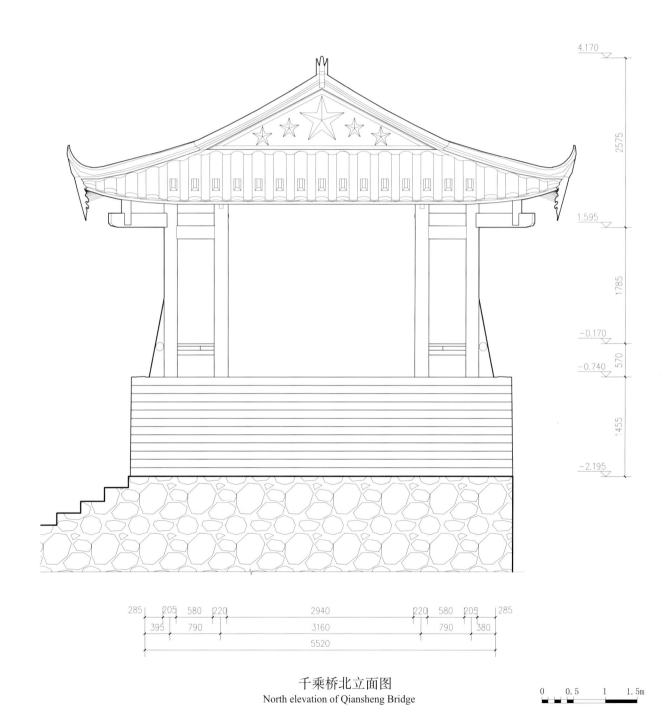

千乘桥北立面图
North elevation of Qiansheng Bridge

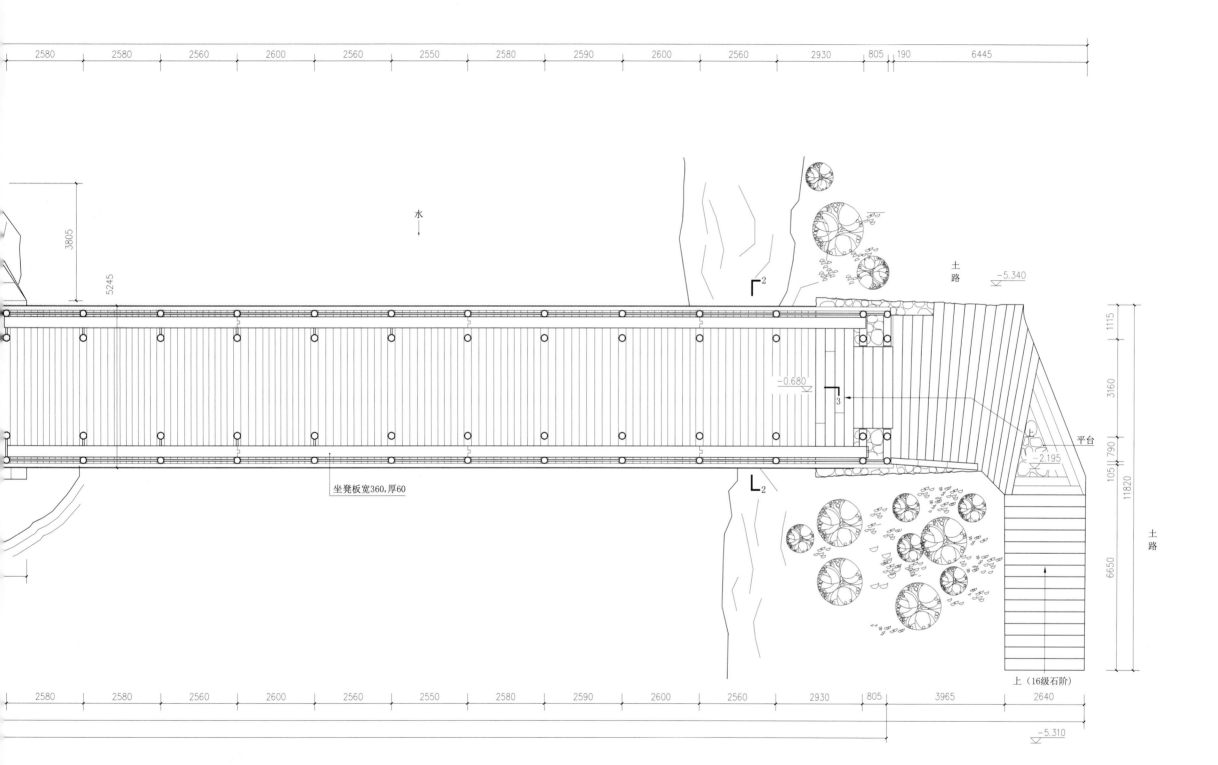

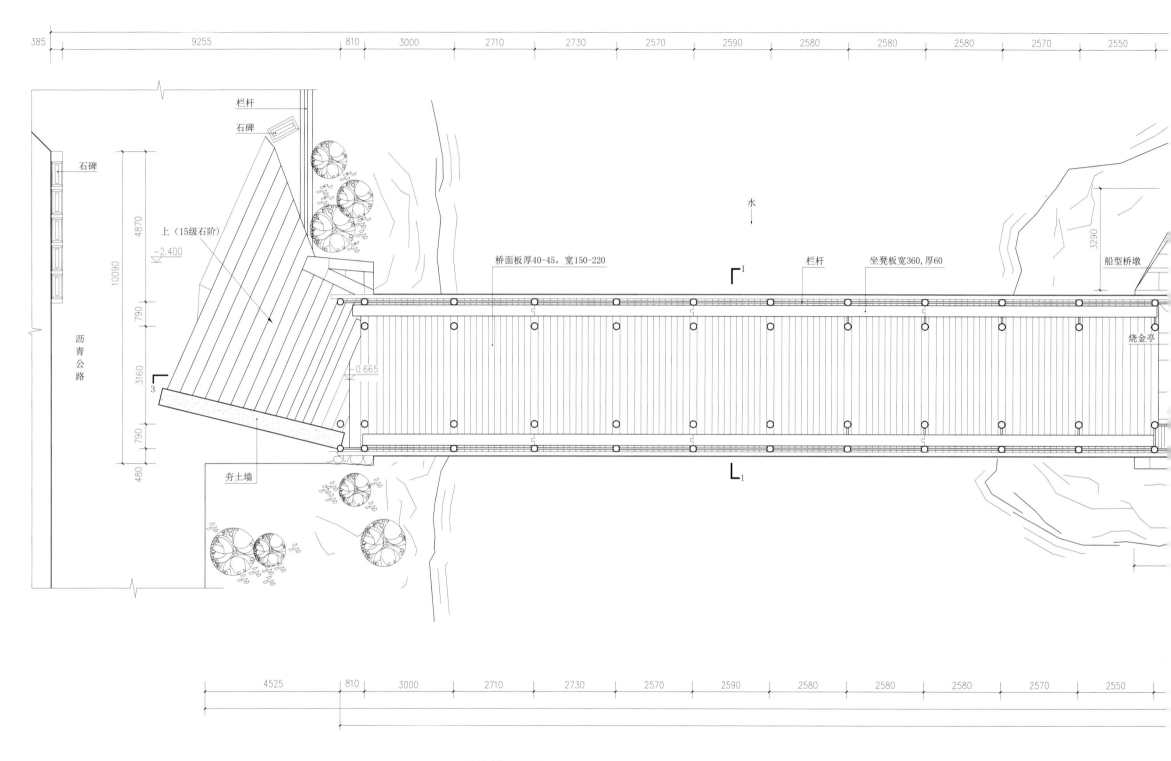

千乘桥平面图
Surface floor plan of Qiansheng Bridge

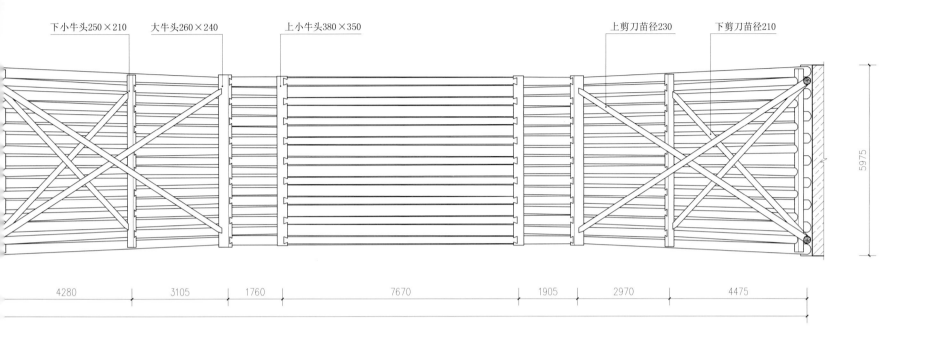

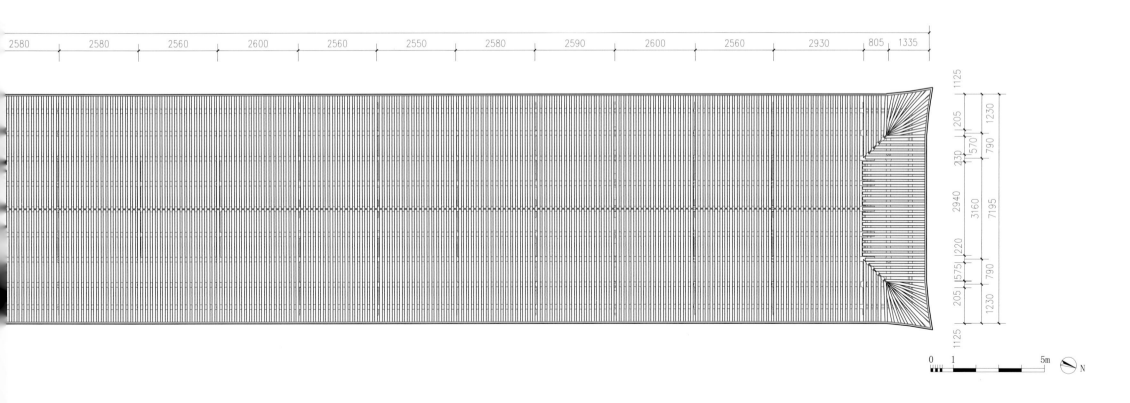

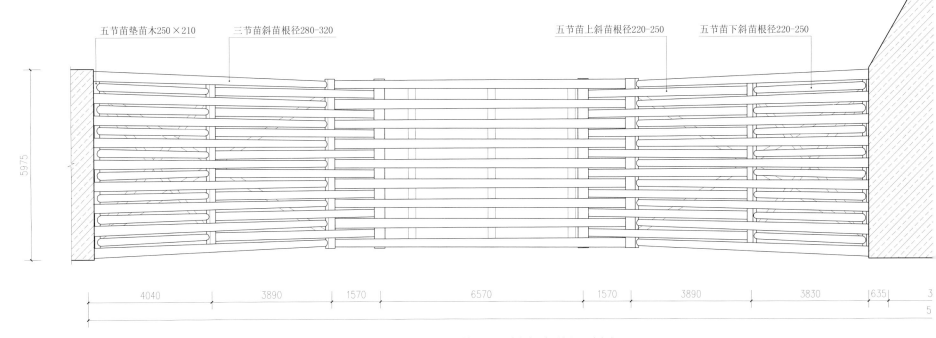

千乘桥桥梁拱骨系统仰视（左）与俯视（右）图
Plan of timber arch system of Qiansheng Bridge as seen from below (left) and above (right)

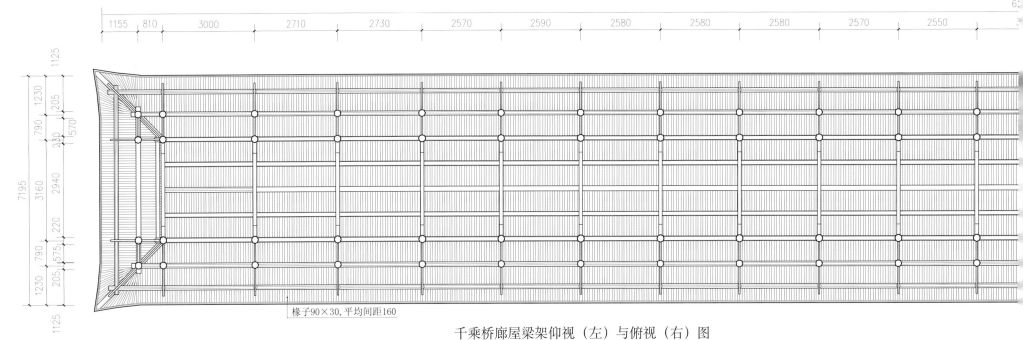

千乘桥廊屋梁架仰视（左）与俯视（右）图
Plan of corridor beam framework of Qiansheng Bridge as seen from below (left) and above (right)

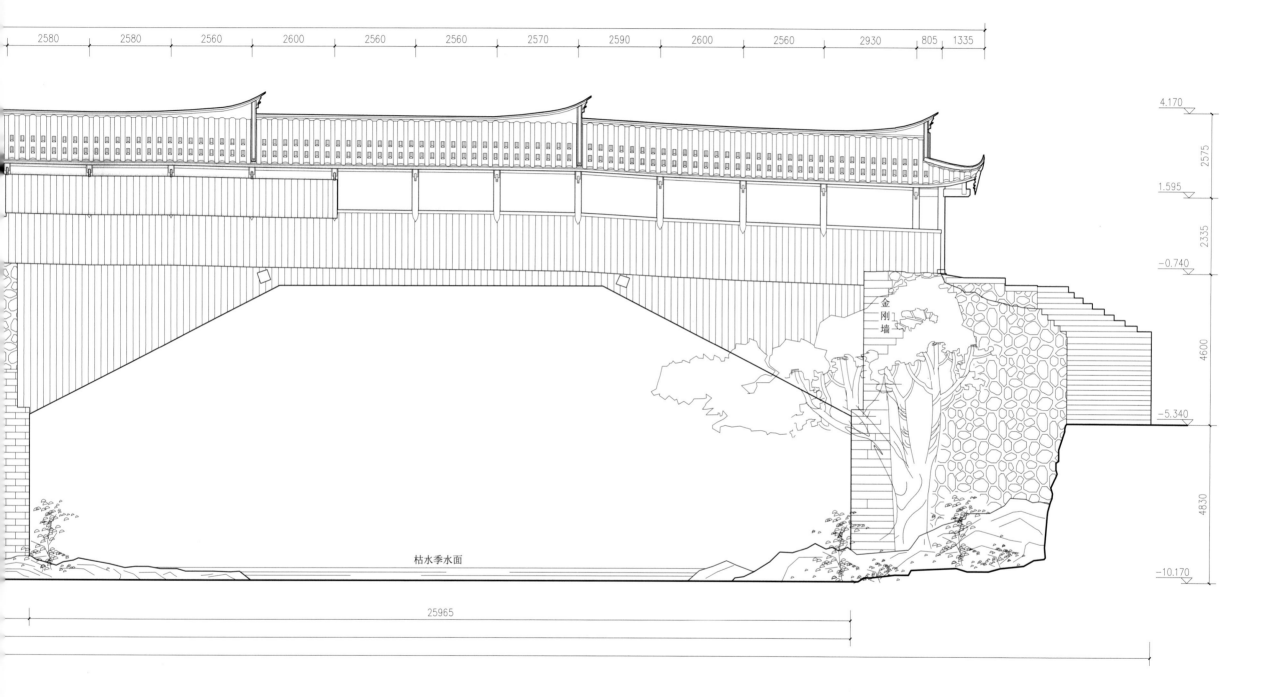

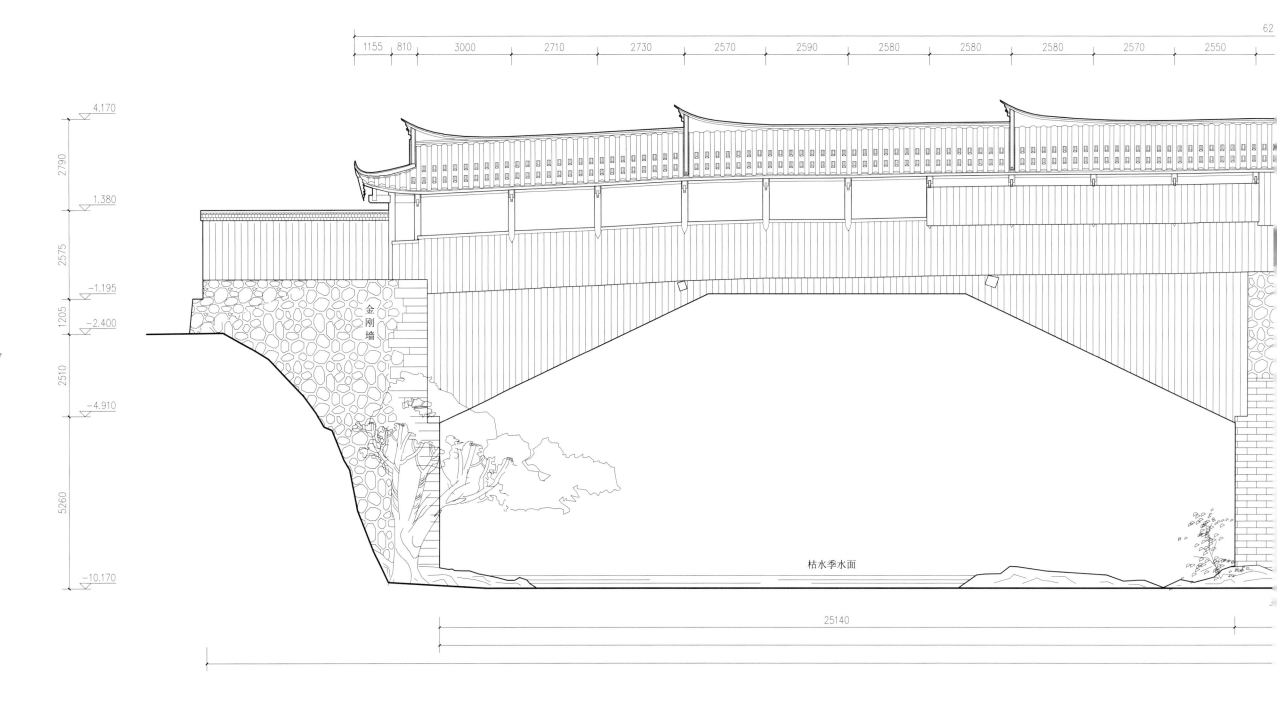

千乘桥东立面图
East elevation of Qiansheng Bridge

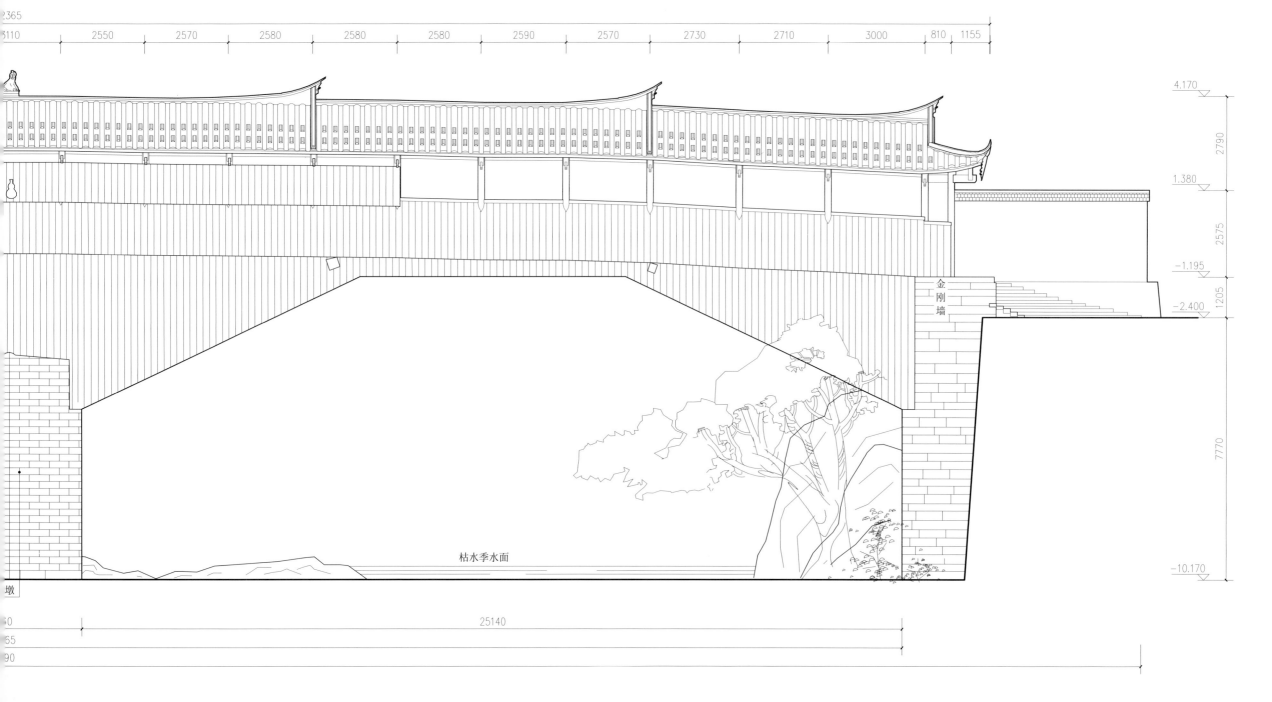

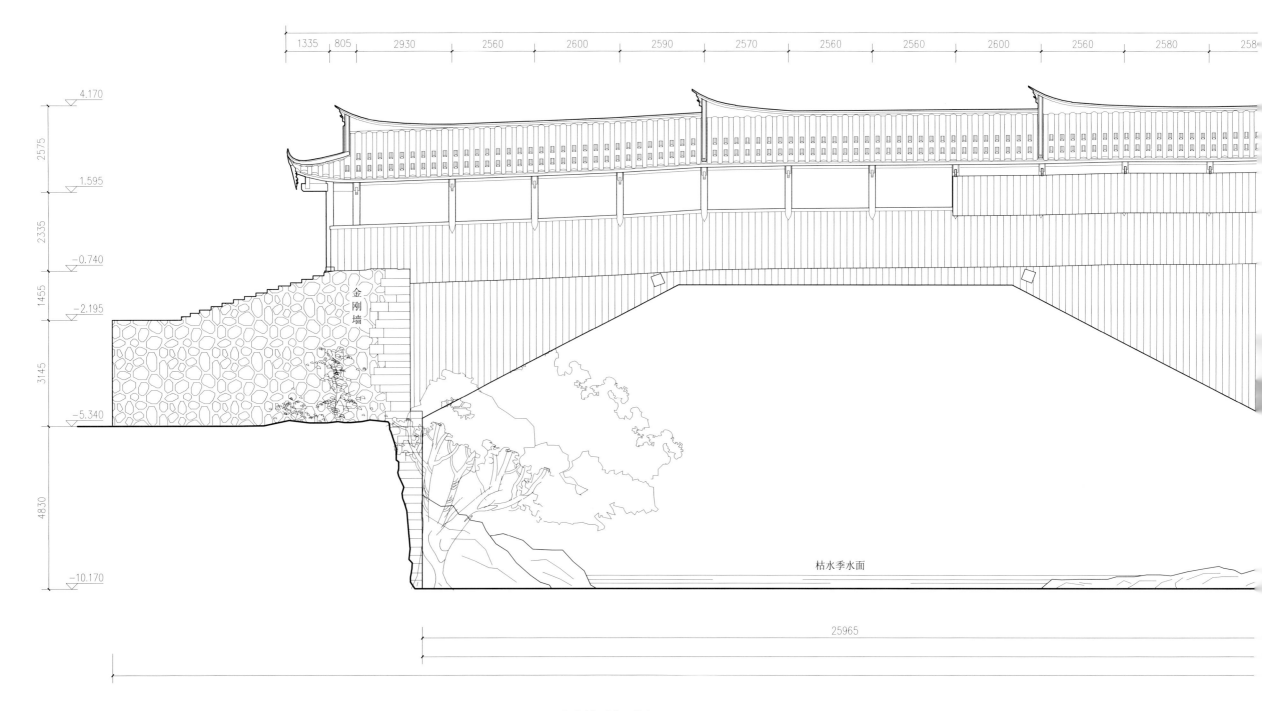

千乘桥西立面图
West elevation of Qiansheng Bridge

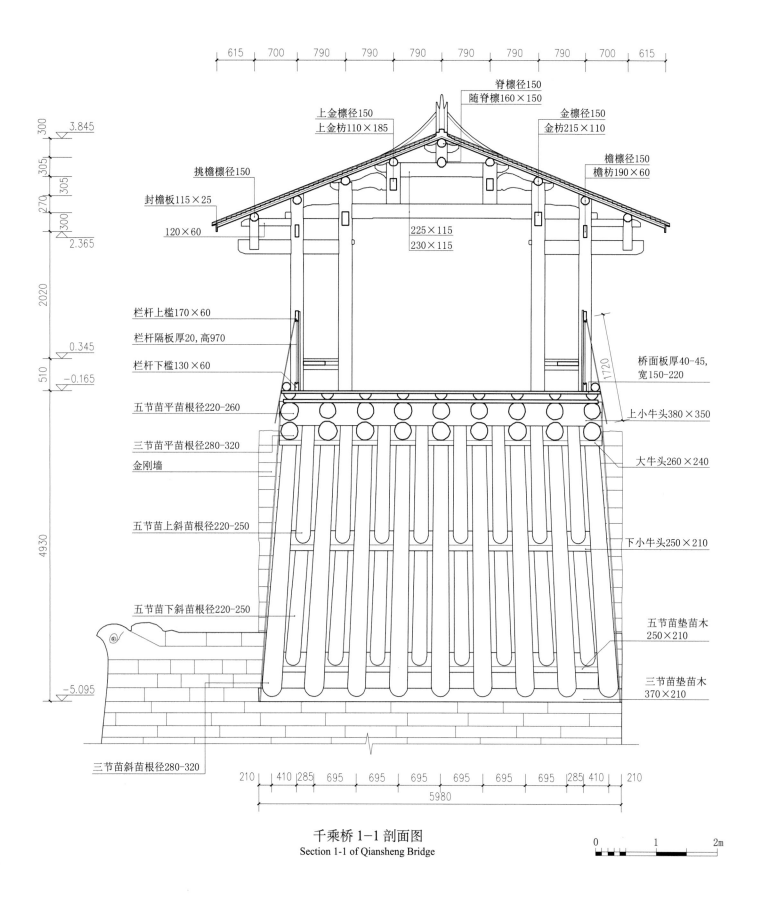

千乘桥 1-1 剖面图
Section 1-1 of Qiansheng Bridge

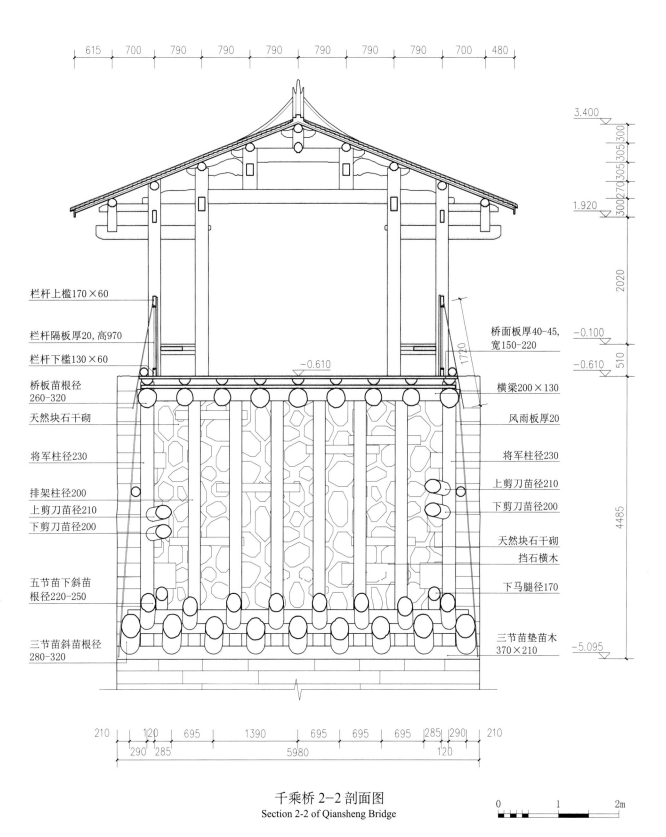

千乘桥 2-2 剖面图
Section 2-2 of Qiansheng Bridge

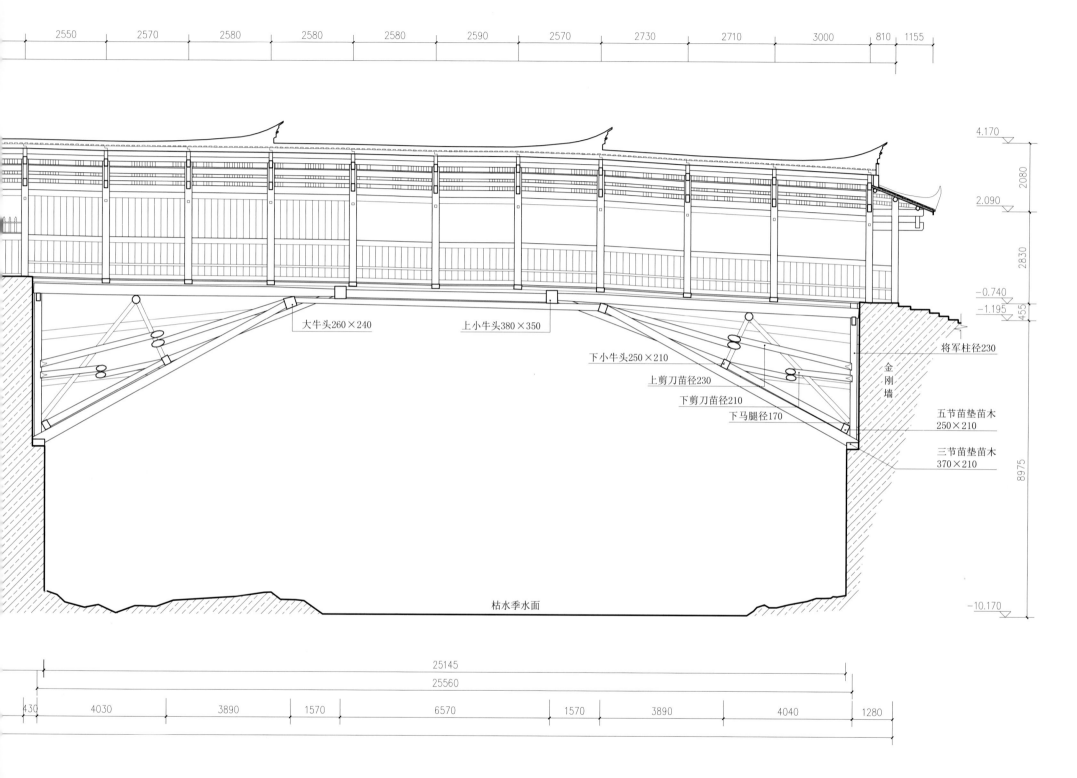

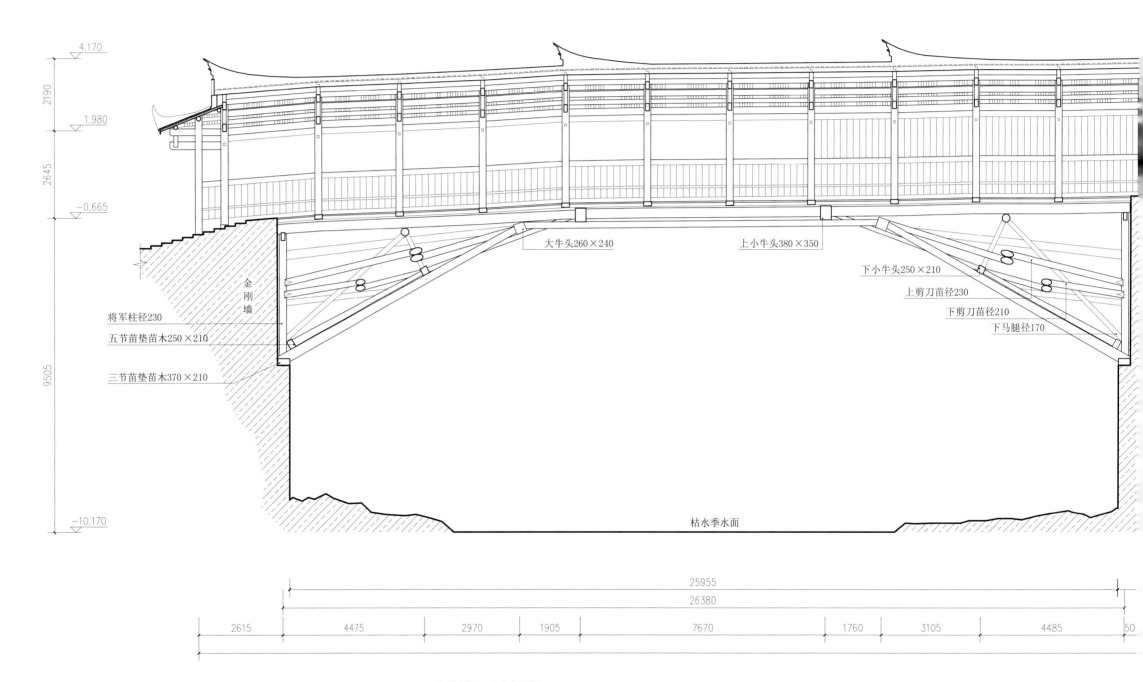

千乘桥 3-3 剖面图

Section 3-3 of Qiansheng Bridge

广福桥

Guangfu Bridge

Guangfu Bridge, also known as Xiyuan Bridge or Kaiyuanchang Bridge, was first built in 1333, the first year of the Yuantong reign period of the Yuan Dynasty. Located between Lingxia village and Kaiyuan village of Lingxia township, Guangfu Bridge spans east to west across Lingxia Stream in a single span. Wooden boards are mounted to form a deck that is then covered with pebbles. A shrine is installed in the middle of the covered corridor to worship Wuxian Lingjun alternative name for (Emperor Wuxian, also know as Wutong Dadi, Mawangye).

广福桥，又称『溪源桥』『开源长桥』，始建于元代元统元年（1333年），位于岭下乡岭下村与开源村之间，单孔跨越岭下溪，东西走向。桥体拱架系统上铺木板，再上铺卵石为桥面。廊屋中部设神龛，祀五显灵君。

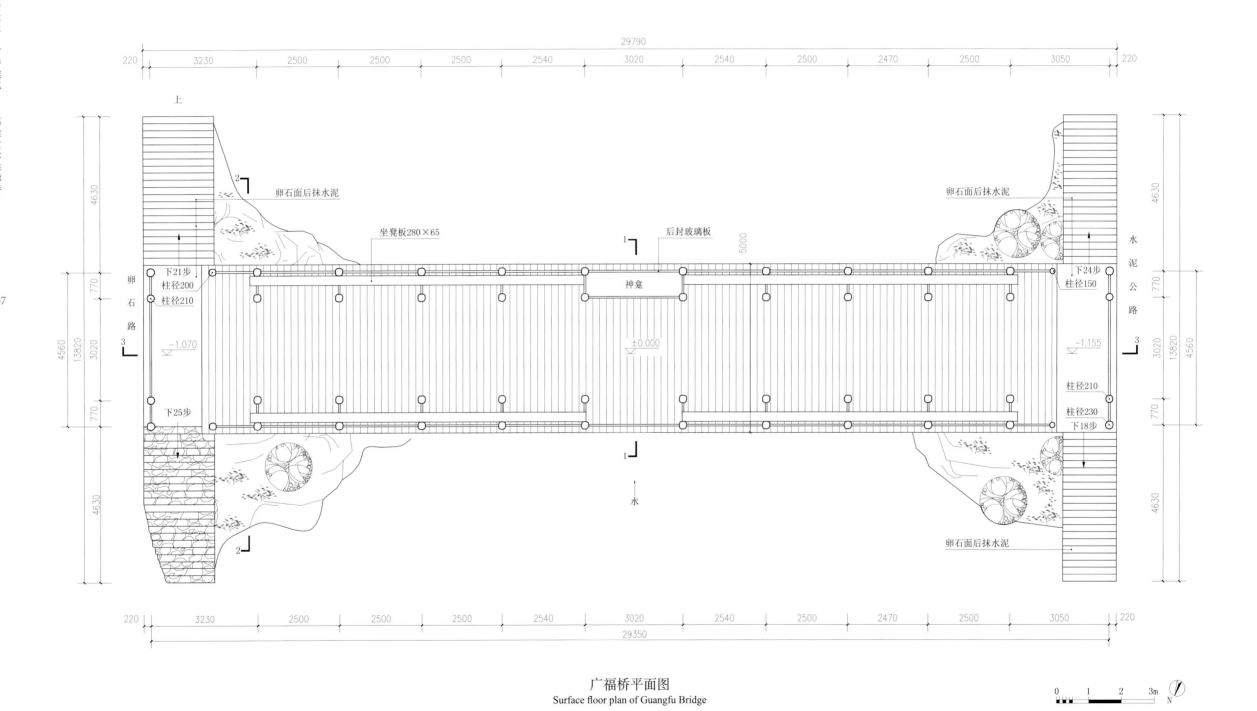

广福桥平面图
Surface floor plan of Guangfu Bridge

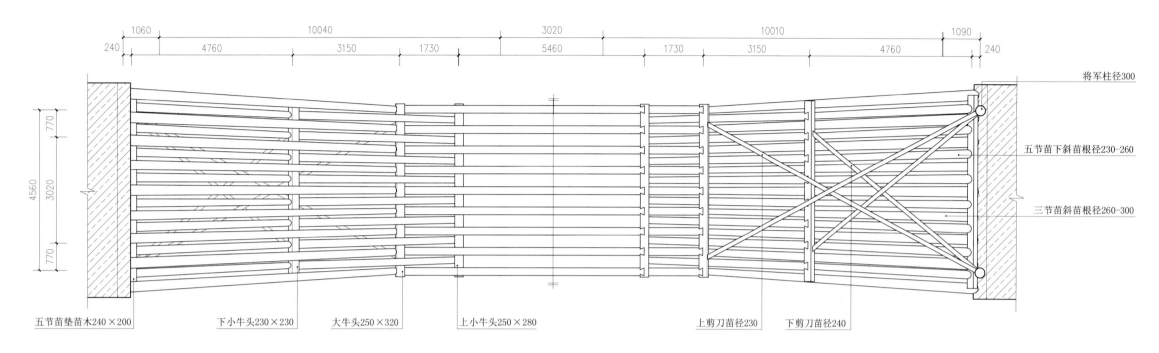

广福桥桥梁拱骨系统仰视（左）与俯视（右）图
Plan of timber arch system of Guangfu Bridge as seen from below (left) and above (right)

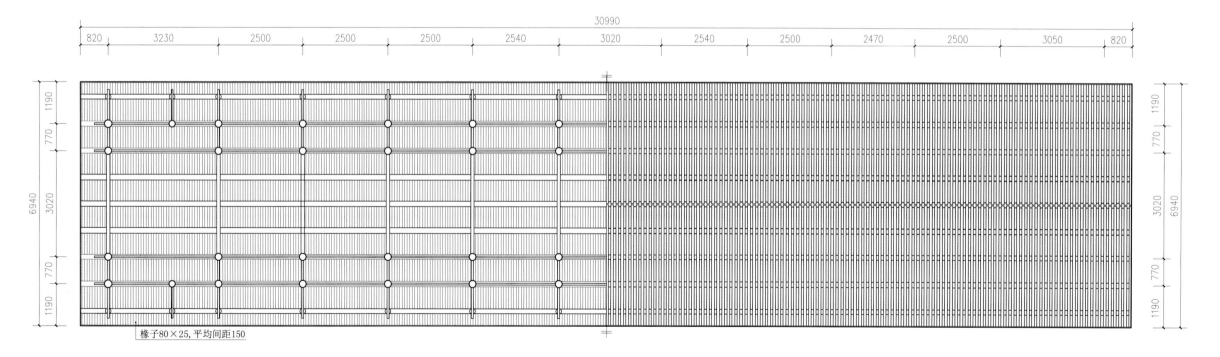

广福桥廊屋梁架仰视（左）与俯视（右）图
Plan of corridor beam framework of Guangfu Bridge as seen from below (left) and above (right)

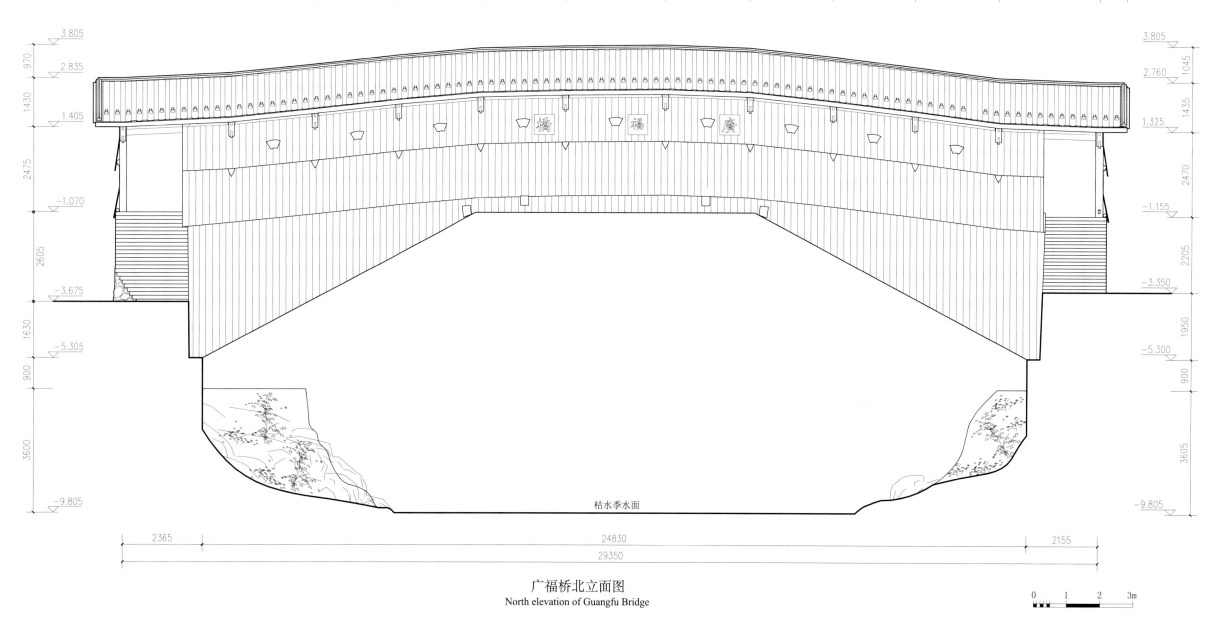

广福桥北立面图
North elevation of Guangfu Bridge

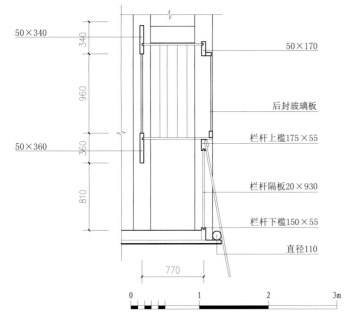

广福桥神龛剖面图
Section of shrine of Guangfu Bridge

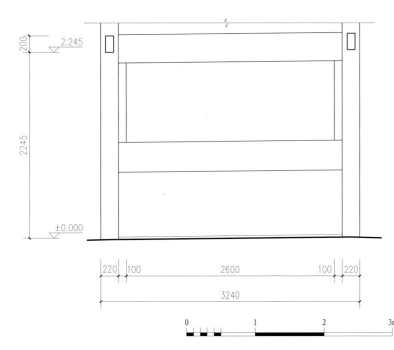

广福桥神龛立面图
Elevation of shrine of Guangfu Bridge

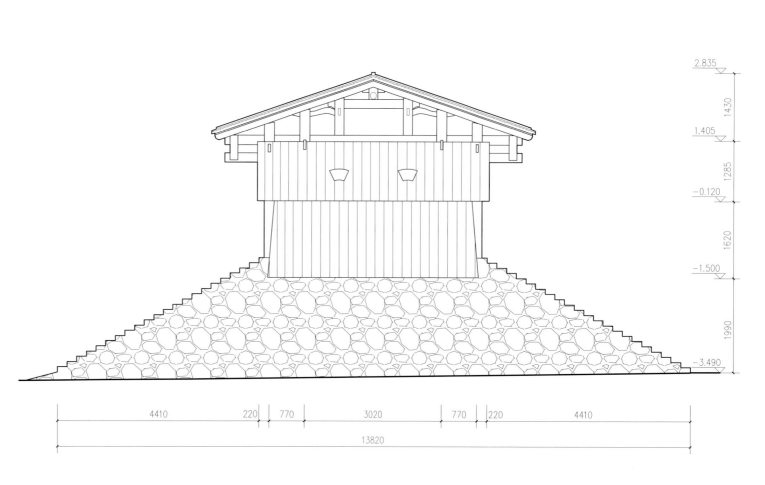

广福桥东立面图
East elevation of Guangfu Bridge

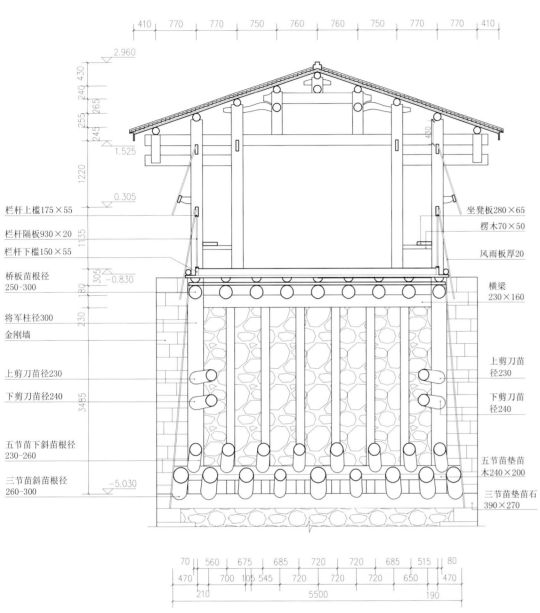
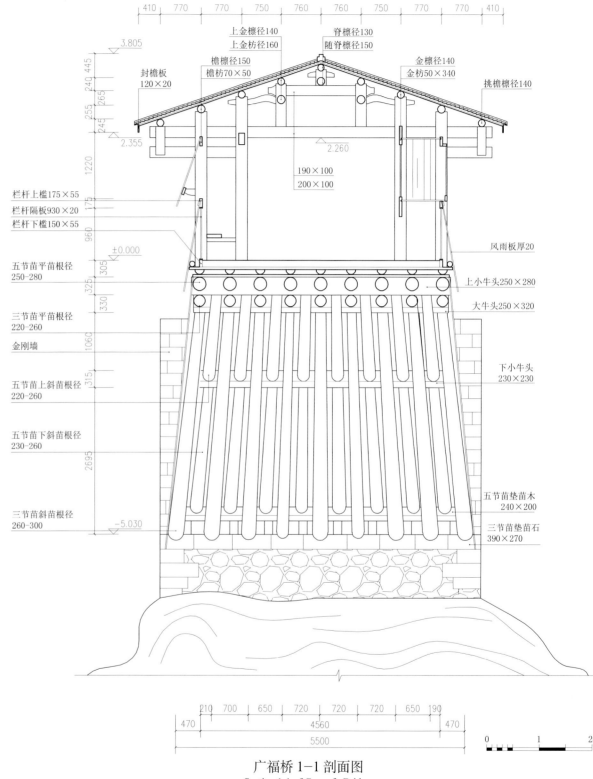

广福桥 2-2 剖面图
Section 2-2 of Guangfu Bridge

广福桥 1-1 剖面图
Section 1-1 of Guangfu Bridge

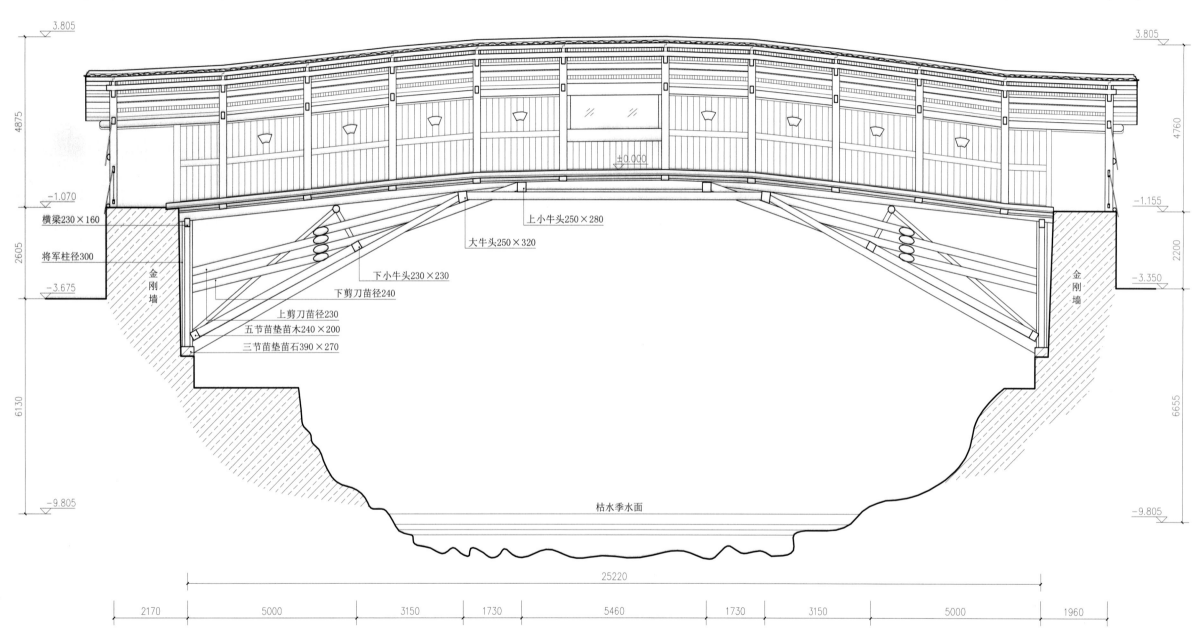

广福桥 3-3 剖面图
Section 3-3 of Guangfu Bridge

惠风桥

Huifeng Bridge

Huifeng Bridge, also known as Huangzhai Bridge or Pandi Bridge, was built in the Kangxi reign period of the Qing Dynasty (1662-1722), but rebuilt in 1941, the thirtieth year of the Republican era. Located in Pandi village of Daixi township, the bridge spans northwest to southeast across Daixi Stream in a single span. Wooden boards are mounted to form a deck.

惠风桥，又称『黄宅桥』『泮地桥』，始建于清代康熙年间（1662—1722年），中华民国三十年（1941年）重建，位于黛溪镇泮地村，单孔跨越黛溪，东南—西北走向，桥体拱架系统上铺木板为桥面。

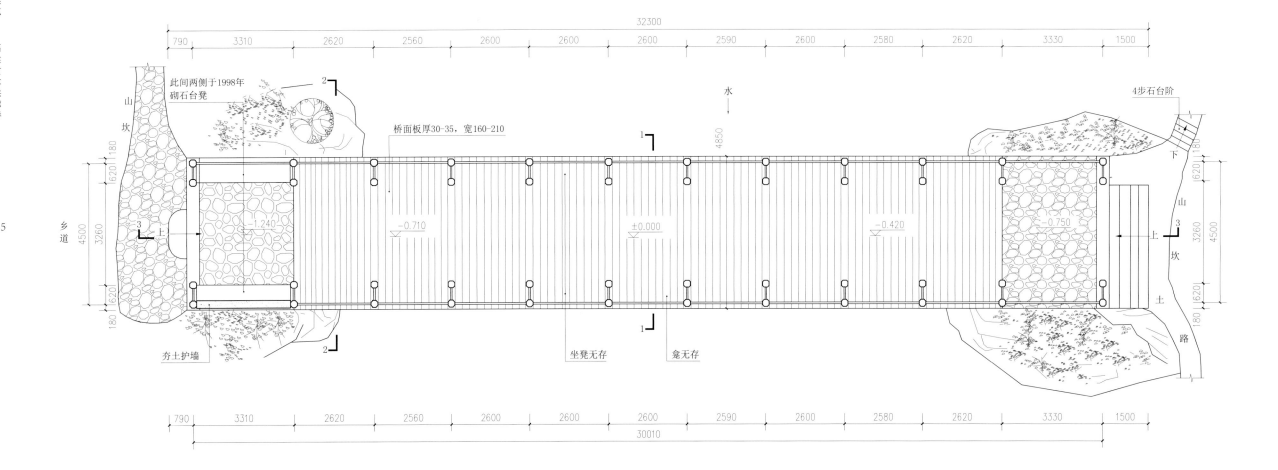

惠风桥平面图
Surface floor plan of Huifeng Bridge

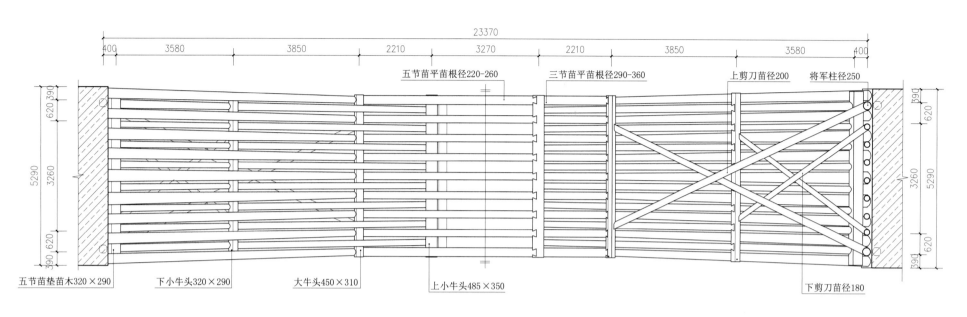

惠风桥桥体拱架系统仰视（左）与俯视（右）图

Plan of timber arch system of Huifeng Bridge as seen from below (left) and above (right)

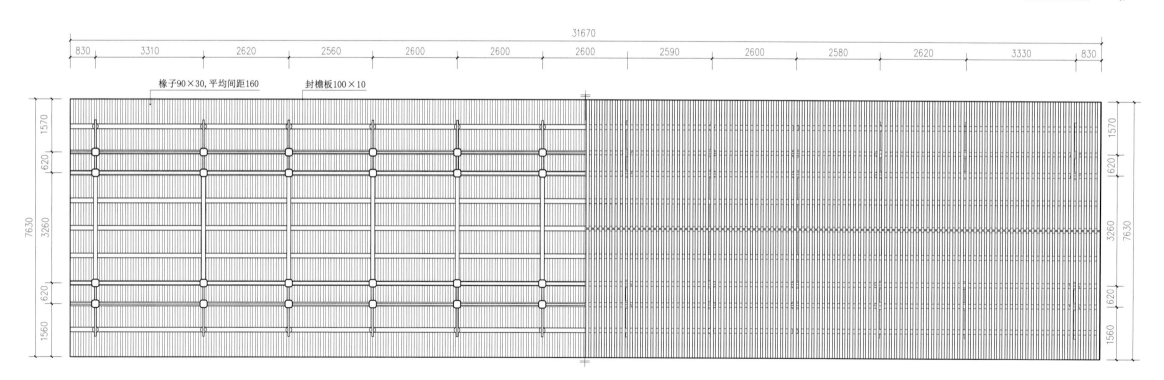

惠风桥廊屋梁架仰视（左）与俯视（右）图

Plan of corridor beam framework of Huifeng Bridge as seen from below (left) and above (right)

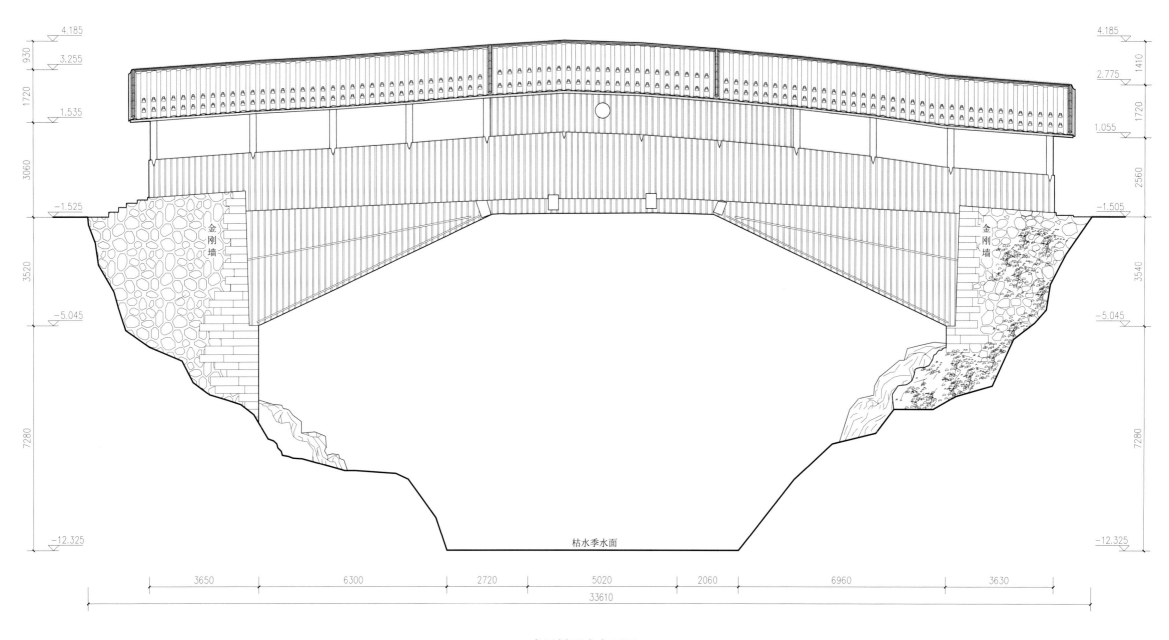

惠风桥西南立面图
Southwest elevation of Huifeng Bridge

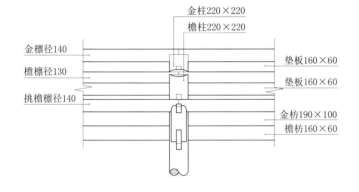

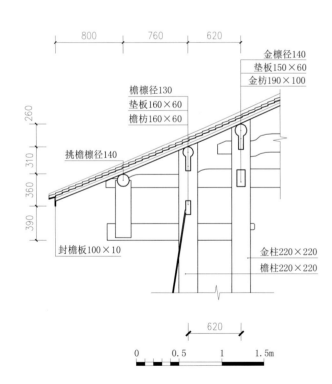

惠风桥出檐大样图
Roof eaves of Huifeng Bridge

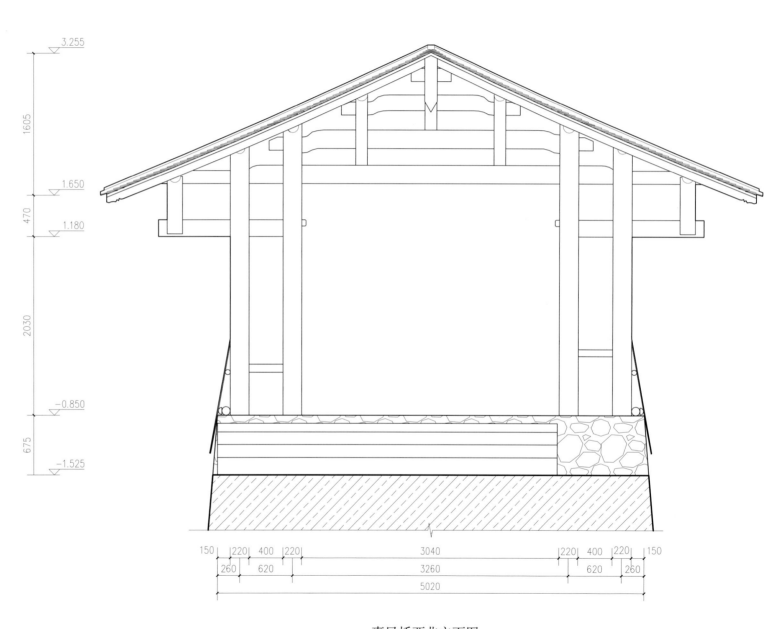

惠风桥西北立面图
Northwest elevation of Huifeng Bridge

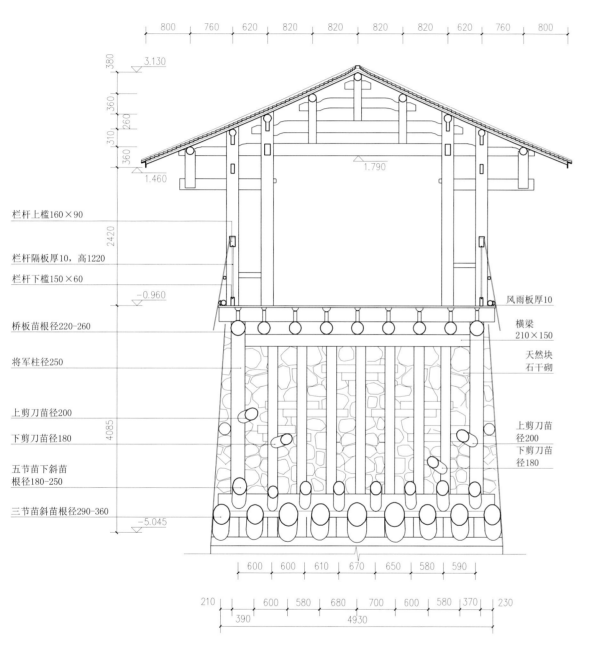

惠风桥 2-2 剖面图
Section 2-2 of Huifeng Bridge

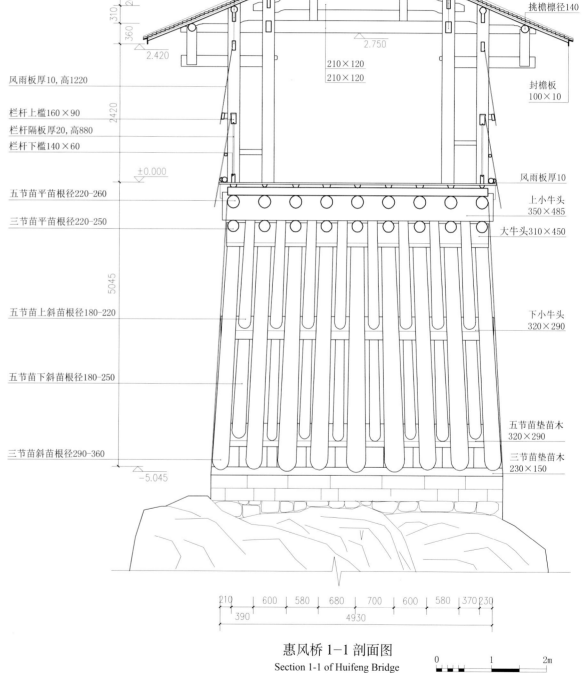

惠风桥 1-1 剖面图
Section 1-1 of Huifeng Bridge

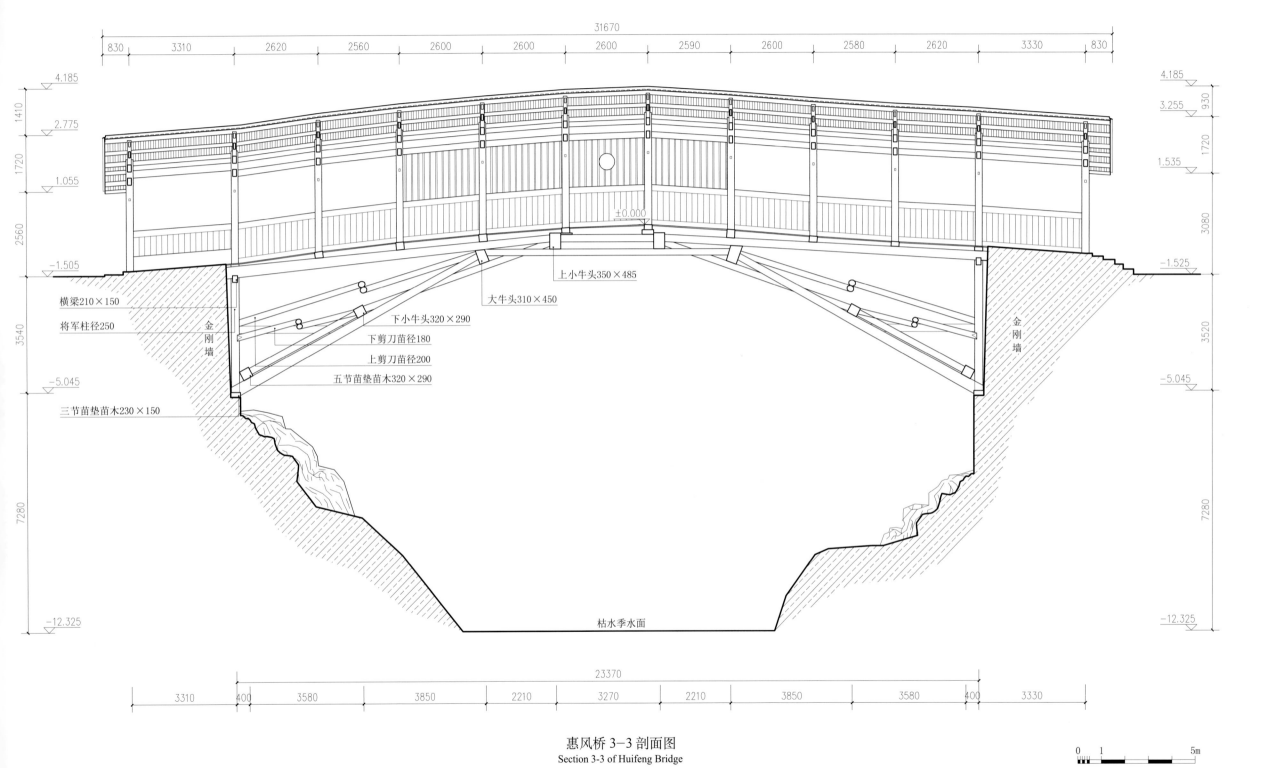

惠风桥 3-3 剖面图
Section 3-3 of Huifeng Bridge

龙津桥

Longjin Bridge

Longjin Bridge, also known as Yusuo Bridge or Xiwei Bridge, was built in the early Qing Dynasty. Located in Houlong village of Pingcheng township, the bridge spans east to west across Houlong Stream in a single span. Wooden boards form a deck covered with pebbles. A shrine was built in the center of the covered corridor to worship Wuxian Dadi (Emperor Wuxian, also know as Wutong Dadi, Mawangye). Longjin Bridge is one of the Eight Scenes of *Houlong* and known as Qiaosuo ("Bridge Lock") Longjin. Two stone steles stand at the head of the bridge. Chenjinggu Temple is located nearby.

龙津桥，又称『玉锁桥』、『溪尾桥』，始建于清代初期，位于屏城乡后垄村，单孔跨越后垄溪，东西走向。桥体拱架系统上铺木板，再上铺卵石为桥面。廊屋中部设神龛，祀五显大帝。龙津桥是『后垄八景』之一，名为『桥锁龙津』。桥头立两方石碑，附近有陈靖姑庙。

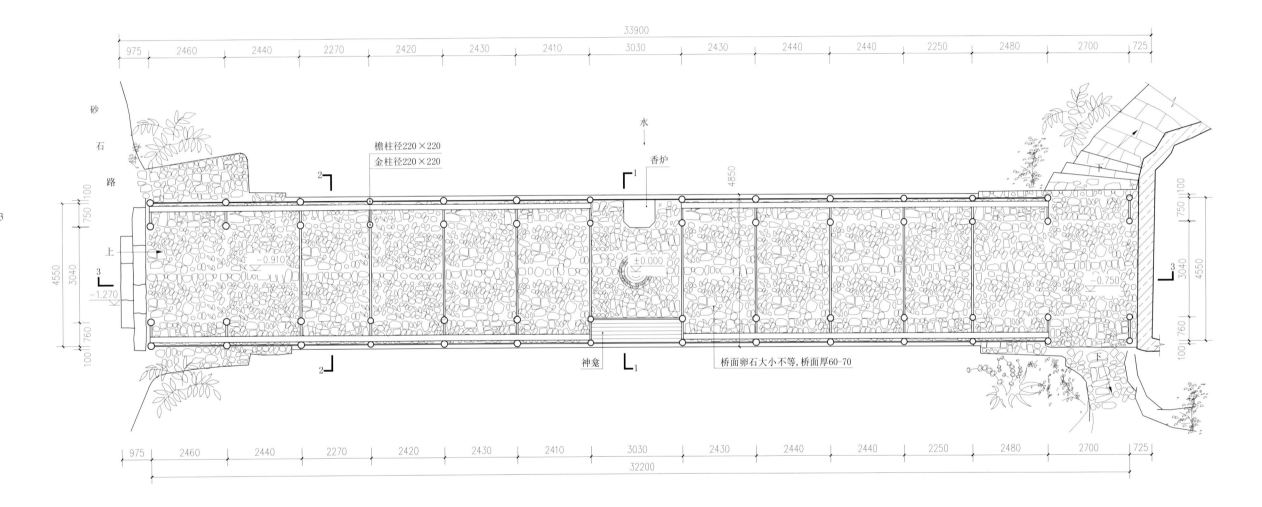

龙津桥平面图
Surface floor plan of Longjin Bridge

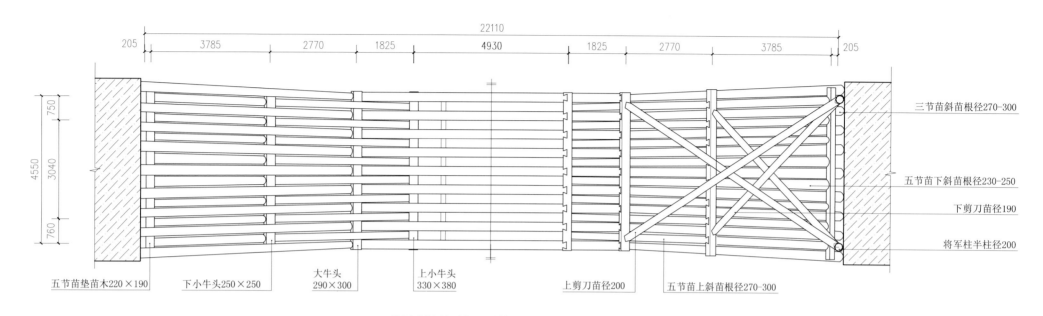

龙津桥桥梁拱骨系统仰视（左）与俯视（右）图
Plan of timber arch system of Longjin Bridge as seen from below (left) and above (right)

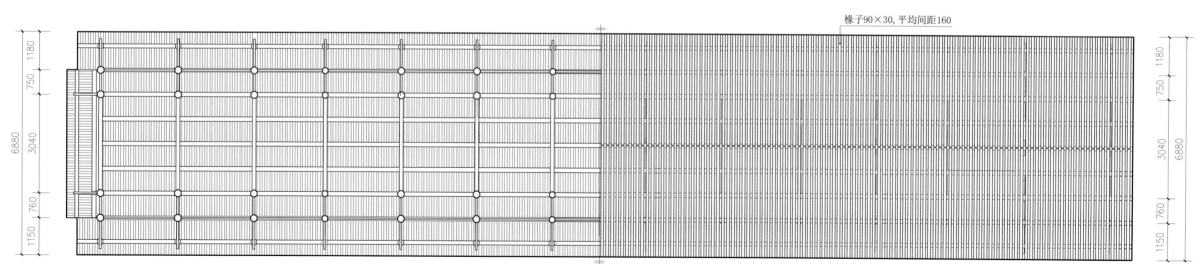

龙津桥廊屋梁架仰视（左）与俯视（右）图
Plan of corridor beam framework of Longjin Bridge as seen from below (left) and above (right)

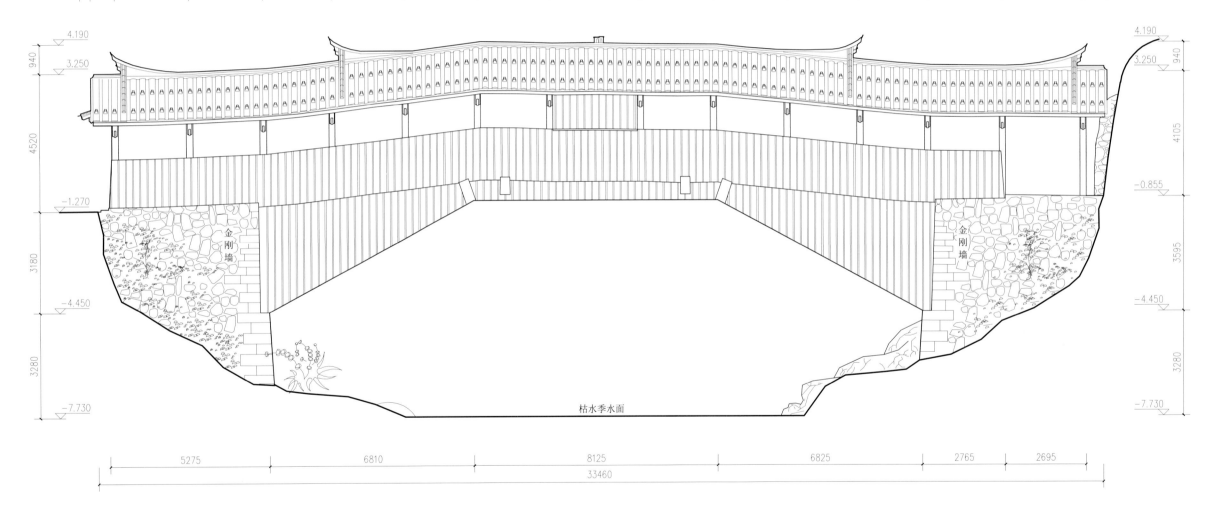

龙津桥南立面图
South elevation of Longjin Bridge

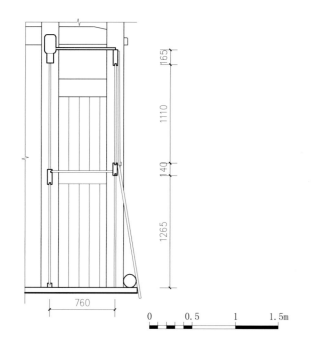

龙津桥神龛剖面图
Section of shrine of Longjin Bridge

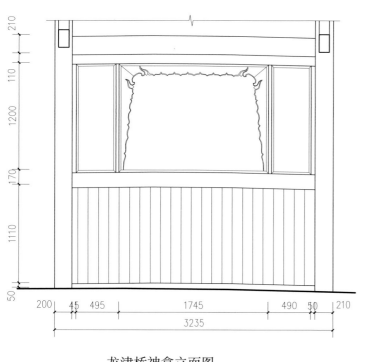

龙津桥神龛立面图
Elevation of shrine of Longjin Bridge

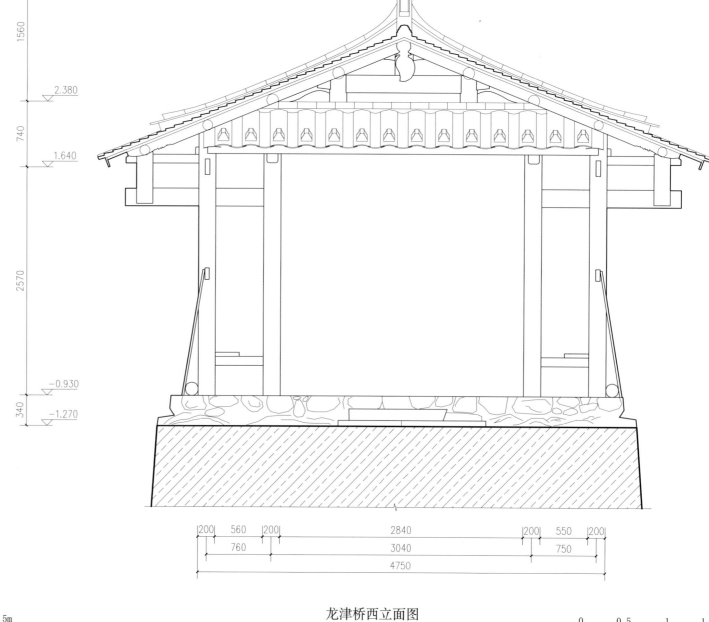

龙津桥西立面图
West elevation of Longjin Bridge

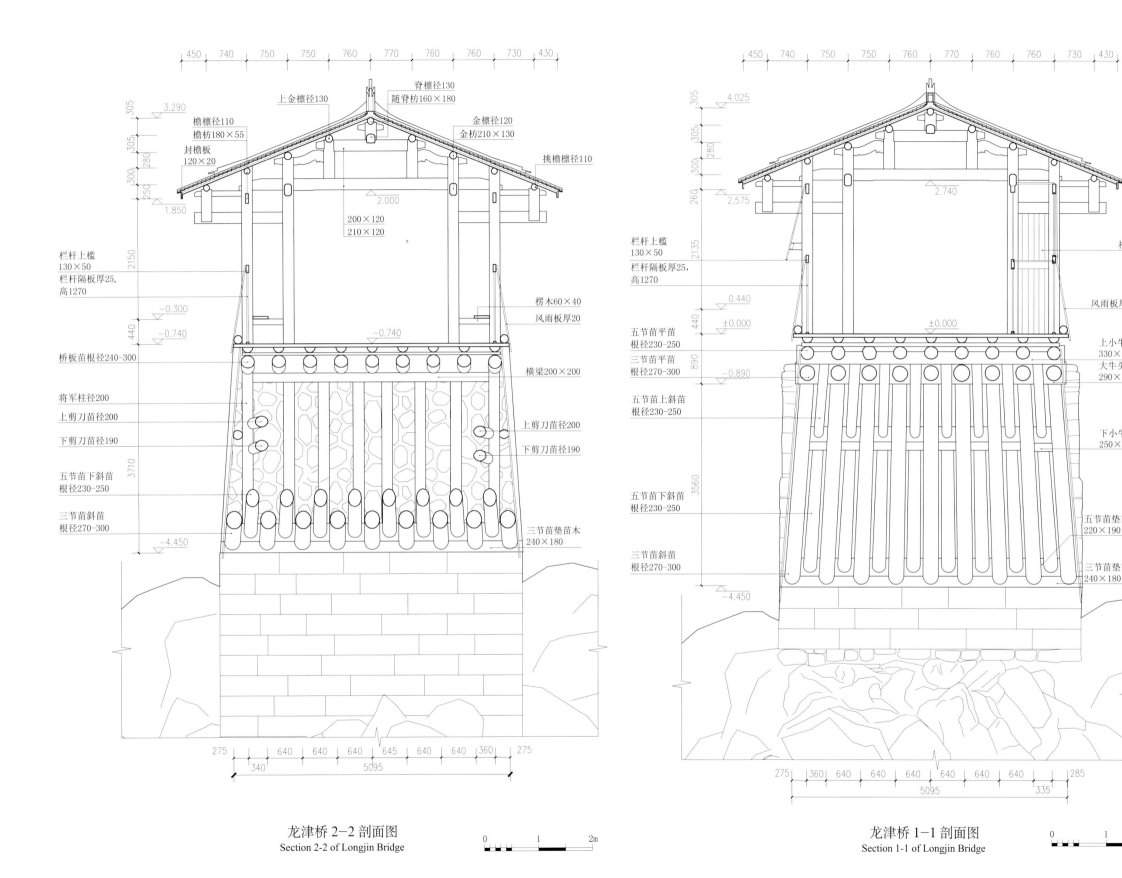

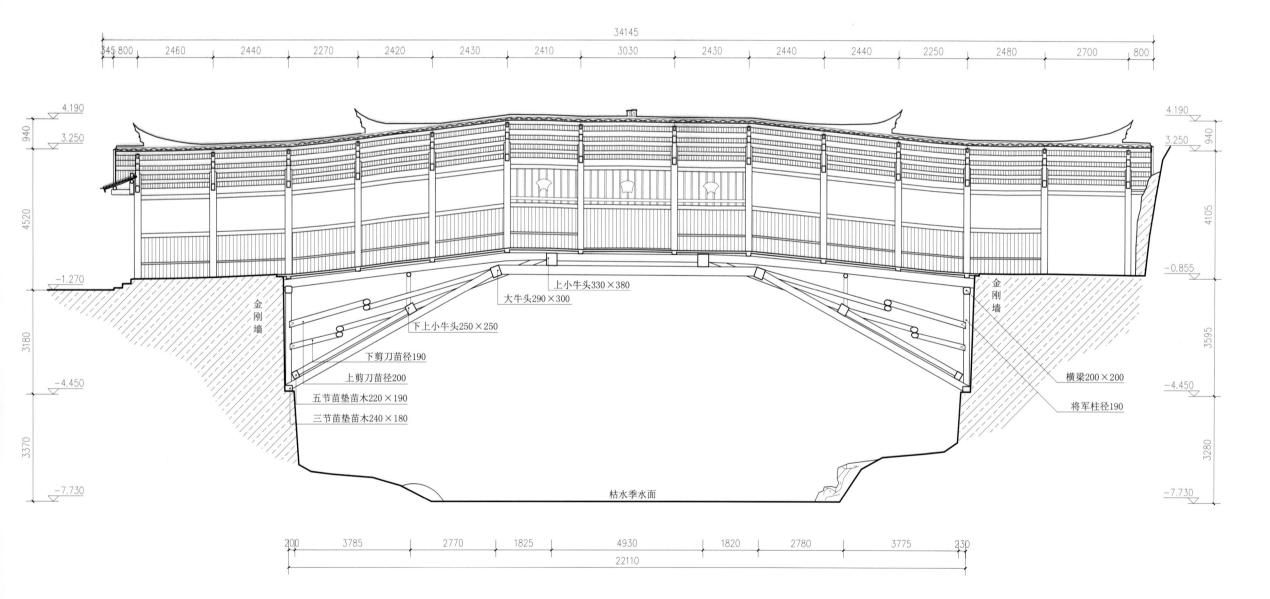

龙津桥 3-3 剖面图
Section 3-3 of Longjin Bridge

清晏桥

Qingyan Bridge

Qingyan Bridge, also known as An Bridge, was built in 1852, the second year of the Xianfeng reign period of the Qing Dynasty, but was rebuilt in 1905, the thirty-first year of the Guangxu reign period. Originally located on the old path from Qiantang village in Xiling township to Jitou village in Tangkou district, the bridge was moved to a new location on the west of Qianlin village because the bridge would have been submerged by the rising levels of water in the Jinzaoqiao Hydropower Station built. The bridge spans northeast to southwest across the valley in a single span. Wooden boards are mounted as a deck, and a shrine has been built in the middle of the covered corridor to worship Guanyin. Two stone steles stand to the side of the bridge.

清晏桥，又称『暗桥』，始建于清代咸丰二年（1852年），清代光绪三十一年（1905年）重建，原位于熙岭乡前塘村通往棠口乡漈头村的古道上，后因建造金造桥水电站，桥处于水库淹没区，被搬迁至前林村西边，单孔跨越山谷，东北—西南走向。桥体拱架系统上铺木板为桥面，廊屋中部设神龛，祀观音。桥边立两方石碑。

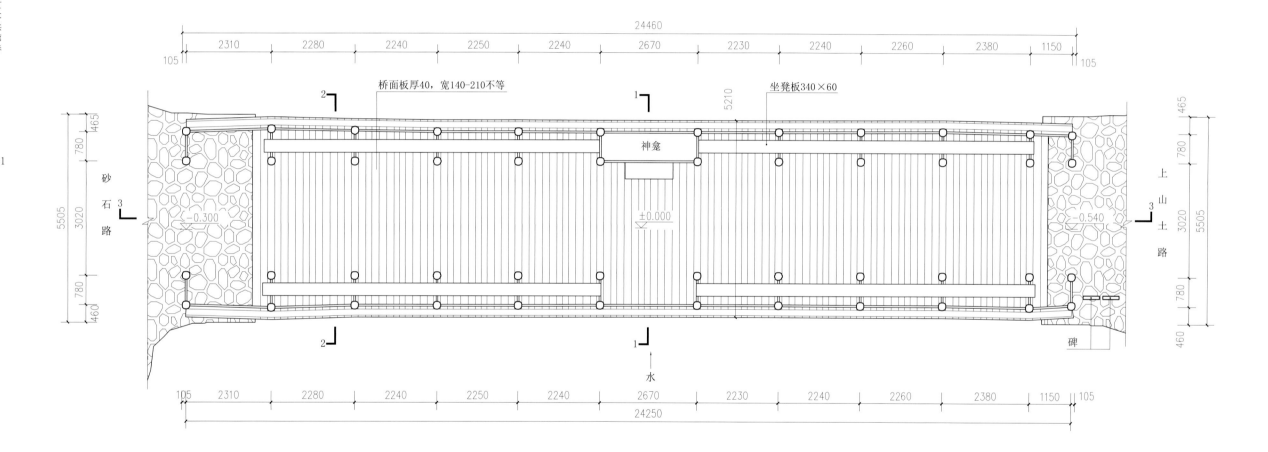

清晏桥平面图
Surface floor plan of Qingyan Bridge

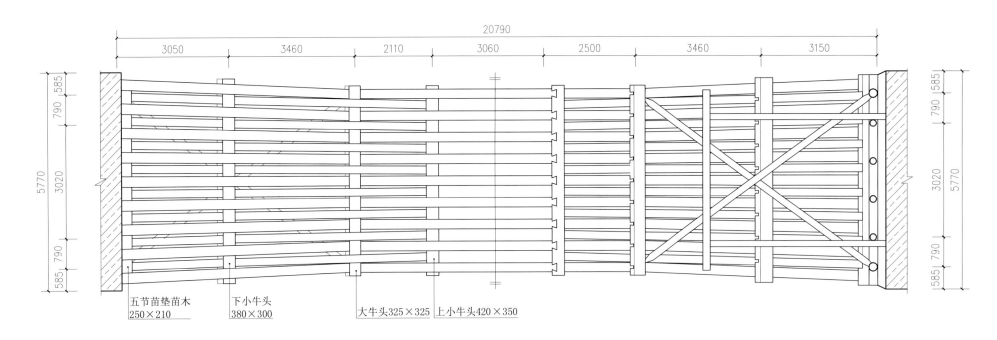

清晏桥桥体拱架系统仰视（左）与俯视（右）图
Plan of timber arch system of Qingyan Bridge as seen from below (left) and above (right)

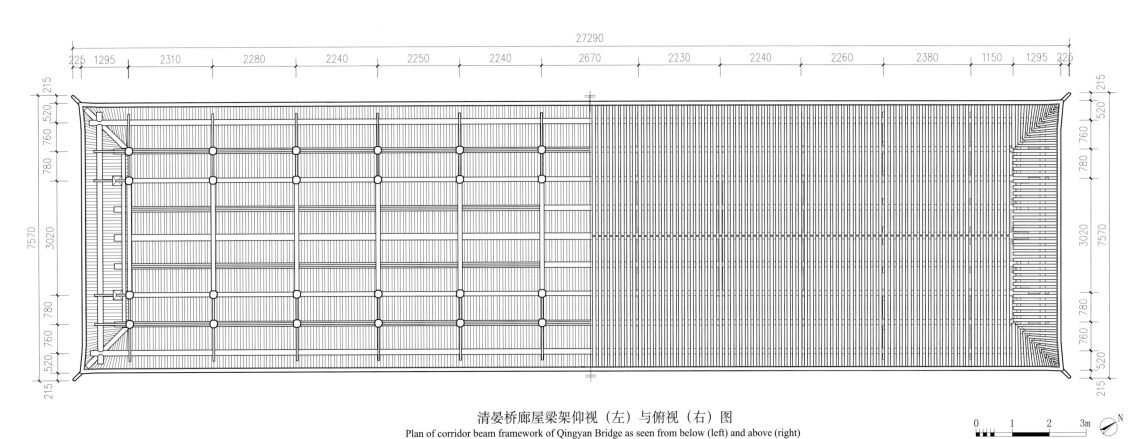

清晏桥廊屋梁架仰视（左）与俯视（右）图
Plan of corridor beam framework of Qingyan Bridge as seen from below (left) and above (right)

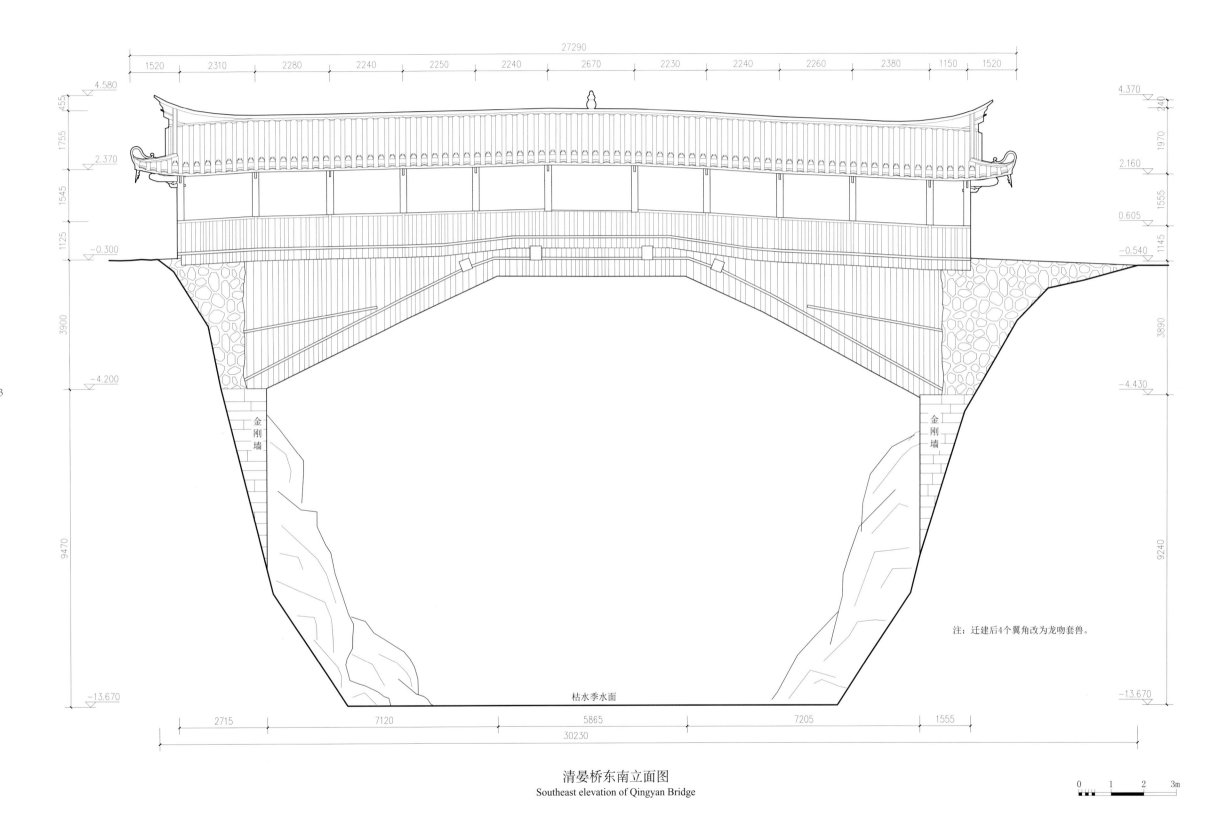

清晏桥东南立面图
Southeast elevation of Qingyan Bridge

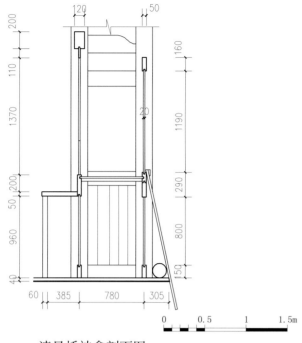

清晏桥神龛剖面图
Section of shrine of Qingyan Bridge

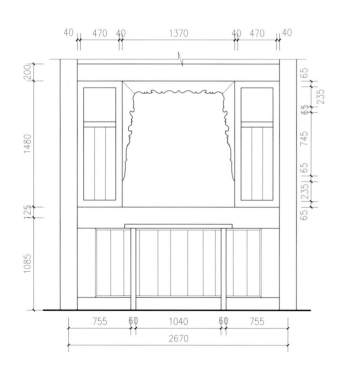

清晏桥神龛立面图
Elevation of shrine of Qingyan Bridge

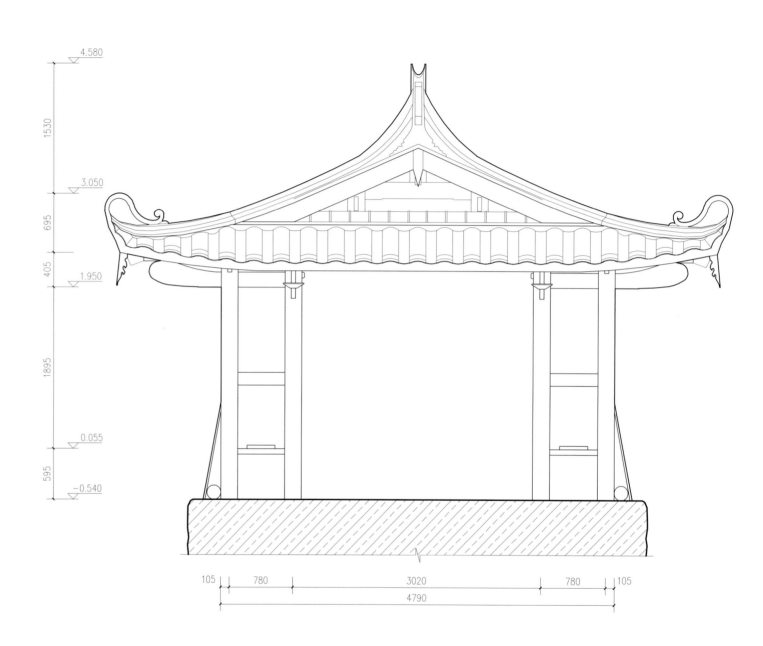

清晏桥东北立面图
Northeast elevation of Qingyan Bridge

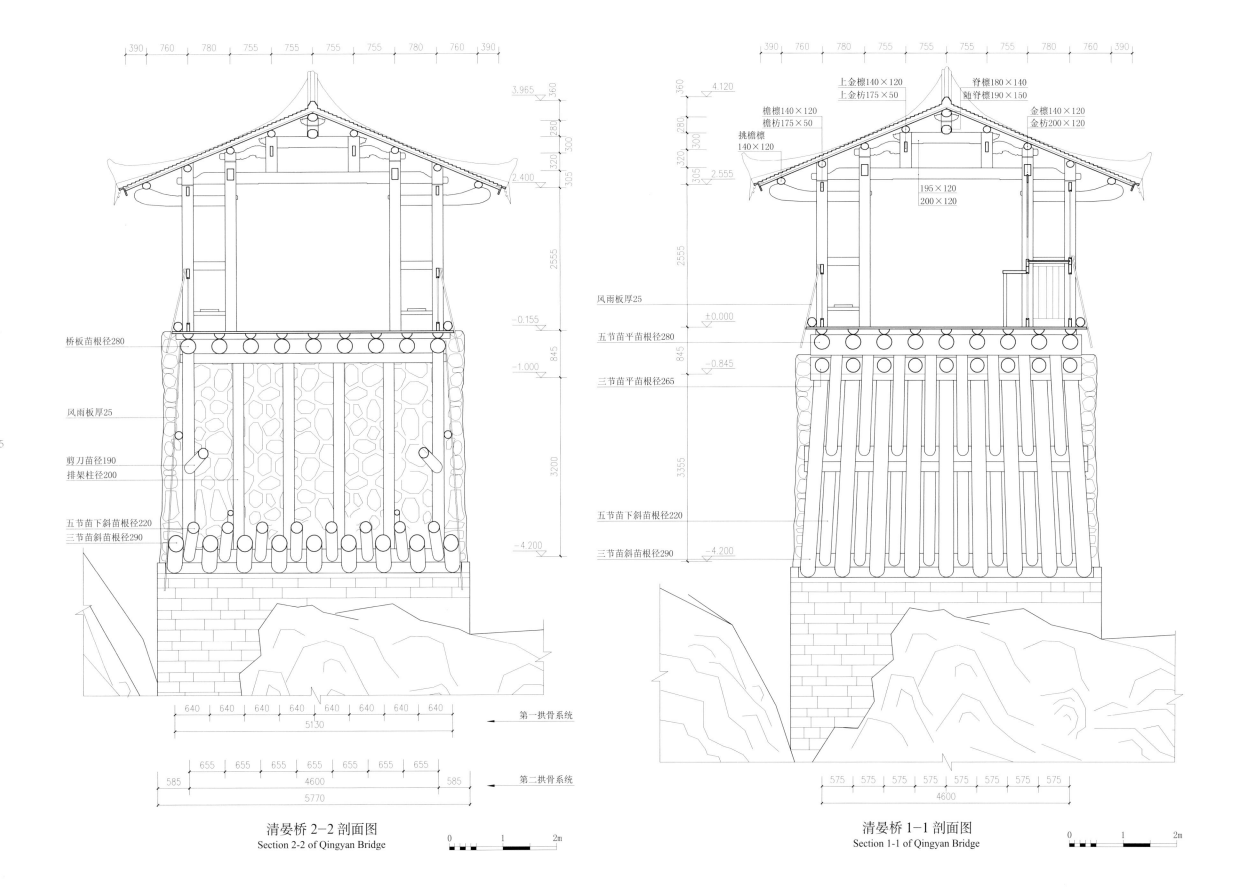

清晏桥 2-2 剖面图
Section 2-2 of Qingyan Bridge

清晏桥 1-1 剖面图
Section 1-1 of Qingyan Bridge

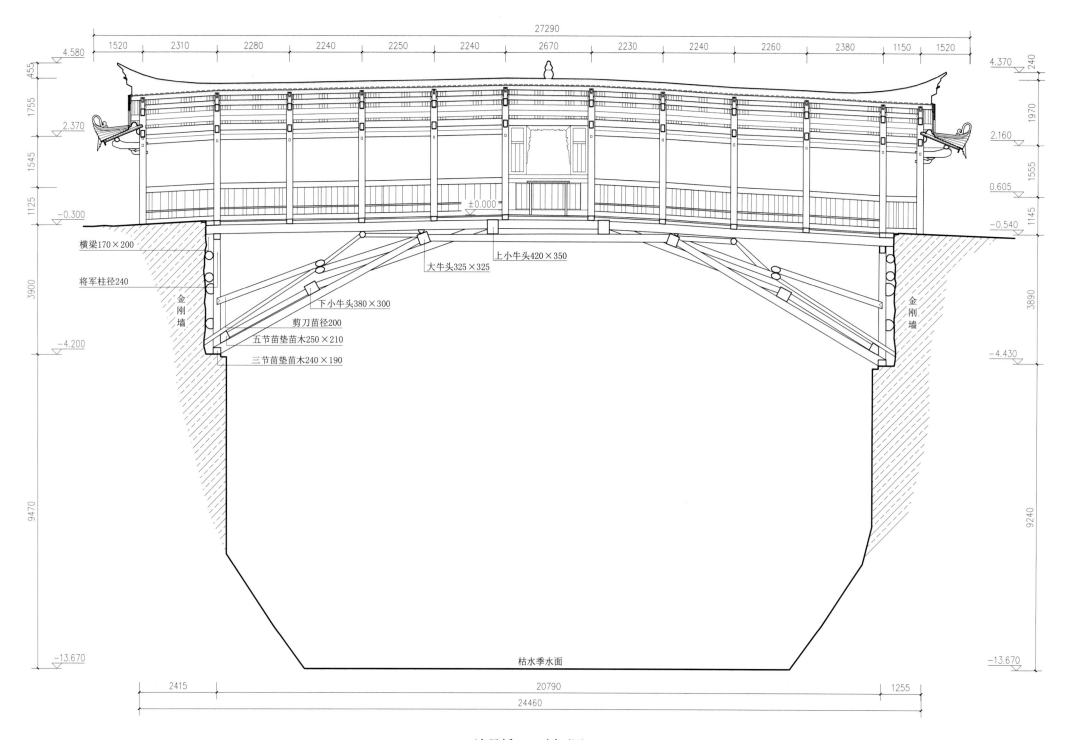

清晏桥 3-3 剖面图
Section 3-3 of Qingyan Bridge

龙井桥

Longjing Bridge

Longjing Bridge was built in the Song Dynasty but rebuilt in 1820, the twenty-fifth year of the Jiaqing reign period of the Qing Dynasty. Located on the old path of the southeast of Baiyu village of Shoushan township, the bridge spans northeast to southwest across Jinzao stream in a single span. The name Longjing (Dragon Well) Bridge derives from the deep pool of water that was once under the bridge, a scene like that of a dragon spouting water. Wooden boards form a deck covered with bricks. There is a shrine dedicated to the worship of the bodhisattva Guanyin at the center of the covered corridor. The bridge was once elevated 20m above the surface of the water and is one of the steepest bridges in southeastern China, as recorded in *Zhongguo Guqiao Jishu Shi* (*History of traditional Chinese bridge technology*). The construction of the hydropower station downstream, however, caused the water level to rise 14m (so that the bridge is now elevated only 6m above the water surface).

龙井桥，始建于宋代，清代嘉庆二十五年（1820年）重建，位于寿山乡白玉村东南的古道上，单孔跨越金造溪，东北—西南走向。原桥下有一深潭，似龙喷浪如雪，故称"龙井"，桥以此得名。桥体拱架系统上铺木板，再上铺砖为桥面。廊屋中部设神龛，祀观音。桥离溪水高度曾达20m左右，是我国东南险桥之一，被载入《中国古桥技术史》。现因下游建电站，水位升高，离水高度仅6m左右。

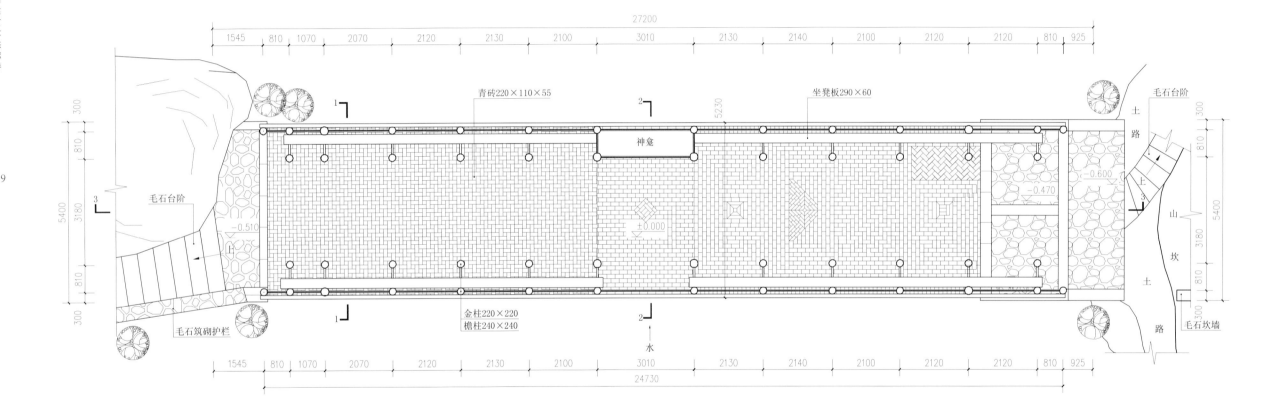

龙井桥平面图
Surface floor plan of Longjing Bridge

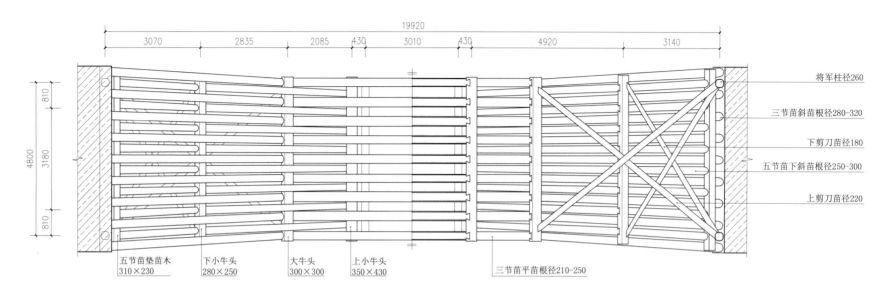

龙井桥桥梁拱骨系统仰视（左）与俯视（右）图
Plan of timber arch system of Longjing Bridge as seen from below (left) and above (right)

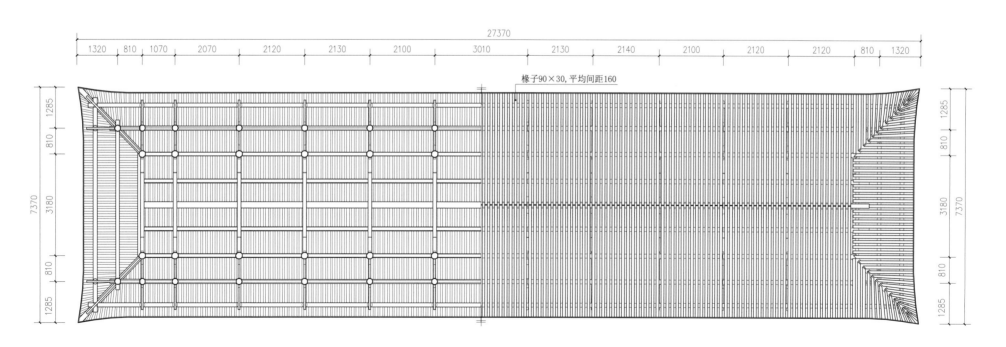

龙井桥廊屋梁架仰视（左）与俯视（右）图
Plan of corridor beam framework of Longjing Bridge as seen from below (left) and above (right)

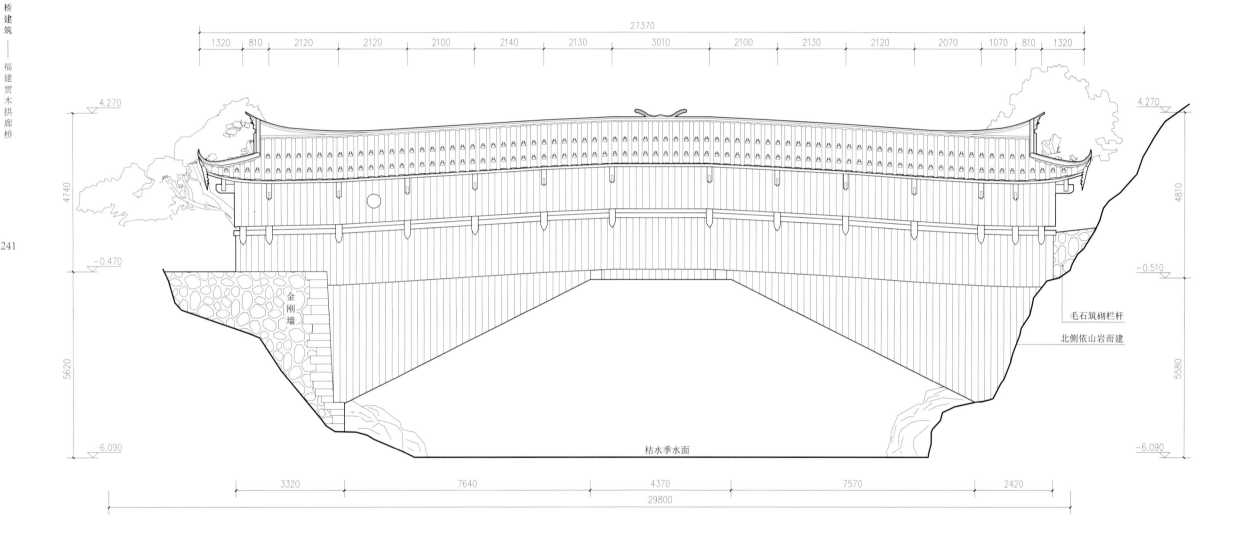

龙井桥东南立面图
Southeast elevation of Longjing Bridge

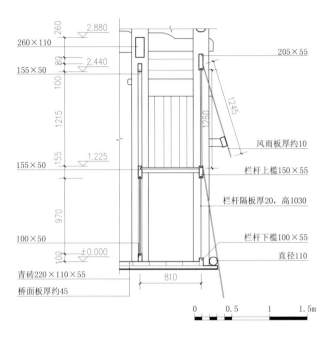

龙井桥神龛剖面图
Section of shrine of Longjing Bridge

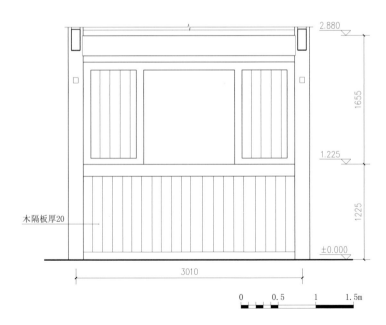

龙井桥神龛立面图
Elevation of shrine of Longjing Bridge

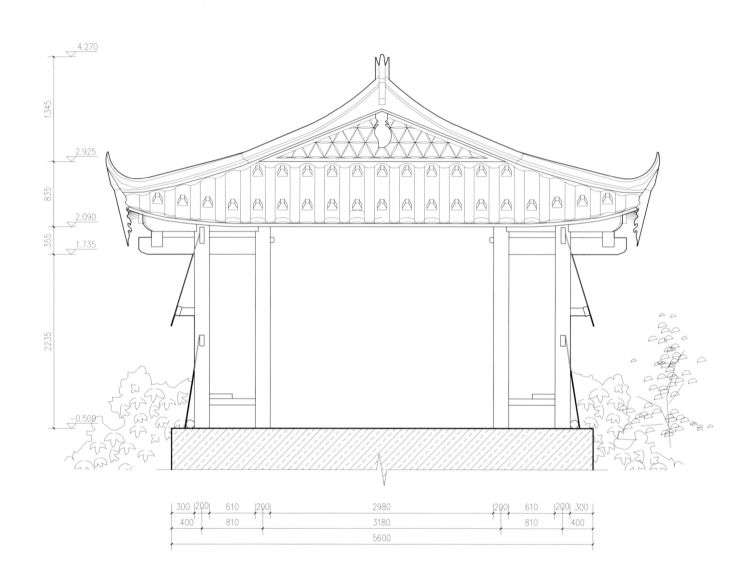

龙井桥西南立面图
Southwest elevation of Longjing Bridge

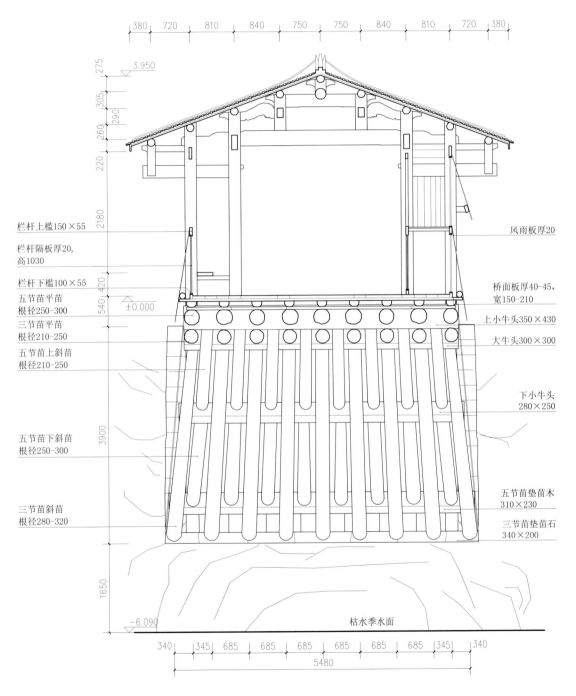
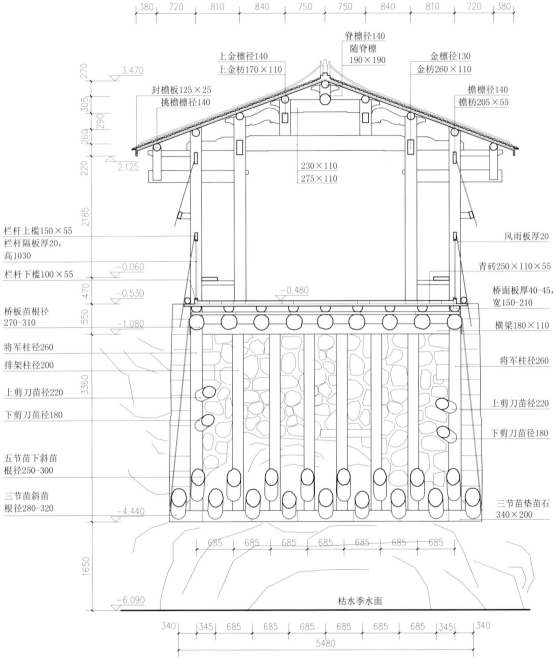

龙井桥 2-2 剖面图
Section 2-2 of Longjing Bridge

龙井桥 1-1 剖面图
Section 1-1 of Longjing Bridge

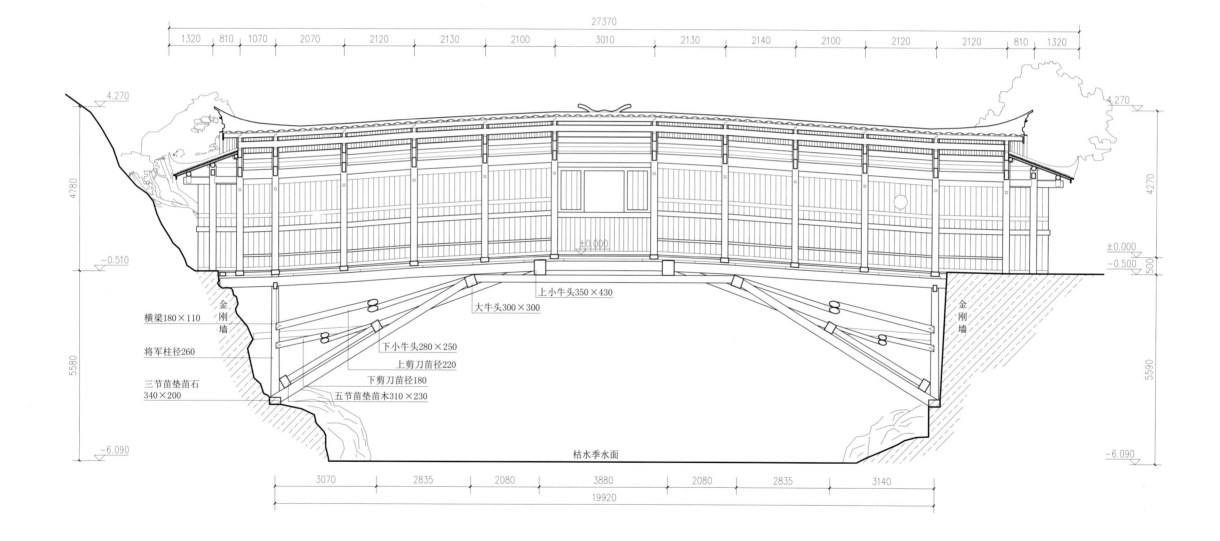

龙井桥 3-3 剖面图
Section 3-3 of Longjing Bridge

广利桥

Guangli Bridge

Guangli Bridge, also known as Huaqiao Bridge, was first built in the Song dynasty. Located in the south of Lingxia village of Lingxia township, the bridge spans east to west across Lingxia Stream (originally known as Jinxia Stream) in a single span. Wooden boards form a deck covered with pebbles. A shrine in the middle of the covered corridor is dedicated to the worship of Zhenwudi. Along both sides of the stream grow precious old trees of the species Taxus chinesis (*Hongdoushan*) and Cryptomeria fortunei (*Liu shan*). Guangli Bridge and Guangfu Bridge are located merely half a kilometer away, and since they both cross Lingxia Stream, they are regarded as twin bridges, which is rare in this region.

广利桥，又称「花桥」，始建于宋代，位于岭下乡岭下村南，单孔跨越岭下（古称「锦厦」）溪，东西走向。桥体拱架系统上铺木板，再上铺卵石为桥面。廊屋中部设神龛，祀真武帝，两岸有红豆杉、柳杉等古树名木林。广利桥与广福桥相距里许，由岭下溪贯穿，是远近不可多得的姐妹桥。

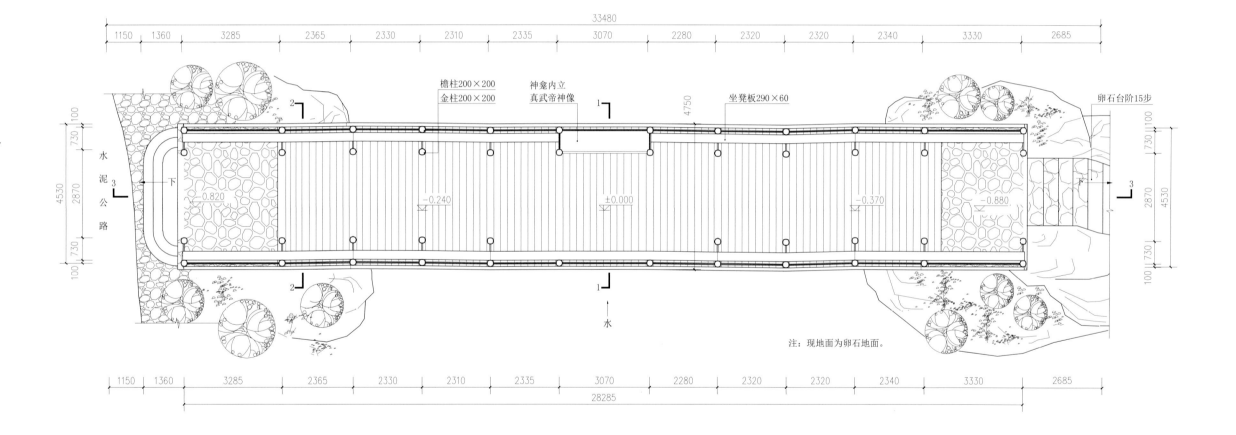

广利桥平面图
Surface floor plan of Guangli Bridge

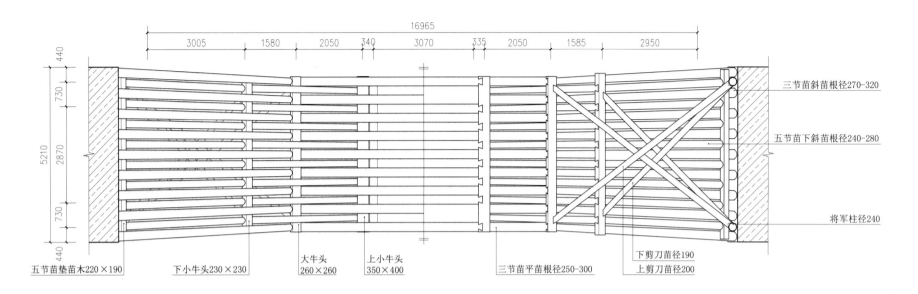

广利桥桥体拱架系统仰视（左）与俯视（右）图
Plan of timber arch system of Guangli Bridge as seen from below (left) and above (right)

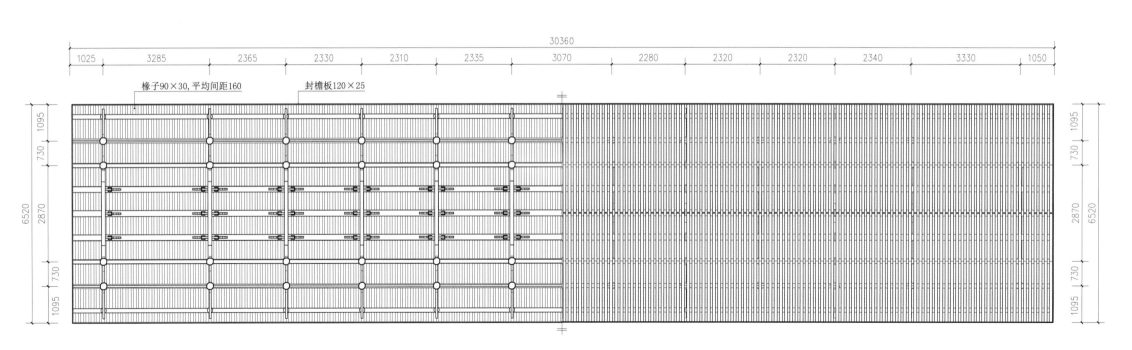

广利桥廊屋梁架仰视（左）与俯视（右）图
Plan of corridor beam framework of Guangli Bridge as seen from below (left) and above (right)

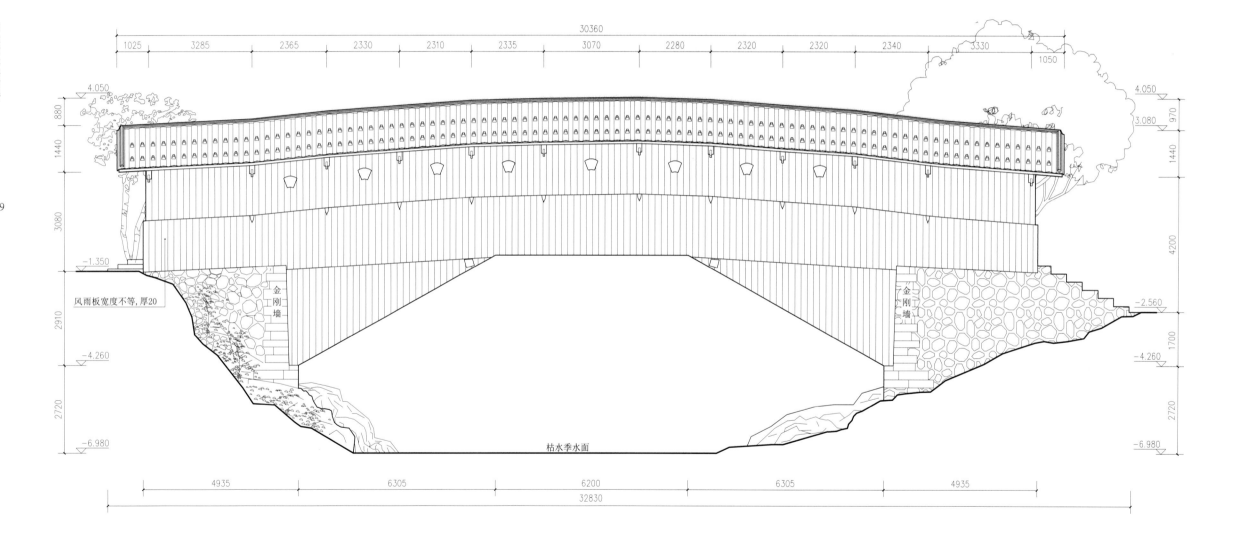

广利桥北立面图
North elevation of Guangli Bridge

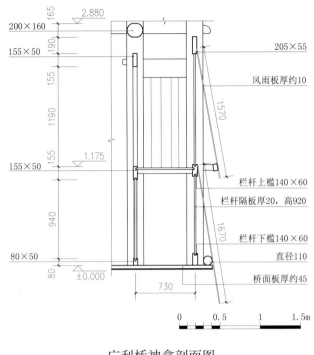

广利桥神龛剖面图
Section of shrine of Guangli Bridge

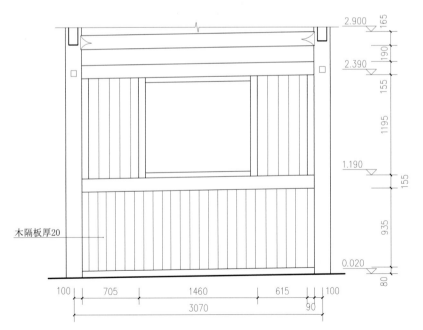

广利桥神龛立面图
Elevation of shrine of Guangli Bridge

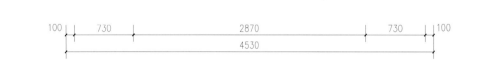

广利桥东立面图
East elevation of Guangli Bridge

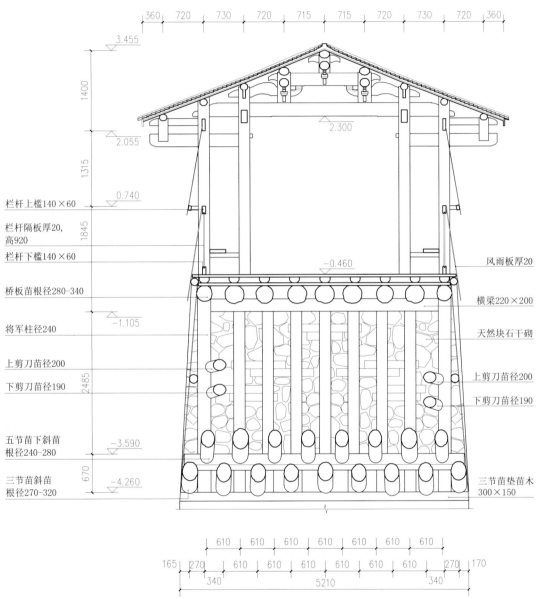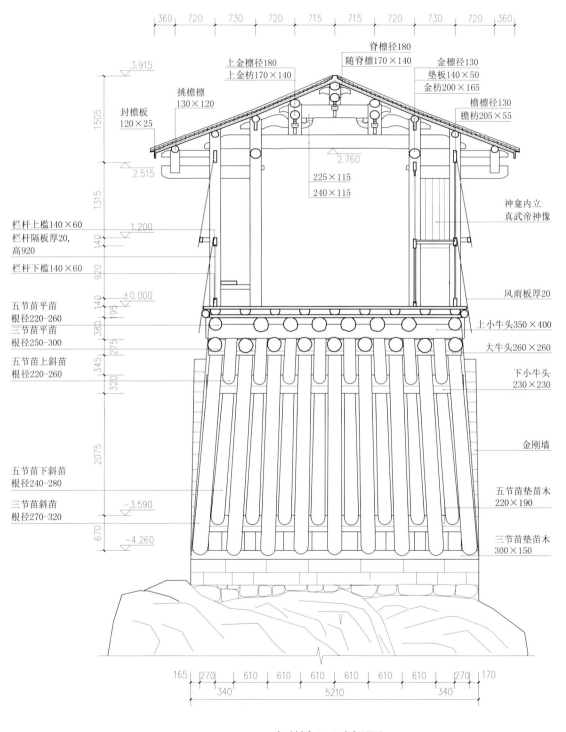

广利桥 2-2 剖面图
Section 2-2 of Guangli Bridge

广利桥 1-1 剖面图
Section 1-1 of Guangli Bridge

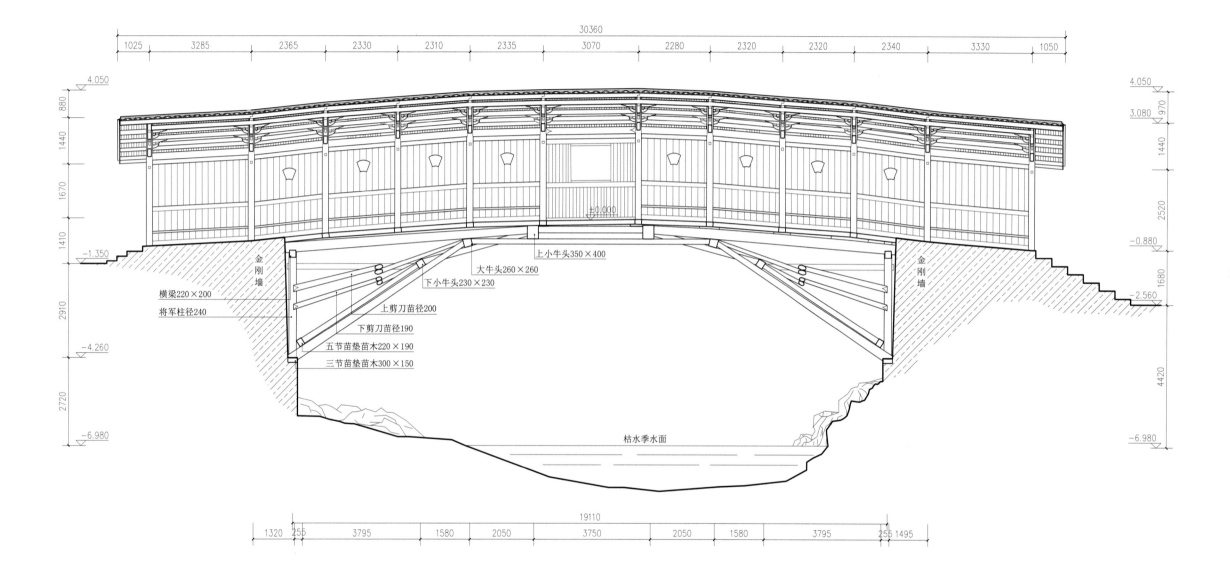

广利桥 3-3 剖面图
Section 3-3 of Guangli Bridge

溪里桥

Xili Bridge

The date of the first construction of Xili Bridge also known as Jinxi Bridge remains unknown, but it was rebuilt in the early Qing Dynasty, destroyed in 1969, and rebuilt again in 1970. Located in Xili village of Xiling township, the bridge spans north to south across Xili Stream in a single span. Wooden boards are mounted to form a deck, and a shrine is installed in the middle of the covered corridor dedicated to Guanyin. Two hundred-year-old trees of the species Taxus chinesis (*Hongdoushan*) grow on either side of the bridge, and an old temple with a plaque saying "*Jinxi Baozhang*" (guarded by Jinxi Stream) stands the west of the bridge.

溪里桥，又称『锦溪桥』，始建年代不详，清代初期重建，1969年毁掉，1970年重建；位于熙岭乡溪里村，单孔跨越溪里溪，南北走向。桥体拱架系统上铺木板为桥面，廊屋中部设神龛，祀观音。桥两岸各有一株百年树龄的红豆杉，桥西不远处有一座匾额为『锦溪保障』的古庙。

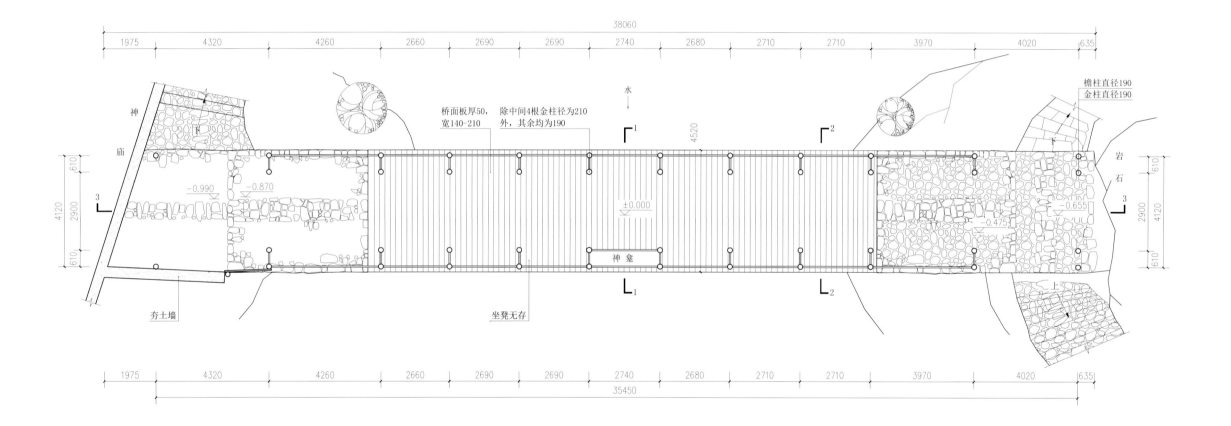

溪里桥平面图
Surface floor plan of Xili Bridge

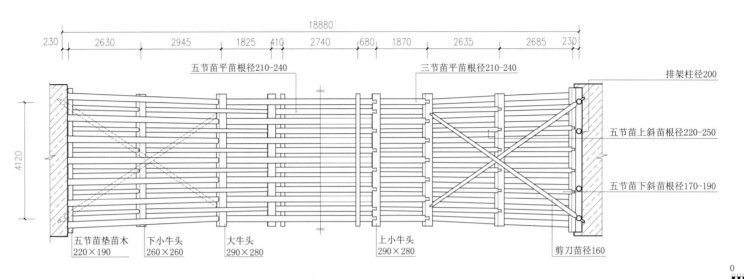

溪里桥桥体拱架系统仰视（左）与俯视（右）图

Plan of timber arch system of Xili Bridge as seen from below (left) and above (right)

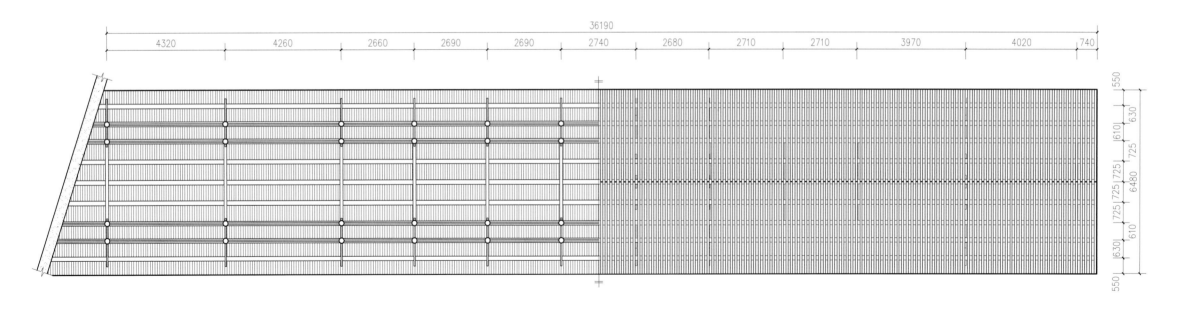

溪里桥廊屋梁架仰视（左）与俯视（右）图

Plan of corridor beam framework of Xili Bridge as seen from below (left) and above (right)

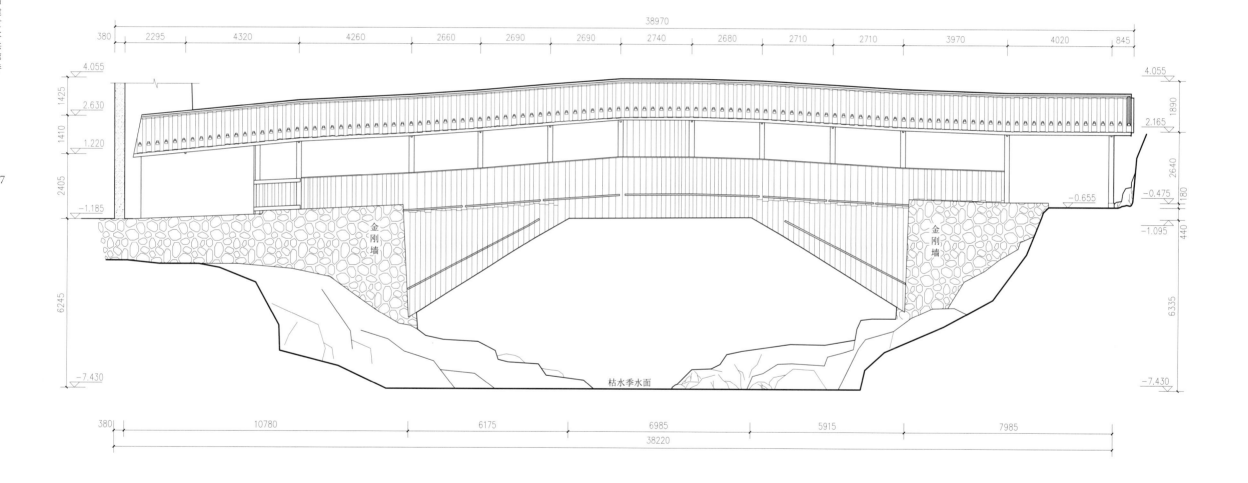

溪里桥东立面图
East elevation of Xili Bridge

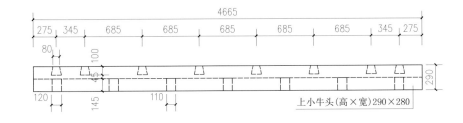

溪里桥牛头大样图
Niutou of Xili Bridge

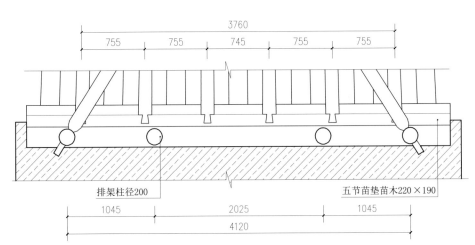

溪里桥垫苗木大样图
Dianmiaomu of Xili Bridge

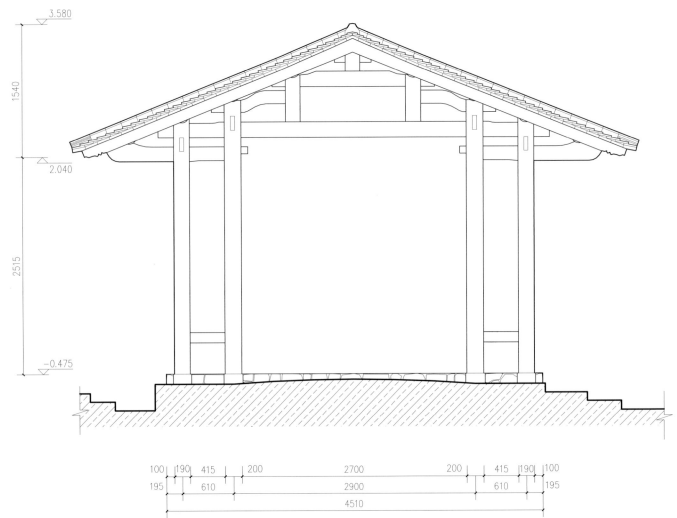

溪里桥南立面图
South elevation of Xili Bridge

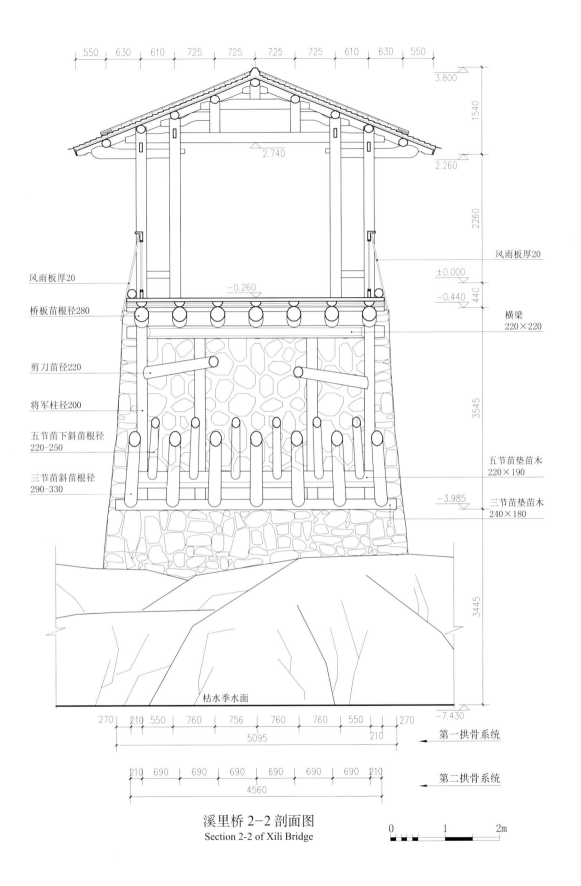

溪里桥 2-2 剖面图
Section 2-2 of Xili Bridge

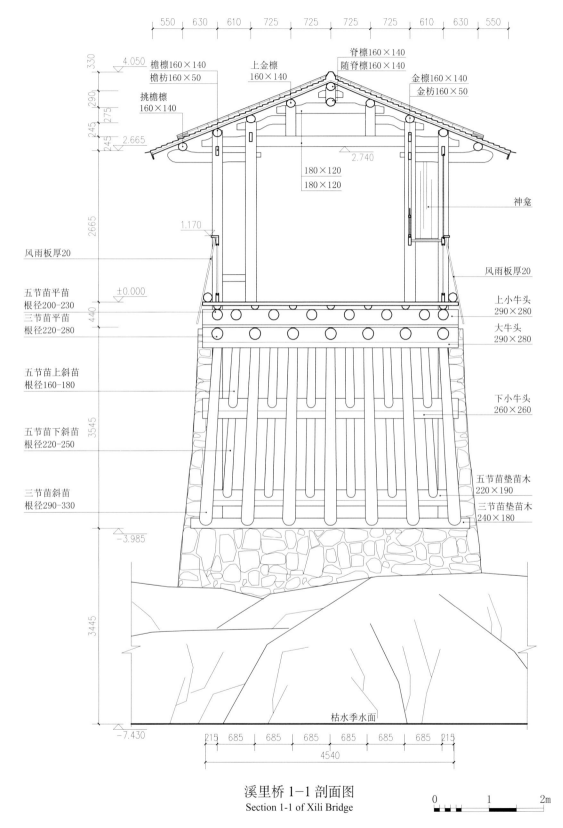

溪里桥 1-1 剖面图
Section 1-1 of Xili Bridge

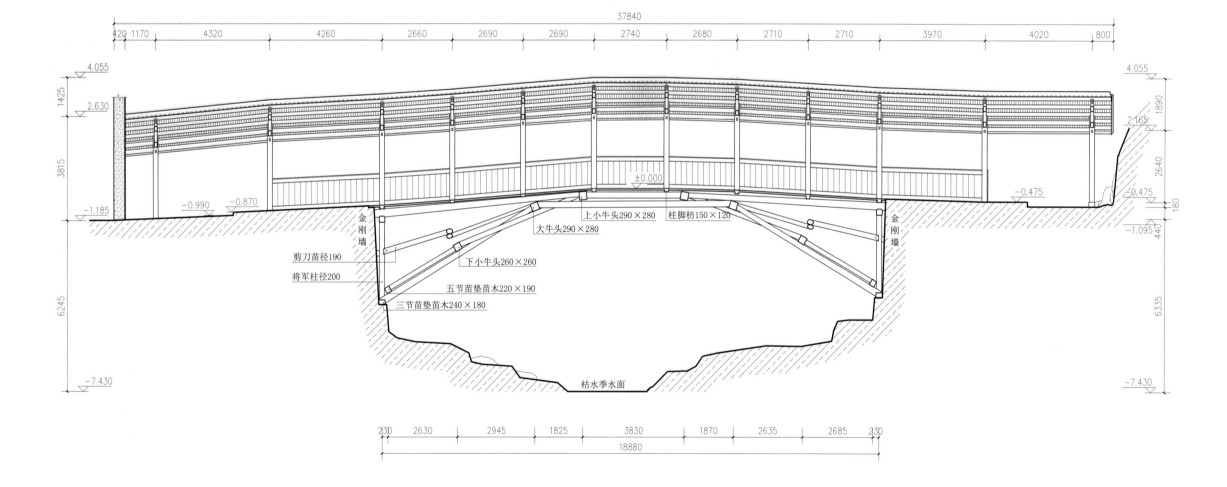

溪里桥 3-3 剖面图
Section 3-3 of Xili Bridge

樟口桥

Zhangkou Bridge

樟口桥，又称「樟源桥」，始建年代不详，清代咸丰五年（1855年）重修，1955年重建，位于黛溪镇漳源村，单孔跨越黛溪，东北—西南走向。桥体拱架系统上铺木板、再上铺卵石为桥面。廊屋中部设神龛，祀真武帝。

Zhangkou Bridge, also known as Zhangyuan Bridge, was rebuilt in 1855, the fifth year of the Xianfeng reign period of the Qing Dynasty. The first construction date remains unknown. It was rebuilt in 1955. Located in Zhangyuan village of Daixi township, the bridge spans northeast to southwest across Daixi Stream in a single span. Wooden boards form a deck covered with pebbles. A shrine is installed in the middle of the covered corridor dedicated to Zhenwudi.

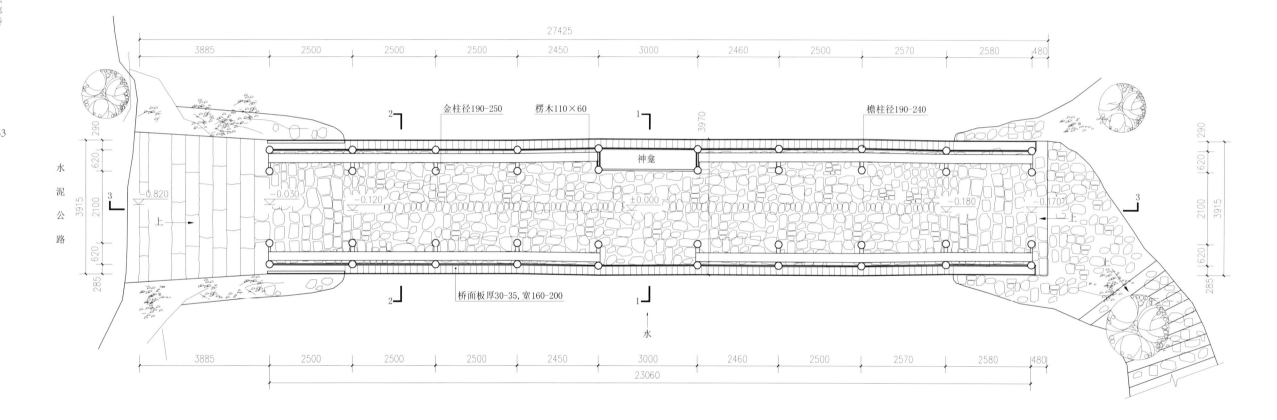

樟口桥平面图
Surface floor plan of Zhangkou Bridge

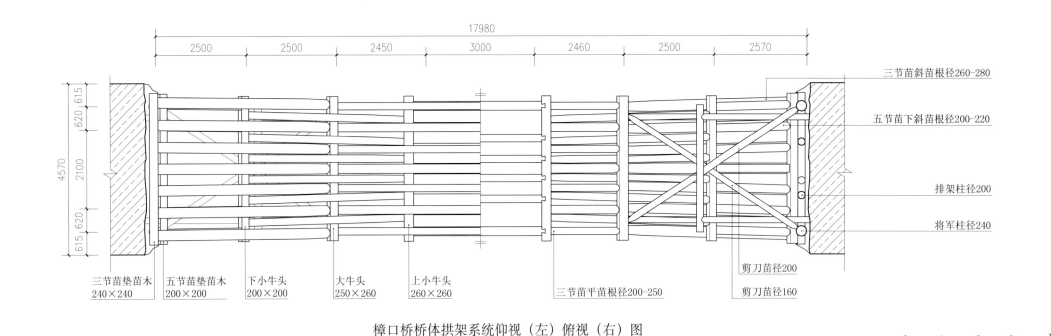

樟口桥桥体拱架系统仰视（左）俯视（右）图
Plan of timber arch system of Zhangkou Bridge as seen from below (left) and above (right)

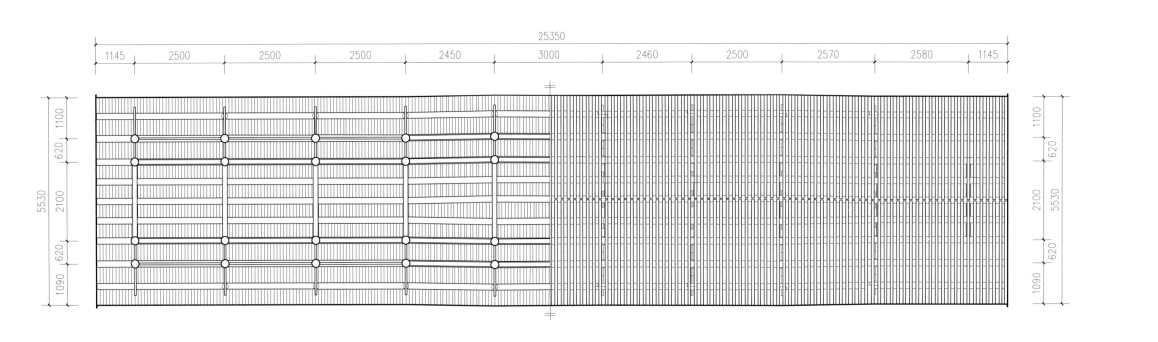

樟口桥廊屋梁架仰视（左）与俯视（右）图
Plan of corridor beam framework of Zhangkou Bridge as seen from below (left) and above (right)

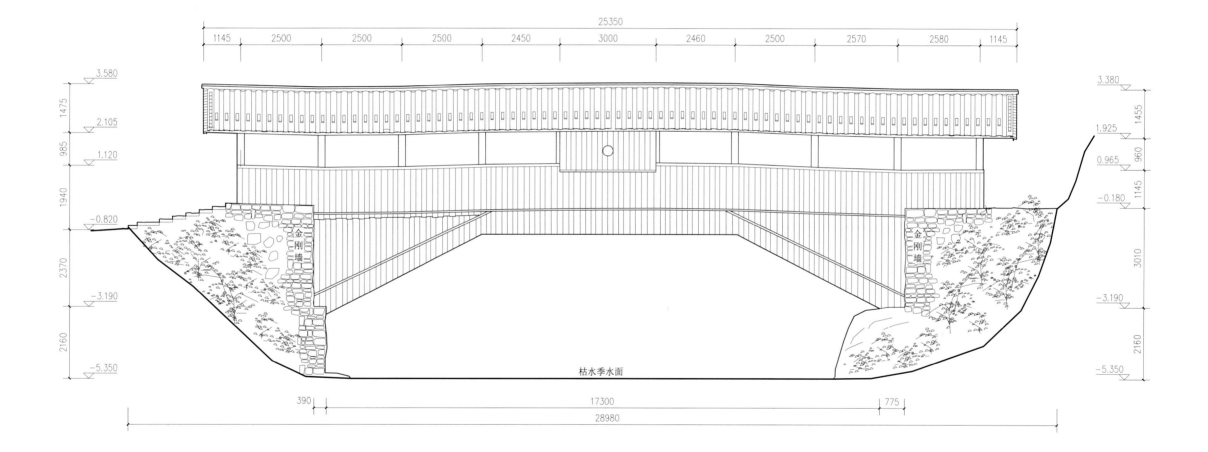

樟口桥东南立面图
Southeast elevation of Zhangkou Bridge

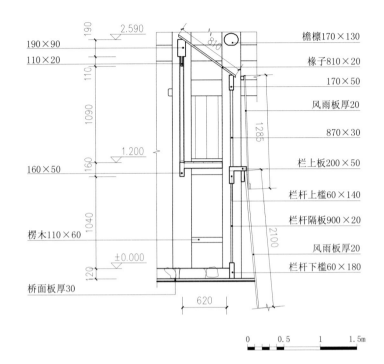

樟口桥神龛剖面图
Section of shrine of Zhangkou Bridge

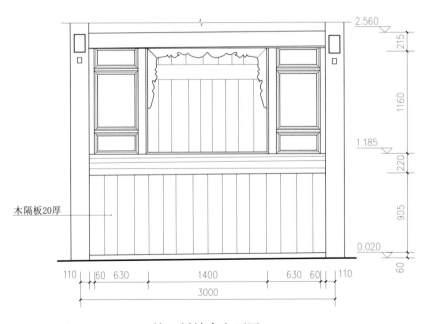

樟口桥神龛立面图
Elevation of shrine of Zhangkou Bridge

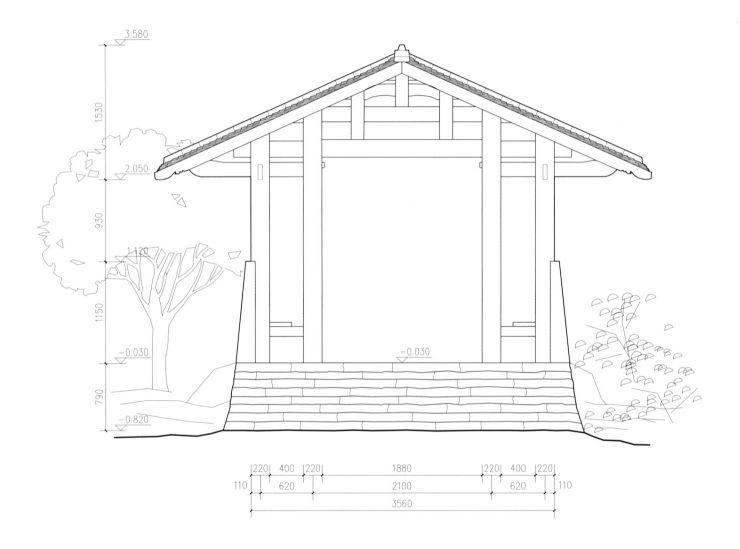

樟口桥西南立面图
Southwest elevation of Zhangkou Bridge

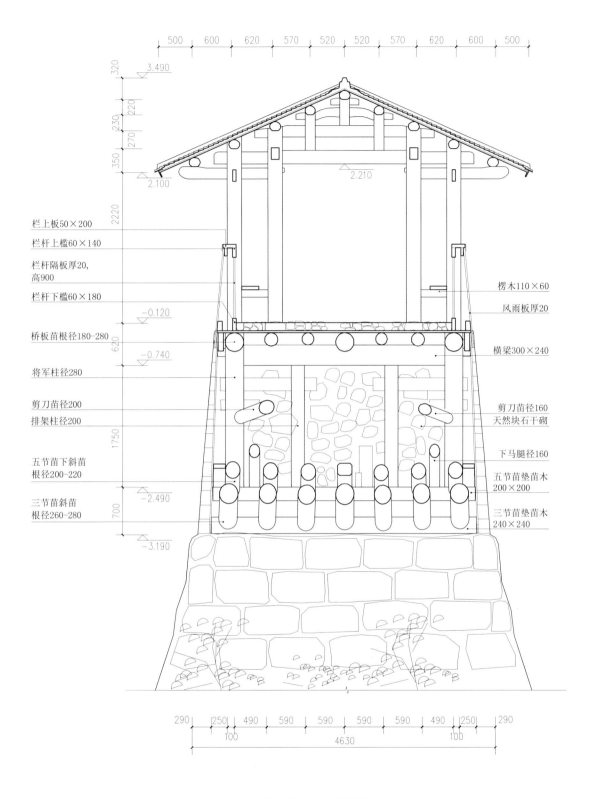

樟口桥 2-2 剖面图
Section 2-2 of Zhangkou Bridge

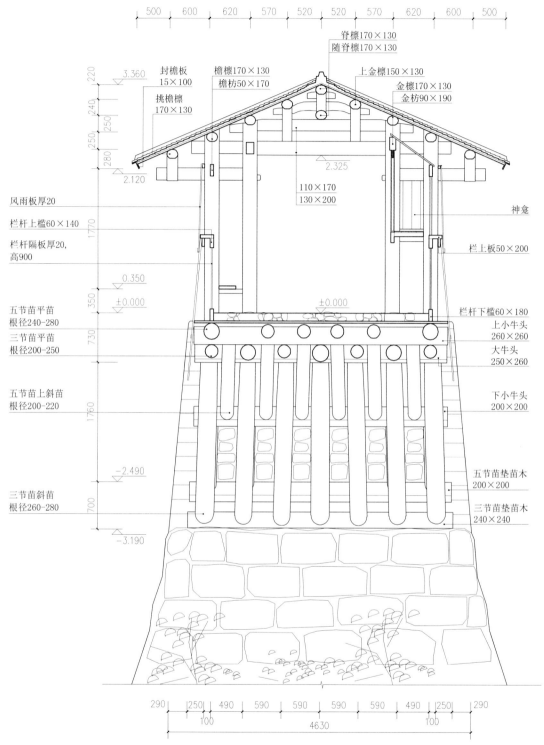

樟口桥 1-1 剖面图
Section 1-1 of Zhangkou Bridge

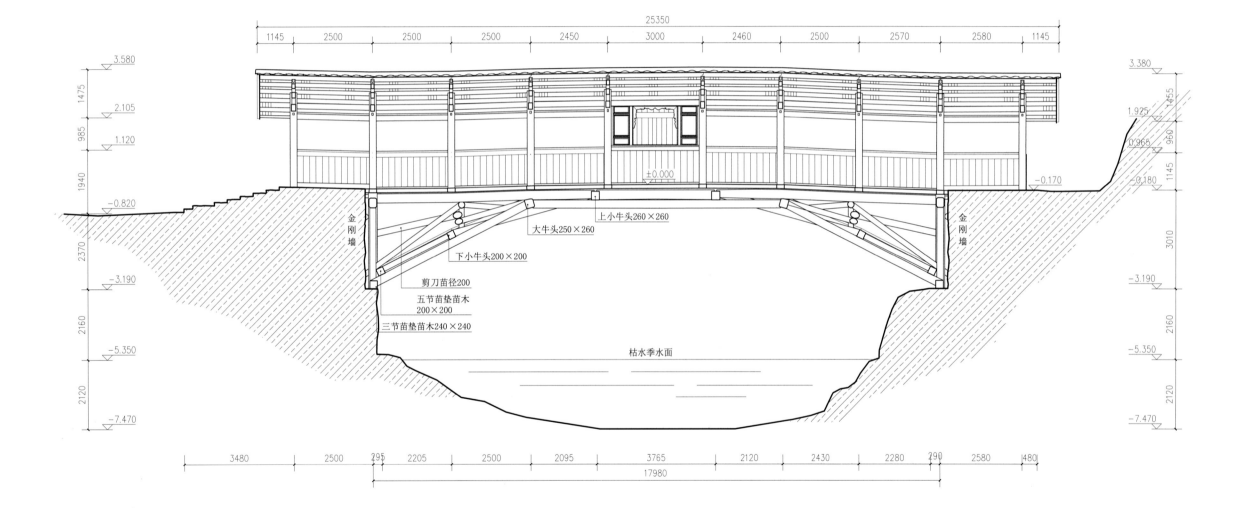

樟口桥 3-3 剖面图

Section 3-3 of Zhangkou Bridge

万安桥

Wan'an Bridge

Wan'an Bridge, also known as Changqiao Bridge, Caihong Bridge, or Longjiang Gongji Bridge, was first built in 1090, the fifth year of the Yuanyou reign period of the Northern Song Dynasty. It was rebuilt twice in imperial times during the Qing Dynasty, in 1742, the seventh year of the Qianlong reign period, and in 1845, the twenty-fifth year of the Daoguang reign period, and once in the Republican era in 1932. When the bridge rebuilt for the last time, the double-eave pavilion was built on the northwest of the bridge. In 1953, the two northwestern spans of the bridge and the pavilion were destroyed by the flood. The former was rebuilt the following year, while the latter was not. Located in Changqiao village of Changqiao township, the bridge spans northwest to southeast across the Changqiao Stream (also known as Longjiang River). Wan'an Bridge has six unequal spans and five piers that are shaped like a boat. Wooden boards are mounted as a deck. According to the present documentation, the bridge is the longest interlocked timber-arched covered bridge still extant today, and it is recorded in *Zhongguo Kexue Jishu Shi* (*Chinese History of Science and Technology*) volume on bridges. Southeast of the bridge stands Dasheng Temple.

万安桥，又称『长桥』、『彩虹桥』、『龙江公济桥』，始建于北宋元祐五年（1090年），分别于清代乾隆七年（1742年）、道光二十五年（1845年）、中华民国21年（1932年）重建，最后一次又在西北端加建重檐桥亭。1953年，西北两孔段落和桥亭被冲毁，前者于次年被重建，后者再未被恢复。位于长桥镇长桥村，跨越长桥溪（又称龙江），东南—西北走向。桥五墩六孔，墩呈船形，贯木拱不等跨，桥体拱架系统上铺木板为桥面，是全国现存最长的古代贯木拱廊桥，被载入《中国科学技术史·桥梁卷》。桥东南有大圣庙。

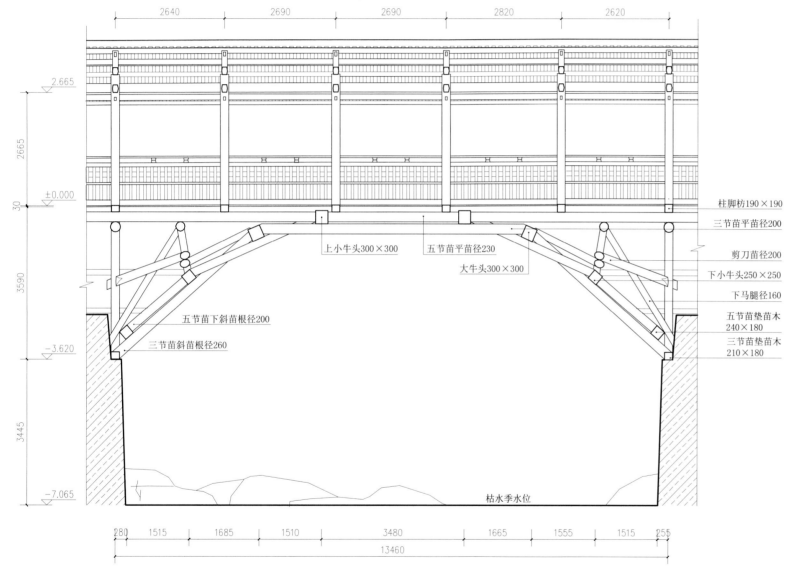

万安桥单跨剖面图
Span section of Wan'an Bridge

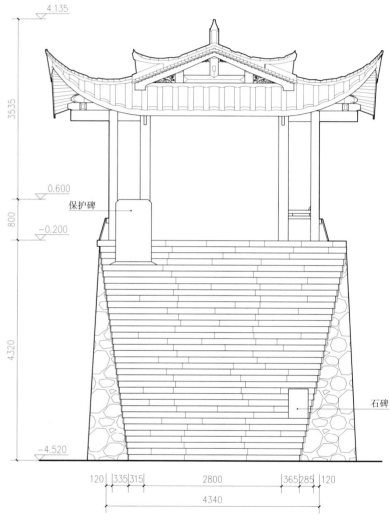

万安桥西北立面图
Northwest elevation of Wan'an Bridge

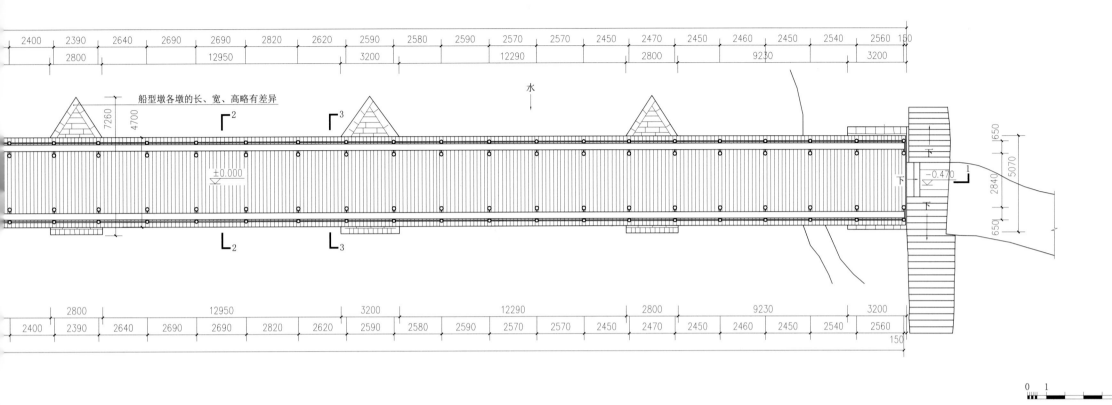

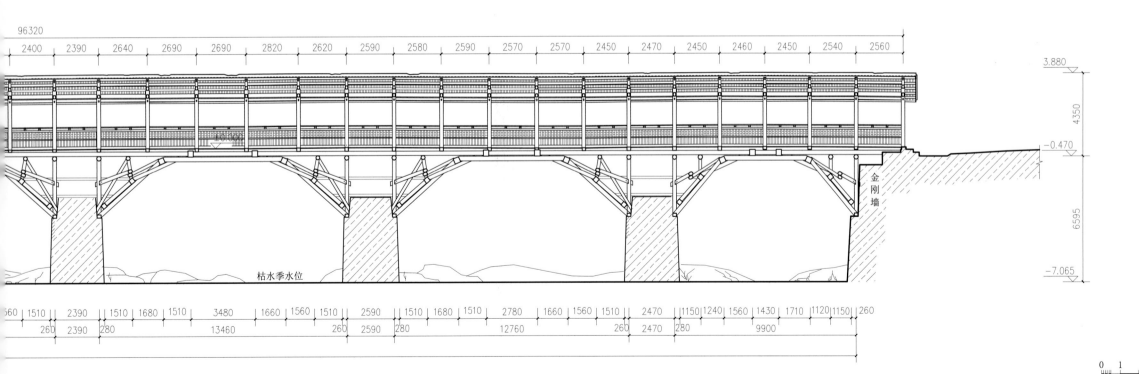

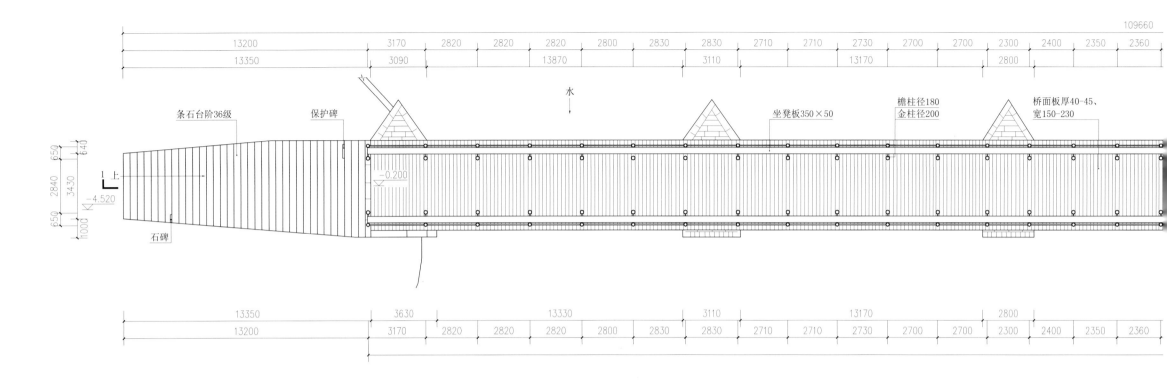

万安桥平面图
Surface floor plan of Wan'an Bridge

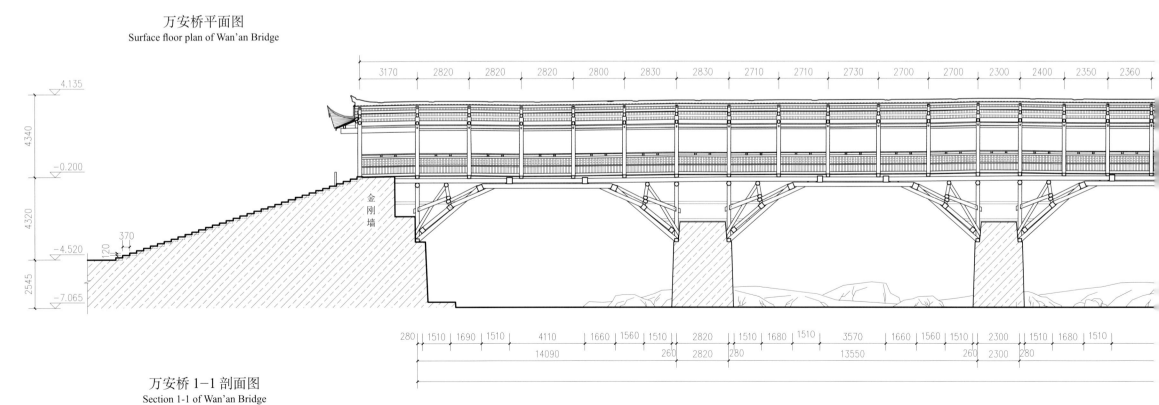

万安桥 1-1 剖面图
Section 1-1 of Wan'an Bridge

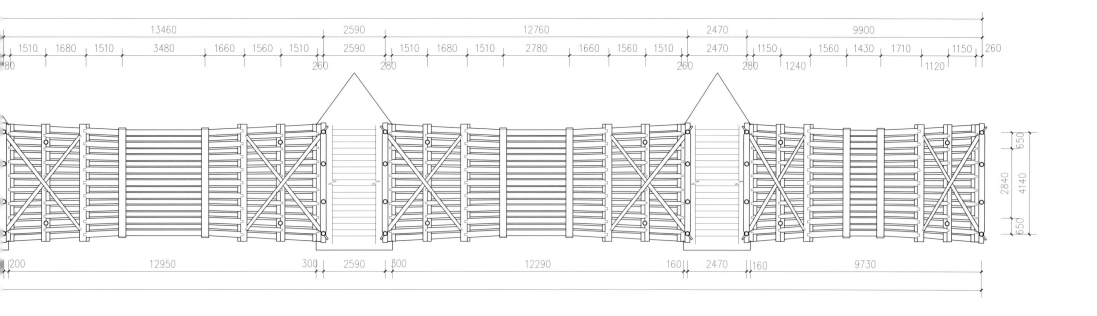
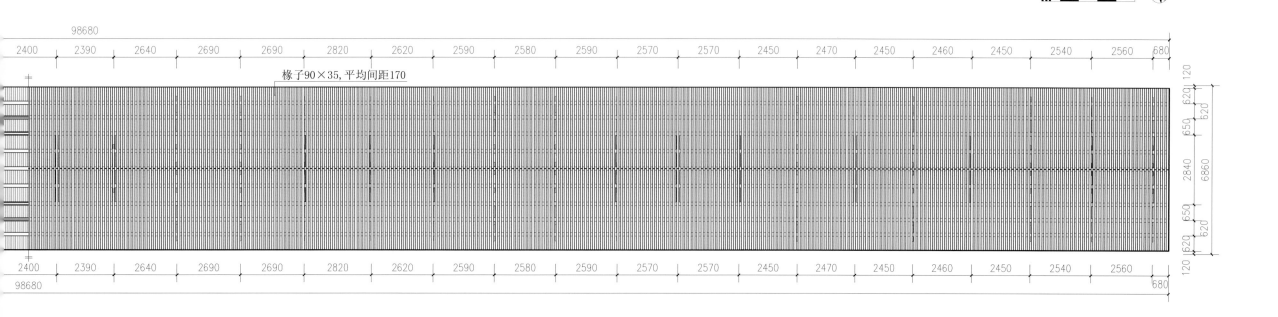

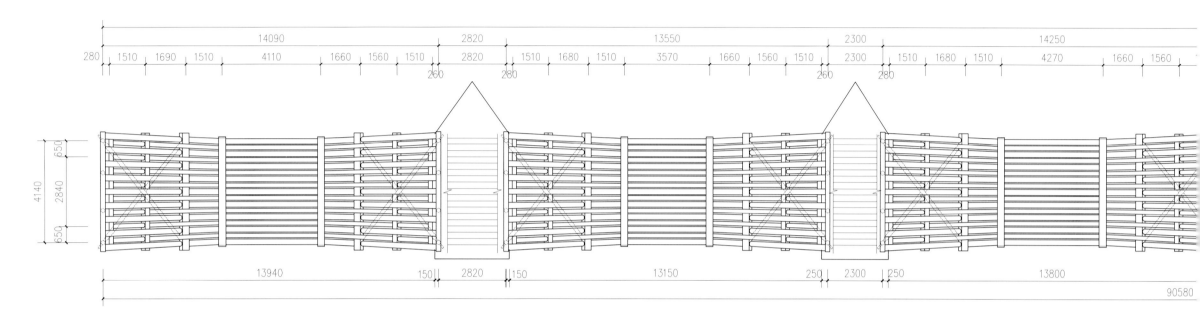

万安桥廊屋梁架仰视（左）与俯视（右）图
Plan of corridor beam framework of Wan'an Bridge as seen from below (left) and above (right)

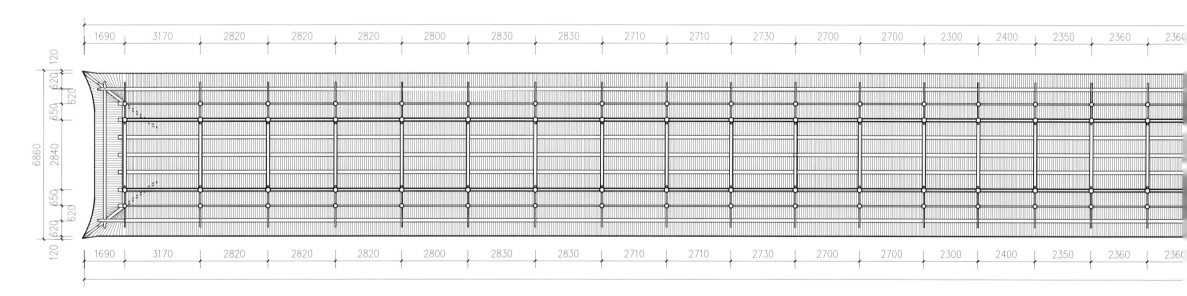

万安桥桥梁拱骨系统仰视（左）与俯视（右）图
Plan of timber arch system of Wan'an Bridge as seen from below (left) and above (right)

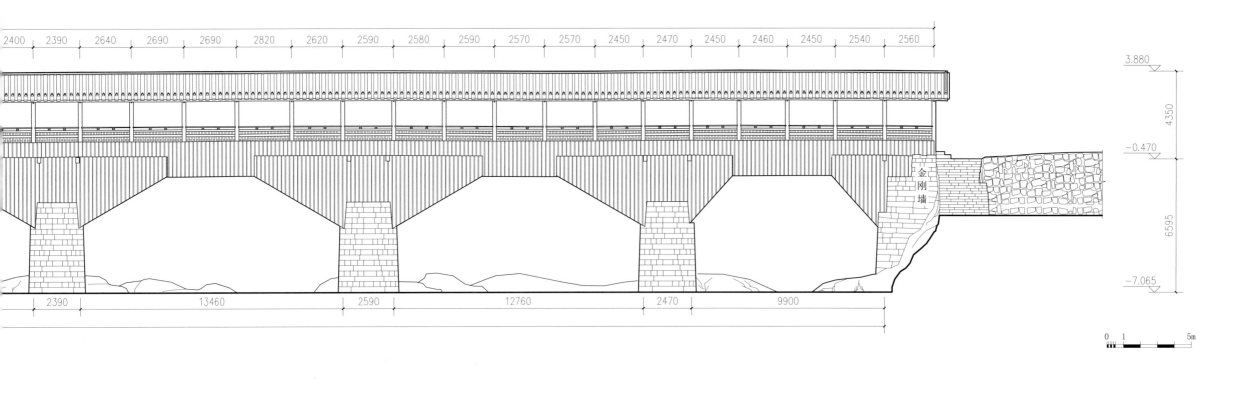

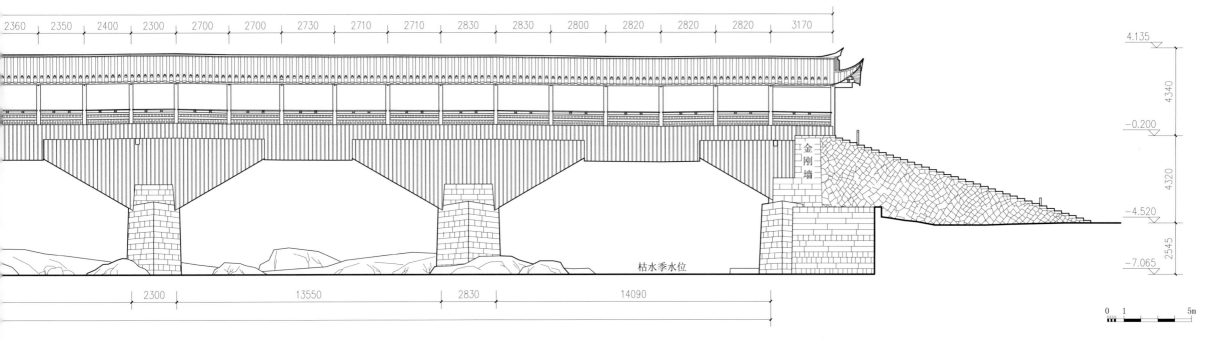

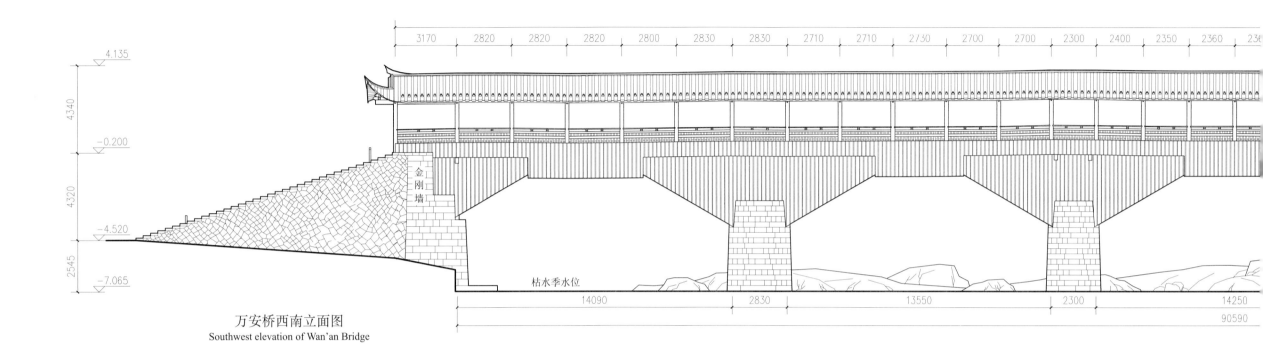

万安桥西南立面图
Southwest elevation of Wan'an Bridge

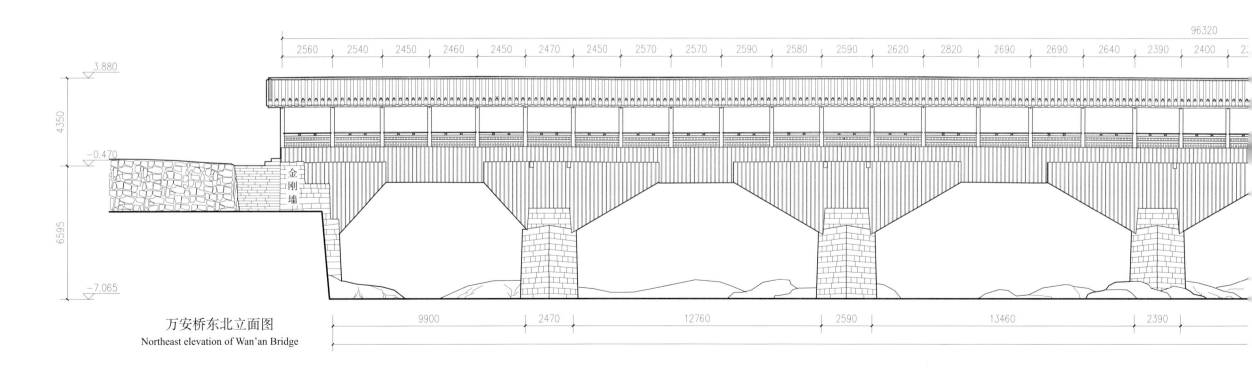

万安桥东北立面图
Northeast elevation of Wan'an Bridge

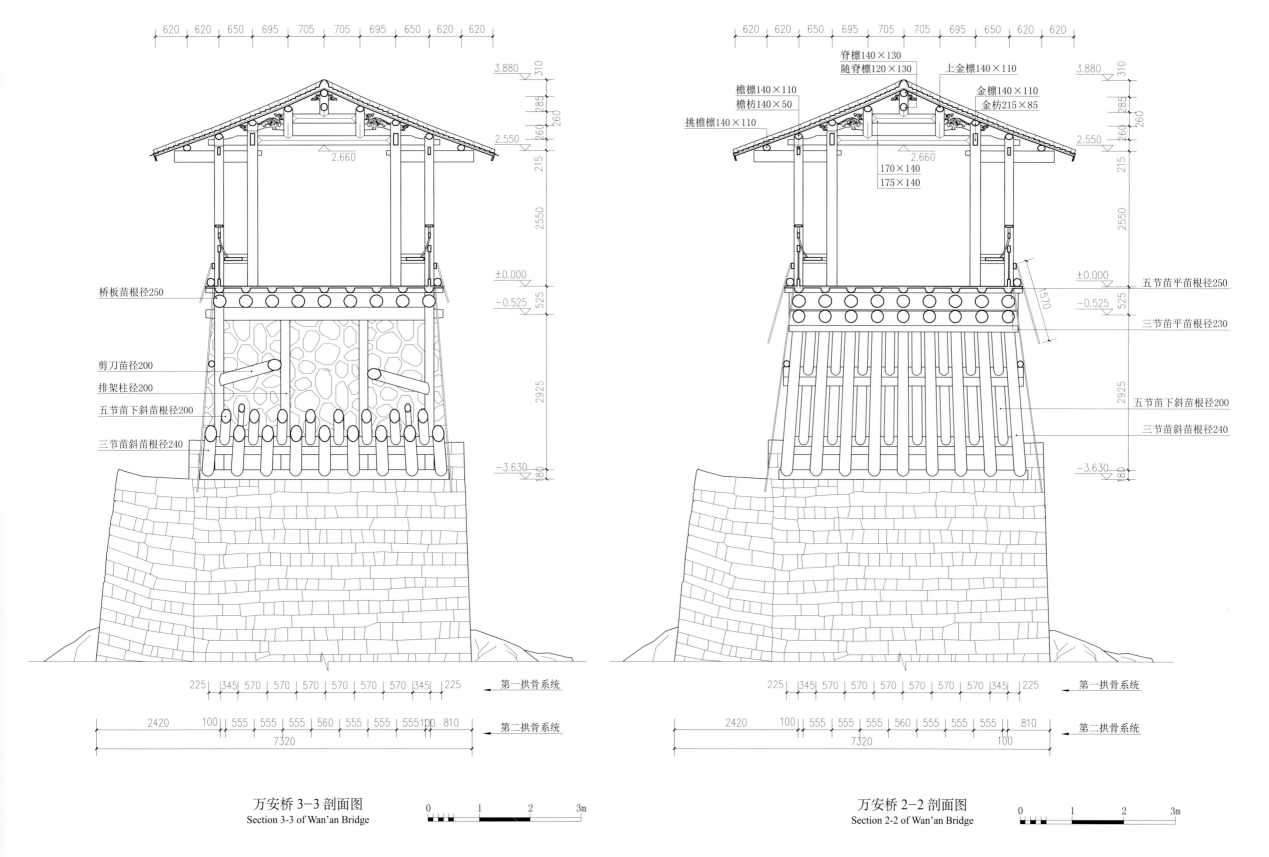

迎风桥

Yingfeng Bridge

Yingfeng Bridge, also known as Ludi Bridge, located in Ludi village of Pingcheng township, was first built in 1854, the fourth year of the Xianfeng reign of the Qing Dynasty. According to hearsay, it dates roughly to the same period as the nearby Liantai Baota Bridge built in 1823, the third year of the Daoguang reign of the Qing Dynasty. Yingfeng Bridge spans east to west across Ludi Stream in a single span, and the deck is paved with wooden boards, and a shrine is installed in the middle of the covered corridor. The bridge was a primary thoroughfare in the past, serving as a link between Ludi village situated in the deep mountains with the outside world. But today, few people use the bridge because a modern highway was built near the western end of the bridge.

迎风桥，又名『陆地桥』，始建于清代咸丰四年（1854年），位于屏城乡陆地村，据悉与距此不远建于清代道光三年（1823年）的莲台宝塔桥属同一年代，单孔跨越陆地溪，东西走向，桥体拱架系统上铺木板为桥面，廊屋中部设神龛。旧时此桥是处于深山中的陆地村出村要道，现进村公路从其西桥头通过，已少有人经桥通行。

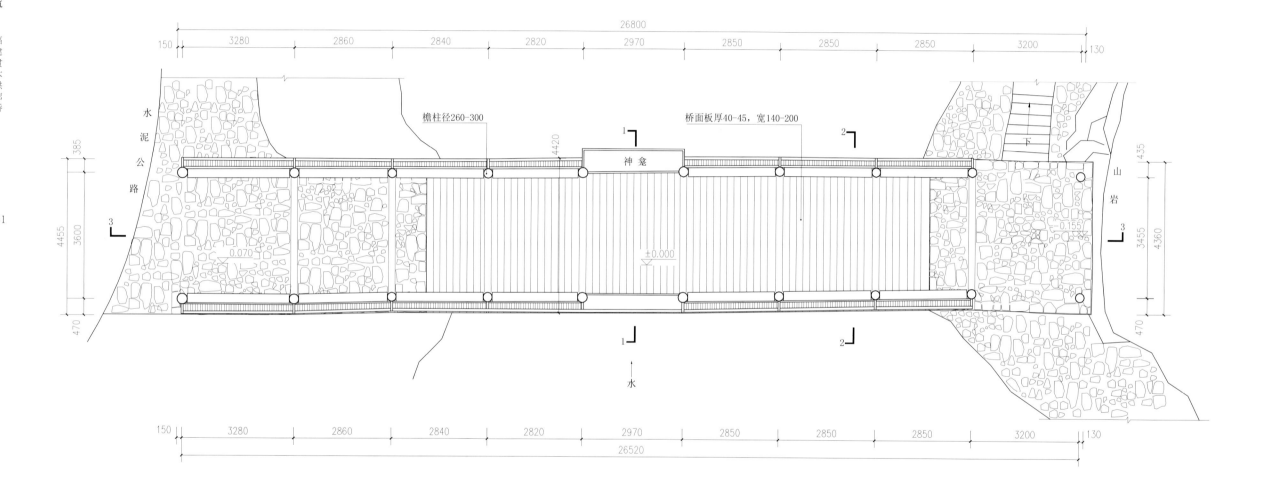

迎风桥平面图
Surface floor plan of Yingfeng Bridge

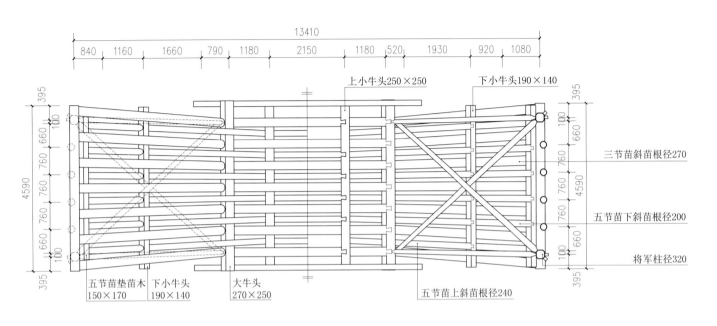

迎风桥桥体拱架系统仰视（左）俯视（右）图
Plan of timber arch system of Yingfeng Bridge as seen from below (left) and above (right)

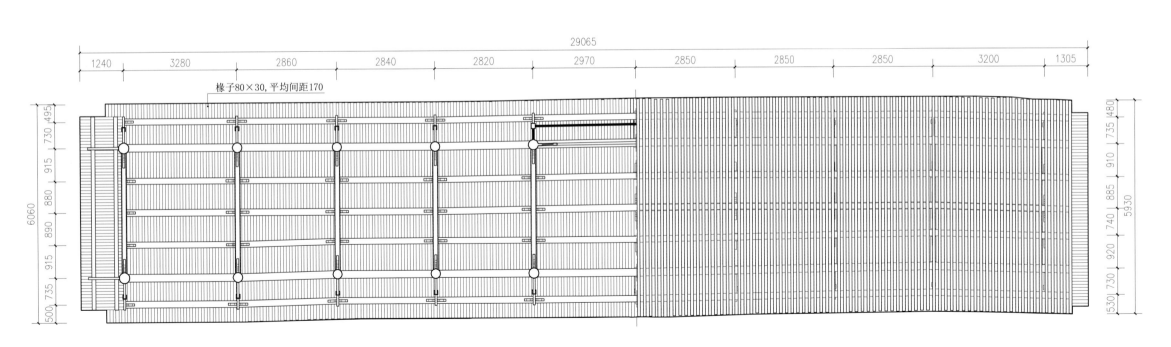

迎风桥廊屋梁架仰视（左）俯视（右）图
Plan of corridor beam framework of Yingfeng Bridge as seen from below (left) and above (right)

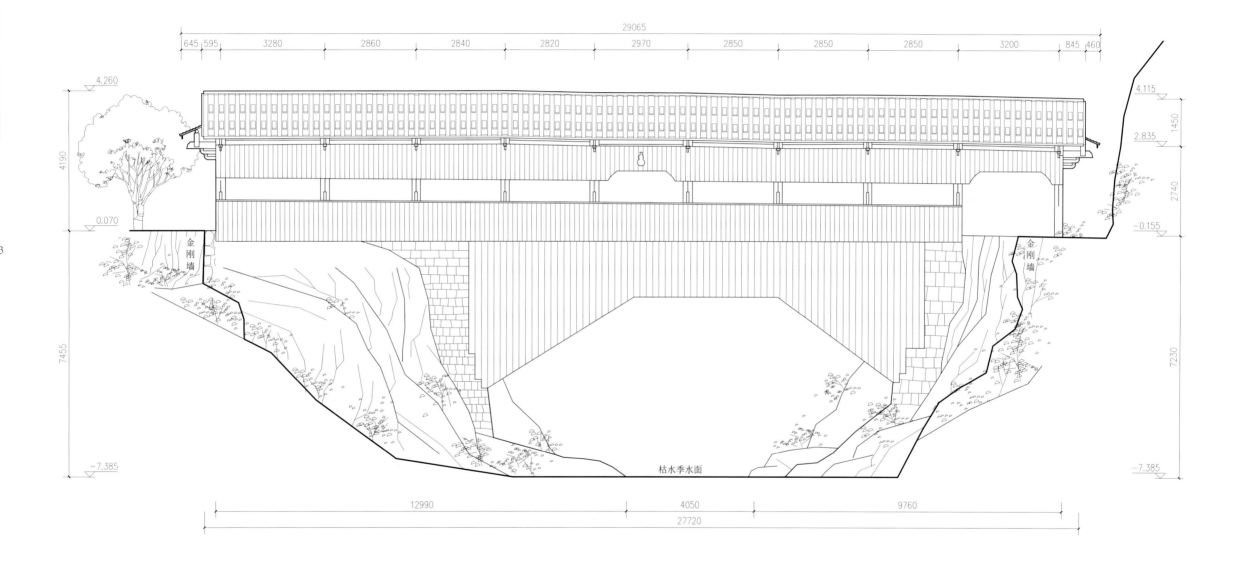

迎风桥南立面图
South elevation of Yingfeng Bridge

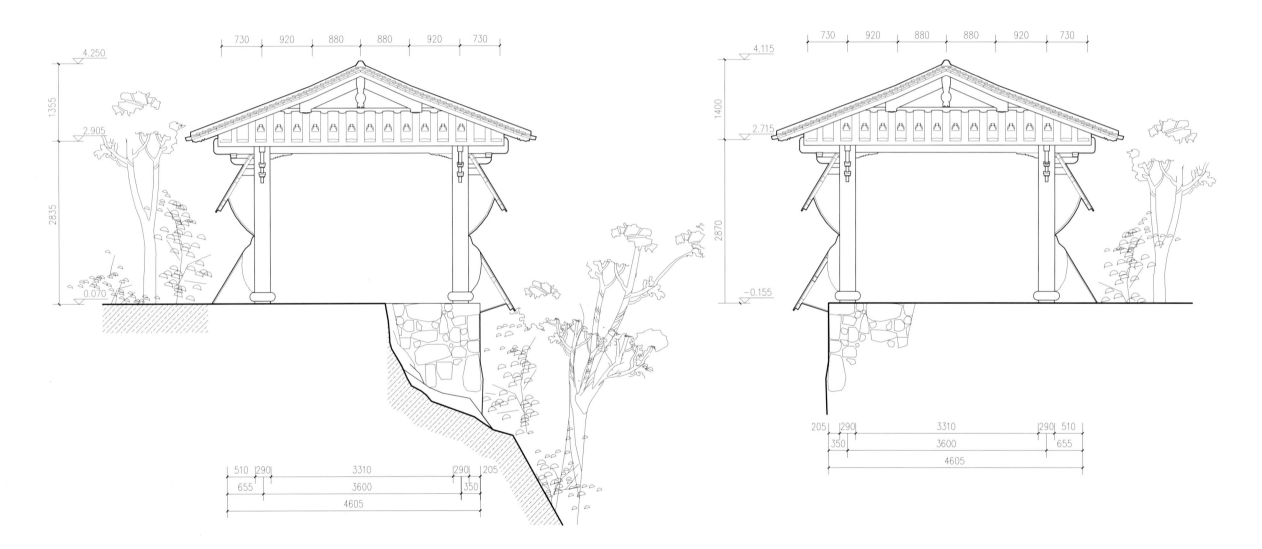

迎风桥西立面图
West elevation of Yingfeng Bridge

迎风桥东立面图
East elevation of Yingfeng Bridge

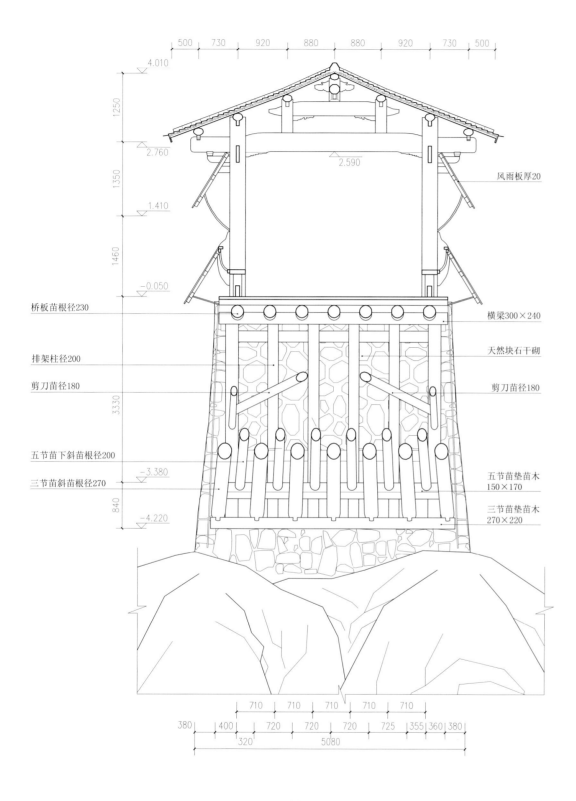

迎风桥 2-2 剖面图
Section 2-2 of Yingfeng Bridge

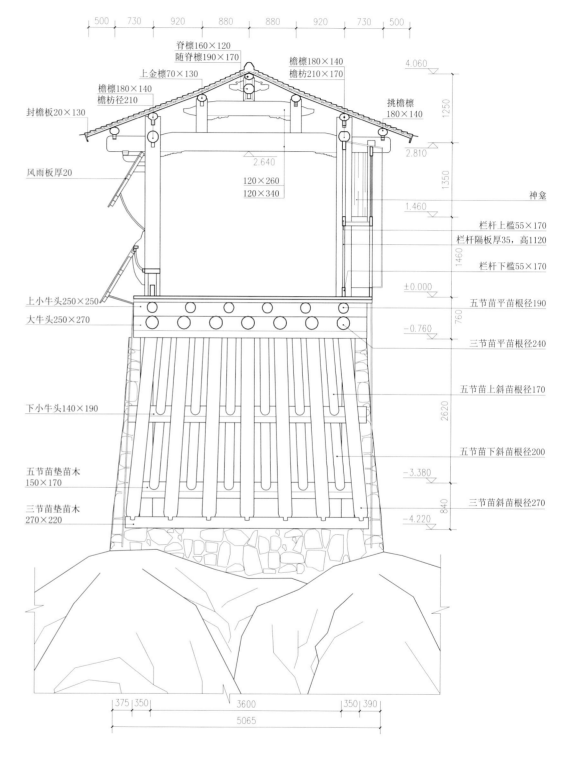

迎风桥 1-1 剖面图
Section 1-1 of Yingfeng Bridge

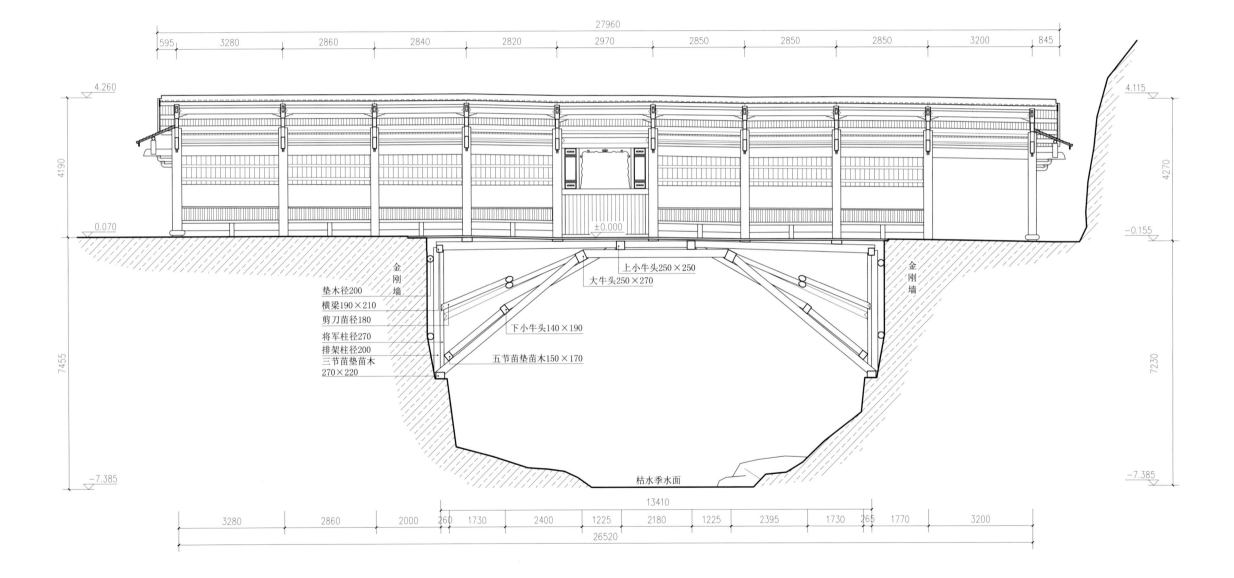

迎风桥 3-3 剖面图
Section 3-3 of Yingfeng Bridge

参与测绘及相关工作的单位及人员名单

支持单位：
中国文化遗产研究院　中国艺术研究院
福建省文物局　泉州市文物保护研究中心
寿宁县文体和旅游局　寿宁县博物馆
屏南县文体和旅游局　屏南县博物馆

参与人员：
肖　东　姚洪峰　程　霏　程潞潞　陈艺军　郑剑峰　黄婷婷
吴燕萍　杨华翔　黄伟娥　林宏淦　谢清燕　康巧妹　张　璠
黄日承　林炳文　陈志毅　丛　薇　张海利　曾　灵　杜雅芬

测绘时间：
2005 年 3 月至 2008 年 11 月、2011 年 3 月至 2015 年 11 月

英文翻译：
程　霏

英文校对：
曾　灵

特别致谢：
郑国珍　周芬芳　黄春财　康　健　何经平　楼建龙　常　浩
龚迪发　龚　健　陆世飞　苏旭东　张世带　黄闽辉　缪　正

List of Participants Involved in Surveying and Related Works

Support Departments

Chinese Academy of Cultural Heritage, Chinese Academy of Arts, Cultural Relics Bureau of Fujian Province, Cultural Relics Protection Research Center of Quanzhou, Culture, Sports and Tourism Bureau of Shouning County, Shouning Museum, Culture, Sports and Tourism Bureau of Pingnan County, Pingnan Museum.

Participants

XIAO Dong, YAO Hongfeng, CHENG Fei, CHENG Lulu, CHEN Yijun, ZHENG Jianfeng, HUANG Tingting, WU Yanping, YANG Huaxiang, HUANG Wei'e, LIN Honggan, XIE Qingyan, KANG Qiaomei, ZHANG Pan, HUANG Richeng, LIN Bingwen, CHEN Zhiyi, CONG Wei, ZHANG Haili, ZENG Ling, DU Yafen

Survey Time

March, 2005-November, 2008
March, 2011-November, 2015

Translator

CHENG Fei

Proofreader

ZENG Ling

Acknowledgement

ZHENG Guozhen, ZHOU Fenfang, HUANG Chuncai, KANG Jian, HE Jingping, LOU Jianlong, CHANG Hao, GONG Difa, GONG Jian, LU Shifei, SU Xudong, ZHANG Shidai, HUANG Minhui, MIU Zheng

图书在版编目(CIP)数据

福建贯木拱廊桥/肖东，姚洪峰，程霏编著.－北京：中国建筑工业出版社，2018.10
（中国古建筑测绘大系·古桥建筑）
ISBN 978-7-112-22671-9

Ⅰ.①福… Ⅱ.①肖… ②姚… ③程… Ⅲ.①木桥－拱桥－建筑艺术－福建－图集 Ⅳ.①U448.22-64

中国版本图书馆CIP数据核字（2018）第206388号

丛书策划／王莉慧
责任编辑／李 鸽 陈海娇
英文审稿／［奥］荷雅丽（Alexandra Harrer）
书籍设计／付金红
责任校对／王 烨

中国古建筑测绘大系·古桥建筑
福建贯木拱廊桥
肖 东 姚洪峰 程 霏 编著
*

中国建筑工业出版社出版、发行（北京海淀三里河路9号）
各地新华书店、建筑书店经销
北京方舟正佳图文设计有限公司制版
北京雅昌艺术印刷有限公司印刷
*

开本：787×1092毫米 横1/8 印张：39½ 字数：830千字
2020年5月第一版 2020年5月第一次印刷
定价：288.00元
ISBN 978-7-112-22671-9
　　　　（32787）

版权所有　翻印必究
如有印装质量问题，可寄本社退换
（邮政编码 100037）